Apple Training Series
iLife '09

Michael E. Cohen / Michael Wohl
Richard Harrington / Mary Plummer

Apple
Certified

Apple Training Series: iLife '09
Michael E. Cohen, Michael Wohl, Richard Harrington, Mary Plummer
Copyright © 2009 by Peachpit Press

Published by Peachpit Press. For information on Peachpit Press books, contact:

Peachpit Press
1249 Eighth Street
Berkeley, CA 94710
(510) 524-2178
Fax: (510) 524-2221
http://www.peachpit.com
To report errors, please send a note to errata@peachpit.com
Peachpit Press is a division of Pearson Education

Apple Series Editor: Serena Herr
Project Editor: Stephen Nathans-Kelly
Production Coordinator: Kim Wimpsett
Technical Editor: Charlie Miller
Technical Reviewers: Heather Christy, Brendan Boykin
Copy Editor: Dave Awl
Proofers: Karen Seriguchi, Dave Awl, Darren Meiss
Compositor: Chris Gillespie, Happenstance Type-O-Rama
Media Producer: Eric Geoffroy
Indexer: Jack Lewis
Cover Illustration: Kent Oberheu
Cover Production: Happenstance Type-O-Rama

ISBN 13: 978-0-321-61850-4
ISBN 10: 0-321-61850-5
9 8 7 6 5 4 3 2 1
Printed and bound in the United States of America

Contents at a Glance

Table of Contents

iMovie: Making Great Movies

GarageBand: A Musical Sampler

Getting Started

Welcome to the official Apple training course for the iLife '09 suite of products: iPhoto, iMovie, GarageBand, iWeb, and iDVD. You don't need to have any special background to get started, other than having a Mac (and perhaps a healthy curiosity about what you can do with it).

Learning iLife really means learning to live digitally; you're not so much learning to use new software as learning how to integrate your Mac comfortably into your home, school, and work. The iLife tools are only part of the picture—and this book is not so much a training manual as it is a way to show you how to enrich your world by weaving digital audio, photos, videos, and the web into many aspects of your life.

So instead of teaching you all the geeky details of these hip tools, we concentrate in this book on how real people really use them. We may even skip entire areas of functionality, all with an eye toward having fun, achieving quick success, and forming a foundation of confidence on which you can build.

What iLife Does for You

There was a time when your photographs were in one part of your house; your music collection was somewhere else; and VHS videotapes were scattered around the television. Each medium was tricky to keep organized.

But when all your media is digital—in the form of digital snapshots, digital audio (CDs, MP3s, and so on), and digital video (DVDs and DV cassettes)—keeping it organized is pretty easy, sharing content is streamlined, and using the material interchangeably between formats is both simple and kind of fun.

A Macintosh is designed to sit at the heart of your digital home. It's just a computer, but it's designed to make managing and combining all this content effortless. Better than that, Apple provides—free on all Macs—software that orchestrates the commingling of all this content. iLife is a family of products made up of applications designed to stand alone but also tuned to work together in remarkable ways.

What iLife teaches you is *media literacy:* the ability to communicate in a variety of powerful ways that are different from speaking or writing. Making professional-quality videos, podcasts, and websites, and being able to combine picture and sound effectively, is a skill that can be applied throughout your life. Once you have it, you'll be stunned by how often you use it, whether for personal pleasure or to commercial advantage.

It's too simplistic to say that iPhoto is the picture software and iMovie is the video software. iPhoto handles the organization of your pictures, true, but once your images are there, using them in slideshows and videos and on the web is very easy. You can't build a box around each component of iLife. So rather than focus on each product in turn, this book helps you create real-world projects, which sometimes involves dipping into several applications in a single lesson. Learning software is seldom fun. But making movies or podcasts, promoting your business, or building a creative report for school can be. You'll end up learning the software along the way.

The Methodology

This book moves through lessons by progressively increasing the complexity of the media you're using. You start by managing still images alone, then move to publishing still images, turning still images into moving *(dynamic)* images, and exploring the possibilities of video and sound. With digital content and the five core iLife applications (iPhoto, iMovie, iWeb, GarageBand, and iDVD), you can create everything from photobooks to DVDs, podcasts to dynamic websites, and polished movies.

Above all, these lessons are meant to be practical—not esoteric projects to show off the software, but real-life projects for real-life people with time constraints, well-worn equipment, and concerns about budget. The lessons cover four general areas: still images, movies, music, and publishing.

iPhoto: Great Pictures Made Easy

▶ In Lessons 1 through 4, you'll work with still images. You'll learn how to import images from your digital camera; how to organize, search, keyword, edit, and archive your pictures; and how to share your pictures in slideshows, cards, picture books, calendars, and on a web gallery.

iMovie: Making Great Movies

▶ In Lessons 5 through 10, you'll work mostly with video—though you'll also combine still photos, music, special effects, graphics, and titles in iMovie. You'll learn to shoot video creatively and edit to maximum effect; add narration to your videos; mix sound with picture; and finish your movie by fine-tuning color, contrast, and audio.

GarageBand: A Musical Sampler

▶ In Lesson 11 you'll learn your way around GarageBand, connect your instruments, and take a music lesson within GarageBand. In Lessons 12 and 13, you'll jam with a virtual band and create original music—in the form of an iPhone ringtone—with GarageBand.

iWeb and iDVD: Publishing with iLife

▶ In Lessons 14 through 16, you'll put it all together, using iWeb, iPhoto, iMovie, and GarageBand to record and produce a sophisticated podcast, build a website with dynamic content, and create and publish blogs and web albums. Finally, in Lesson 17, you'll use iDVD to build a DVD menu for your movie project.

A Word About the Lesson Content

Often, training materials are professionally created—using actors and complicated productions with multiple cameras, lights, microphones, tripods, and a crew. The resulting material is of high quality but bears little similarity to the kind of projects you will be working on.

To make this training as real-world and practical as possible, virtually all the media used in this book was made in precisely the way you would make your own videos. The quality of the shots (for better or worse) is comparable to what you can get with typical consumer equipment, and the sophistication of the projects is precisely what you can achieve using the iLife tools, with settings (and challenges) you will commonly encounter yourself.

We tried to make sure the events depicted here were recorded in the way you are being taught to work. Ideally, this will give you clear and realistic expectations about what you can do with your newfound skills.

System Requirements

This book is written for iLife '09, which comes free with any new Macintosh computer. If you have an older version of iLife, you will need to upgrade to the current iLife version to follow along with every lesson. The upgrade can be purchased online at www.apple.com and is available from any store that sells Apple software.

Before you begin the lessons in this book, you should have a working knowledge of your Mac and its operating system. You don't need to be an expert, but you do need to know how to use the mouse and standard menus and commands, and how to open, save, and close files. You should have a working understanding of how OS X helps organize files on your computer, and you should also be comfortable opening applications (from the Dock or at least the Applications folder). If you need to review any of these techniques, see the printed or online documentation that came with your computer.

For a list of the minimum system requirements for iLife, please refer to the Apple website at: www.apple.com/ilife/systemrequirements.html.

Copying the iLife Lesson Files

The *Apple Training Series: iLife '09* DVD-ROM includes all the project files and media you'll need to complete the lessons in this book. You must install the iLife '09 software before you install the lesson files.

To install the iLife Lesson files:

1   Insert the *ATS iLife09* DVD into your DVD drive.

2   Double-click the installer on the DVD. When the installation is complete, eject the disc.

    This will copy the iLife09_Book_Files folder to your desktop, and will install certain iMovie and Garageband files in the locations where they need to be on your hard drive.

The iLife09_Book_Files folder contains the lesson files used in this course. Each lesson has its own folder. Note that several lessons use the files from a previous lesson; in those cases, the lesson folder contains a simple text file indicating that there are no new media files for that lesson.

About Apple Training and Certification

Apple Training Series: iLife '09 is part of the official training series for Apple applications, developed by experts in the field and certified by Apple. The lessons are designed to let you learn at your own pace. If you follow the book from start to finish, or at least complete the lessons in each section consecutively, you will build on what you learned in previous lessons.

Apple Certification offers Associate-level certification for the iLife '09 product suites. Professionals, educators and students can earn Apple Certified Associate status to validate entry-level skills in our digital lifestyle and productivity applications. As a special offer, this Apple Training Series book includes a discount code that lets you to take this exam online for $45 (a $65 value). Details appear on the DVD.

For those who prefer to learn in an instructor-led setting, Apple also offers training courses that lead to certification at Apple Authorized Training Centers worldwide in iLife, iWork, Mac OS X, Mac OS X Server, and Apple's Pro applications. These courses are taught by Apple Certified Trainers, and balance concepts and lectures with hands-on labs and exercises.

To learn more about Apple Training and Certification, or to find an Authorized Training Center near you, go to www.apple.com/training.

Resources

Apple Training Series: iLife '09 is not intended to be a comprehensive reference manual, nor does it replace the documentation that comes with the applications. Rather, the book is designed to be used in conjunction with other comprehensive reference guides. These resources include:

▶ Companion Peachpit website: As iLife '09 is updated, Peachpit may choose to update lessons as necessary. Please check www.peachpit.com/ats.ilife09.

▶ Apple's website: www.apple.com.

▶ *Apple Training Series: iWork '09*, by Richard Harrington, is an excellent companion to this book. Learn how to use iLife applications with iWork to create first-class presentations, slideshows, newsletters, publications, and spreadsheets.

▶ *Apple Training Series: GarageBand '09*, by Mary Plummer. This wonderful training book offers a comprehensive introduction to recording, arranging, and mixing music on a Mac.

▶ *The Macintosh iLife*, by Jim Heid (Peachpit Press), an accessible and popular reference guide for the iLife products.

▶ *The Little Digital Video Book*, by Michael Rubin (Peachpit Press), a concise resource on how to make your videos have more impact and look professional. Although the book is not about the iLife software specifically, it expands on many of the concepts touched on in the video lessons.

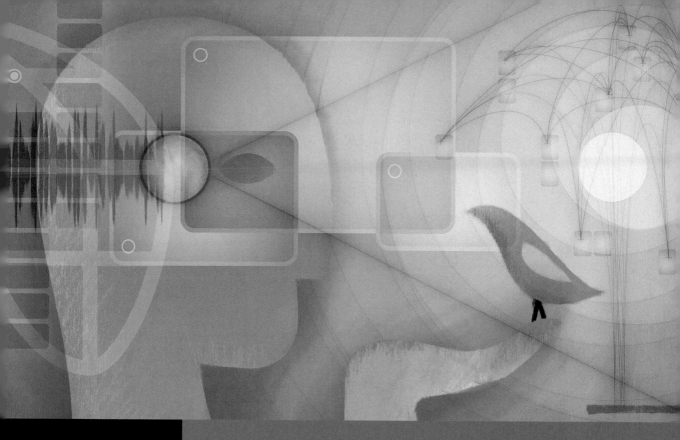

iPhoto: Great Pictures Made Easy

Michael E. Cohen has been a teacher, a programmer, an editor, a Web designer, and a digital media producer. A three-time contributing editor to the *The Macintosh Bible*, Michael is the author or co-author of *Take Control of Syncing Data in Leopard*, *The Mac Xcode 2 Book*, *AirPort and Mac Wireless Networks for Dummies*, *Apple Training Series: iLife '08*, and *Teach Yourself VISUALLY iLife '04*. He lives in Santa Monica, California.

1

Lesson Files	After installation:
	iLife09_Book_Files > Lesson_01 > L1_photos_to_import
Time	This lesson takes approximately 70 minutes to complete.
Goals	Learn basic photographic terms and techniques
	Learn how to connect a camera to your Mac
	Import photos and video from a camera into iPhoto
	Import picture files into iPhoto
	Create and organize Events
	Identify faces in your photos
	Identify your photos by places

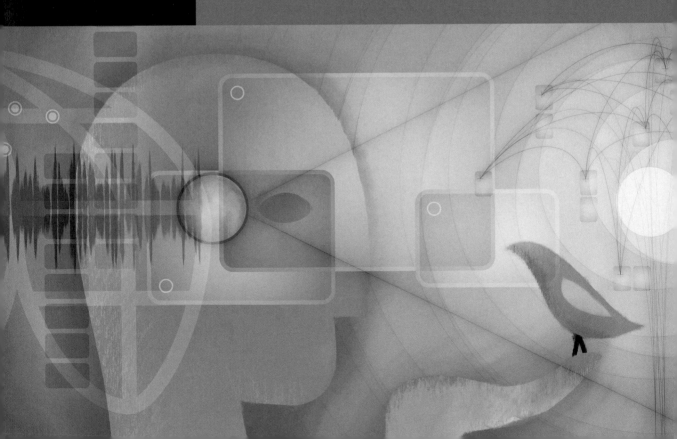

Lesson 1
Importing and Organizing Your Photos

When iPhoto was introduced, it was described as the digital version of the shoebox where you store all your photos.

iPhoto is a pretty amazing shoebox. It can store thousands upon thousands of photos and help you organize them into memorable events and special collections. It can recognize which photos show faces and even identify those faces for you. It can help you track where you took your pictures. It can improve your pictures with its powerful and easy-to-use editing tools. It can send your pictures to a professional printing service so you can order high-quality prints, photo greeting cards, books, or calendars. It can create outstanding animated photo slideshows and web galleries of your pictures, so that your friends and family or the whole world can enjoy them.

But before you can do all these wonderful things, you have to take your photos and get them *into* the shoebox.

That's what this lesson is about.

Shooting Photos

Digital cameras come in all shapes and sizes, from disposable point-and-shoot pocket-size cameras to image-stabilizing, multisensored, super-high-resolution professional models that can cost as much as an automobile. But no matter how simple or how refined the camera, they all have the same job: to capture an instant of light and freeze it in a rectangular frame.

Even the best camera can take a mediocre picture, and even a mediocre camera can take a good one. When it comes to taking a good picture, what's more important than the camera is the photographer behind it.

Getting the Right Shot

Digital cameras have two big advantages over film cameras—you don't have to pay for the film, and you don't have to wait for the film to be developed.

Exploit these advantages: Don't wait for the perfect shot. Instead, take a lot of pictures. Doing so costs nothing, and it may well be that one of your shots will be the perfect shot, or at least something close to it. Keep the good shots, and throw away the rest.

Remember that a camera's sole job is to capture light. If there's more light behind the subject of your picture than on the subject itself, your camera will capture that background light, leaving your subject in darkness. Sometimes you may want that, but usually you don't.

PHOTO: BT FOX

A backlit subject can make or break a shot

Although iPhoto can bring out the detail on a backlit subject, it can only do so much. Try to have the light source behind you, rather than behind your subject. If that's not possible, use the camera's flash if it has one—most cameras do.

TIP ▶ When you use a flash, don't position the camera directly in front of the subject; the flash can reflect back to the camera from shiny surfaces, such as eyeglasses or windows. Instead, place the camera at an angle to the subject and to any reflective surfaces.

A third piece of advice: Exploit the frame.

Each photo you take consists of a view, contained in a frame, of a much larger scene. The first step in exploiting the frame is making sure that everything you want in the picture is within the frame. The next step is arranging the items framed in your picture in a pleasing or interesting way; this is called *composing* the shot.

You can sometimes find natural opportunities that help you compose a shot: For example, you may be able to include a window, a door, or a tree in the frame to help focus attention on the subject or to present it in an interesting way.

PHOTO: BT FOX

Many photographers use the "rule of thirds" when they compose shots. That is, they imagine lines dividing the frame equally into three parts, both horizontally and vertically, and then place the subject on or near one of those lines. This technique puts the subject of the shot slightly above, below, to the left, or to the right of the frame's center.

Also keep in mind that sometimes it's okay for part of your subject to fall outside the frame. Using a close shot that omits part of the subject can add visual interest as well.

Grasping the Technical Details

Three factors combine to affect the quality of the image your camera produces: resolution, exposure, and aperture.

Resolution

Each digital picture consists of thousands of individual colored dots, called *pixels* (short for *picture elements*). The number of pixels that make up the picture is known as the picture's *resolution*. The more pixels, the more detail in the picture; the fewer pixels, the more fuzzy or ragged the picture looks.

Digital cameras are often rated by how many millions of pixels (*megapixels*) they can provide. Two or three megapixels is sufficient to produce attractive snapshots and more than sufficient for pictures on a webpage. You need more megapixels for high-quality full-page pictures in a print publication. However, the more megapixels your camera provides, the more storage space each picture takes up in the camera's memory and on your Mac's hard disk.

A very low-resolution picture

Although the maximum resolution is determined by your camera's optics and can't be changed, you can set many cameras to use a lower resolution to conserve storage space.

Exposure

To capture a picture, your camera briefly opens a shutter to allow the light that makes up the picture to enter the camera. This length of time is called the *exposure* and is usually measured in fractions of a second. The longer the exposure, the more light is captured, but the greater the chance that a small movement of the camera or your picture's subject will cause the image to appear blurred.

Long exposures are useful when shooting in low light, but such pictures require a steady hand (or the use of a tripod) and a stationary subject. Short exposures are usually required for action shots, such as sports photos, but short exposures need a lot of light to illuminate the subject. Many digital cameras can artificially boost their sensitivity to light to compensate for short exposures in low light; however, such pictures may look grainy because of the electronic "noise" that the boost in sensitivity can create.

Pictures taken in very low light look grainy

Aperture

How wide the camera's shutter opens when you take a picture is called its *aperture* setting. The wider the aperture, the more light that can enter the camera when the shutter opens. The exposure and the aperture settings together control how much light a picture captures: A wide aperture with a short exposure lets in the same amount of light as a long exposure and a narrow aperture.

The aperture, however, also controls *depth of field*, the distance between the closest and most distant objects in the picture that are in focus. A narrow aperture gives a wide depth of field, whereas a wide aperture produces a more narrow depth of field.

Digital cameras usually set aperture and exposure automatically. However, you can also adjust these settings manually for greater control with many cameras. If your camera allows you to adjust these settings, experiment with them to learn how each affects the quality of your pictures.

Choosing a Shooting Format

Some cameras offer you a choice between two image formats: *JPEG* and *RAW*.

JPEG (which stands for *Joint Photographic Experts Group*) is a format that reduces the amount of information that makes up a picture. It throws away information that the eye ordinarily can't discern, and uses sophisticated methods to compress the information that does remain so that you can fit more images into the camera's storage.

RAW pictures, on the other hand, retain nearly all of the information that came into the camera when you took them. As a result, RAW images take up considerably more storage space than their JPEG-compressed equivalents: often as much as 10 to 15 times as much storage. The advantage of RAW pictures is that they offer you much finer control when you modify them with image editing tools, such as the ones that iPhoto provides.

For casual photography, or to conserve storage space on your camera or your Mac, you can use the JPEG format with no qualms. Many digital cameras, in fact, offer only the JPEG format.

However, if you plan to make professional use of your pictures, or if you want to have the maximum amount of control when you fine-tune your images, you should consider the RAW format. Just make sure you have plenty of storage space available.

Capturing GPS Data

Courtesy of the U.S. Department of Defense, dozens of satellites circle Earth as part of the *Global Positioning System*, commonly known as *GPS*. These satellites broadcast microwave signals that terrestrial devices can use to pinpoint their locations. The system is used by aircraft, automobile navigation systems, and even digital cameras, such as the one included in the iPhone 3G.

If you have a camera that includes GPS capability, the camera can obtain a precise record of where a picture is taken, and it can store that location information in the picture itself.

Usually, because the GPS receiver in a camera can use up a significant amount of battery power, the GPS receiver can be turned on or off at your discretion.

If you do turn it on, iPhoto's Places feature can use the GPS information in your pictures to show you exactly where you took each shot. You'll find out more about Places later in this lesson.

Opening iPhoto for the First Time

The first time you open a new copy of iPhoto, it asks you to make a number of decisions: whether you want to see the introductory Welcome to iPhoto window every time iPhoto opens, whether you want iPhoto to open automatically whenever you connect a camera to your Mac, and whether you want iPhoto to look up photo locations for you.

1 To begin, open iPhoto.

After a few seconds, iPhoto displays its main window, a dialog attached to the window, another dialog, and the Welcome to iPhoto window. The Welcome to iPhoto window appears in front of the others.

2   In the Welcome to iPhoto window, deselect "Show this window when iPhoto opens," and then click Close.

When the Welcome to iPhoto window closes, a new dialog appears, asking if you want iPhoto to open whenever you connect a camera.

3   Click Yes.

If you click No in this dialog, iPhoto still detects a connected camera when iPhoto is running, but iPhoto won't open automatically when you connect a camera to your Mac.

TIP ▶ If you have an iPhone and regularly connect it to your Mac to sync and charge it, you may want to click No so that iPhoto won't open every time you connect the device.

4   In the dialog attached to the iPhoto window, click Yes.

TIP ▶ You can change the camera connection settings using iPhoto's General preferences, and you can change the location lookup settings using iPhoto's Advanced preferences. You can see the Welcome to iPhoto window at any time by choosing it from iPhoto's Help menu.

Connecting Your Camera to iPhoto

Once you've shot some photos, you need to move them from your camera into iPhoto on your Mac. Connecting a camera is a simple process that actually takes more time to describe than it does to perform. iPhoto can work with the vast majority of digital cameras, including phone cameras like the one in the iPhone, without any other software required.

To connect your camera to your Mac, you need the cable that came with your camera and a free USB port on your Mac. You also should consult the camera manual for the steps you should follow when you connect the camera to a computer. Usually, those steps should be as follows:

1 Turn off your camera and set it in display mode.

Typically, digital cameras have two main modes: a display, or playback, mode in which you use the camera screen to view pictures you've already taken; and a photography mode that you use when taking pictures. Some cameras have three modes: automatic photography, manual photography, and display; or photography, display, and video. Others may have no modes at all and automatically set themselves up properly when connected to your Mac, such as the camera in an iPhone.

2 Connect the cable that came with the camera to its connector on the camera.

3   Connect the other end of the camera's cable to a free USB port on your Mac.

4   Turn your camera on and iPhoto will prepare to import the camera's stored photos. If iPhoto was closed, it will open automatically when you connect a camera.

That's it. iPhoto is ready to import the photos stored in your camera.

TIP ▶ To avoid problems, make sure that your camera is fully charged, or is connected to an external power source, before you connect it to your Mac. You don't want your camera to turn off because of low power while it's in the middle of sending pictures to iPhoto.

Importing Photos from a Camera or Card

When you connect a camera to your Mac, iPhoto lists the camera in its Source list at the left of the iPhoto window under the Devices heading. It also displays small versions (called *thumbnails*) of the photos currently stored in the camera in the main viewing area on the right.

To import all the photos stored in the camera, do the following:

1 Click the Import All button in the lower-right corner of the iPhoto window.

iPhoto imports the pictures, displaying each picture as it imports it.

A dialog appears, asking you if you want to keep the original photos in the camera after you import them.

2   In the dialog, click either Delete Photos or Keep Photos.

> **TIP** ▶ If you select Keep Photos when you import, you can protect your-self from accidentally importing the same photos again the next time you connect your camera by selecting the "Hide photos already imported" checkbox in the lower-left corner of the iPhoto viewing area.

3   Turn off your camera and disconnect it from your Mac.

> **NOTE** ▶ Some cameras can appear on your desktop as a disk drive as well as in iPhoto. If the camera appears on your desktop when you con-nect it, you must eject the camera in the Finder before turning it off and disconnecting.

The photos are added to your iPhoto library.

Importing Selected Photos

As you may have noticed, iPhoto gives you the option of importing either all of the photos in your camera or just a selected group of photos. Here's how you import selected photos from your camera:

1   Connect your camera to your Mac and turn the camera on.

If iPhoto doesn't open automatically, open it.

2   In iPhoto's viewing area, click the first photo you want to import.

3   To select a range of photos, hold down the Shift key and click the last photo you want to import. To select individual photos, hold down the Command key as you click the photos you want to import.

Shift-clicking selects the first and the last photo you clicked and all of the photos in between. Command-clicking adds each photo you click to the selection. The selected photos have a yellow outline.

4   Click the Import Selected button in the lower-right corner of the main iPhoto window.

iPhoto imports the photos you've selected, and then presents a dialog when it finishes.

5   In the dialog, click either Delete Photos or Keep Photos.

6   Turn off your camera and disconnect it from your Mac.

Importing Photos from a Memory Card

Most digital cameras store their photos on a removable memory card. You can purchase additional memory cards for your camera in order to increase the camera's photo capacity. Additional memory cards can come in very handy when you're taking a lot of pictures out in the field: Simply put an empty card in your camera when the card you've been using becomes full.

If you purchase a card reader that's compatible with your camera's memory card and connect the card reader to your Mac, you can import the photos directly from the card using the card reader instead of having to connect your camera. This is useful when you want to conserve your camera's battery charge, or if you have several memory cards on hand from which you want to import pictures. Most card readers connect to a USB port on your Mac, much as a camera does.

To import photos into iPhoto from a memory card, follow these steps:

1   Connect your card reader to your Mac. If iPhoto doesn't open automatically, open it.

2   Insert the memory card into the card reader.

The card appears in iPhoto's Source list under Devices just as a camera does. Note, though, that the Mac also mounts the card on your desktop just as it does an external hard drive or a thumb drive, and that the card in the Source list has an Eject button next to it. You must explicitly eject the card from your Mac before removing the card from the reader.

3   Import the photos from the card using either of iPhoto's Import buttons just as you would when importing photos from a camera.

You can import all the photos on the card or selected photos, and you can choose either to keep or to delete the photos on the card after you import.

4   When you finish importing, click the Eject button beside the card in iPhoto's Source list and wait for the card to vanish from the list.

5   Remove the card from the card reader.

Importing Video from a Camera

Many digital cameras, including some mobile phone cameras, also have the ability to take digital motion video. Such video is often captured at a lower resolution and at a lower frame rate than the video produced by digital video cameras and is usually of shorter duration due to capacity constraints. As you'll see later in this book, iMovie can quite readily use the digital video that you import into iPhoto from your camera.

When you connect a camera or memory card that contains digital video to your Mac, iPhoto can import it into the iPhoto library just as it does still pictures.

1   Connect your camera to your Mac, turn the camera on, and if iPhoto is not set to open automatically, open it.

iPhoto displays the items you can import in its viewing area. Video thumbnails have a small white camera icon in their lower-left corners.

2   Either select the video you want to import and click Import Selected, or click Import All to import everything in the camera, including any video items.

3   In the dialog that appears, click either Keep Photos or Delete Photos.

iPhoto adds the items it imports, including any video items, to the iPhoto library. Videos in the library display the same camera icon on their thumbnails that they did in the viewing area when you imported them.

Importing from Applications

Many applications on your Mac can send images direct to your iPhoto library. For example, you can send image attachments in an email message direct from Mail to iPhoto, you can send any image on a webpage in Safari to iPhoto with a simple Control-click, and you can send any image you view with Leopard's Quick Look feature direct to iPhoto.

Quick Look and Safari can send images direct to iPhoto

To see how this kind of image-friendly partnership between other applications and iPhoto works, you'll use your Mac's Photo Booth application and iSight camera.

1   Open Photo Booth and take a photo with your Mac's iSight camera.

2   In the tray at the bottom of the Photo Booth window, click the photo you just took and then click the iPhoto button above the tray at the left.

iPhoto opens and imports the photo.

Importing Photo Files

iPhoto can import image files in a variety of formats, which makes it useful for storing and arranging all kinds of pictures; they don't even have to have come from a camera. You can drag almost any image file from the Finder to iPhoto to import it.

In this exercise, you'll import the photos you'll use in this lesson and the following lessons from the DVD that accompanies this book. If you haven't already installed the iLife09_Book_Files to your hard disk, please refer to the Getting Started chapter at the beginning of this book to do so now.

1   In iLife09_Book_Files, open the Lesson_01 folder, and drag the entire folder **L1_photos_to_import** to the iPhoto icon in the Dock.

iPhoto opens and imports all of the image files in the folder, including images in any subfolders, into the iPhoto library. When it finishes importing, iPhoto shows you the photos in the last folder that it imported.

TIP If iPhoto is open, you can also drag the files to the iPhoto window.

2   At the left of the iPhoto window, at the top of the Source list, click Events.

The photos in the seven subfolders inside the folder you dragged appear as seven Event thumbnails in the viewing area.

Although it may look as though there are only seven photos in the iPhoto library, each of the Event thumbnails actually represents a collection of photos. Next, you'll learn more about Events, including what they are, how to label them, and how to combine and divide them.

Viewing Events

In iPhoto, an Event contains a group of photos, usually related to one another by time. Suppose, for example, that you take some pictures at a party one evening and, the next day, you take pictures at a swap meet. When you import the photos from your camera, iPhoto automatically groups the photos into several Events based upon when they were taken.

> **NOTE** ▶ iPhoto creates Events by date when you import photos from a camera. However, when you import folders of images, as you've just seen, iPhoto creates an Event for each folder that it imports—regardless of the dates that the photos in the folder were taken. You can change that behavior with iPhoto's Events preferences.

Later in this lesson you'll see how you can move photos from one Event to another, how you can merge Events, and how you can split one Event into two or more Events.

You don't have to use Events to organize your photos by date, though. You can create Events in iPhoto to serve whatever organizational purpose you wish. For example, if you take a bunch of photos while on a hike with your friends, you can split those photos into several Events: one that contains photos of scenic views, one that contains photos of your fellow hikers, and so on.

Looking at Event Key Photos

When you view the Events in your iPhoto library, iPhoto uses a thumbnail of one of the photos in the Event to represent all the photos contained in that Event. iPhoto refers to this thumbnail as the Event's *key photo*. You can adjust how big the Event key photos appear in iPhoto's viewing area:

1   Click Events if something else is selected in iPhoto's Source list.

2   Drag the size slider at the bottom right of the iPhoto window to the left to make the key photos smaller, and drag it to the right to make them larger.

Smaller key photos let you see more Events in the iPhoto viewing area at one time; larger key photos provide more detail so you can more easily recognize them.

Skimming an Event

Large key photos become particularly useful when you want to *skim* the contents of an Event quickly. Skimming an Event shows you the Event's contents without actually opening the Event up. Because all of the Events remain displayed in the viewing area, you can get a look at the contents of several Events quickly and easily.

To locate a photo by skimming an Event, and to display that photo in iPhoto's viewing area, do the following:

1   Move your pointer horizontally over the Event key photo.

As the pointer moves from one side of the key photo area to the other, the area displays the different pictures contained in the Event, one by one. iPhoto also displays the Event's date and the number of pictures it contains.

PHOTO: BT FOX

2   When the photo you want to display appears as the key photo, double-click the Event.

3   Use the scrollers at the right of the viewing area to see more pictures if they don't all fit.

TIP You can change what iPhoto does when you double-click a key photo. Choose iPhoto > Preferences, click Events at the top of the dialog, and click "Magnifies photo." When you set this preference, double-clicking the key photo magnifies the picture that's currently displayed as you skim the Event. This setting also causes a Show Photos button to appear at the bottom of the key photo when your pointer is over the Event. To open the Event, click the Show Photos button.

Navigating the Viewing Area

When a single Event is open, a bar at the top of the viewing area provides the name and the date of the Event you're viewing. The bar also provides Event navigation controls, which you can manipulate as follows:

1   Click the left arrow to view the contents of the previous Event in the library.

2 Click the right arrow to fill the viewing area with the contents of the next Event in your iPhoto library.

3 Click the All Events button to view all of the Event key photos in the viewing area again.

Zooming In

When an Event is open and you see a photo that you want to examine more closely, you can quickly expand it to fill the viewing area without using the size slider at the bottom of the window:

1 Double-click an Event key photo to see all of the Event's photos, then double-click a photo to expand it.

2 Click the picture again to shrink it back down.

TIP If a photo is selected, you can press the spacebar to zoom in and out. Also, when you view an expanded photo, you can move to the other photos in the Event using the arrow keys on your keyboard.

Viewing the Entire iPhoto Library

You're not limited to seeing just the contents of individual Events or to seeing just the key photos that represent all of the Events in your library, either. Here's how to make more photos viewable:

1   Click Photos in the iPhoto Source list.

All the photos in your library appear in the viewing area. Unless your library contains only a few photos, however, they won't all fit in the viewing area.

2   Use the scrollers at the right of the viewing area to see more photos.

3   If Event titles are not visible, choose View > Event Titles.

When Event titles are visible, you can hide or show the photos that belong to individual Events by using the disclosure triangle to the left of an Event's title.

4   Click the disclosure triangle to the left of an Event's title to hide its photos. Click it again to reveal the photos.

TIP ▶ Hold down the Command key when you click the disclosure tri-angle to collapse or expand all of the Events in the viewing area at once.

5   Slide the size slider at the bottom right of the window to shrink or enlarge the photos shown in the viewing area.

TIP ▶ Clicking any of the first three items under the Recent heading in the Source list shows you specific Events and photos quickly. The item at the top of the list displays the Event you most recently opened. The item below it displays all the photos you have imported lately regardless of the Event to which they belong; the default is to show the photos imported over the last 12 months, but you can change the duration using iPhoto's preferences. The third item shows you the Event that you most recently imported.

Organizing Your Events

As the number of Events in your library increases, you may discover that an Event's key photo and date don't provide you with enough information to help you remember what the Event contains or why you created it. Giving an Event a title and providing it with a short description easily solves that problem.

Untitled Events have a date beneath their key photos when iPhoto displays
them in the viewing area. When you move your pointer over an untitled Event,
iPhoto informs you of the Event's lack of a title.

Choosing Meaningful Event Titles

Even if an Event has a title, it may not be a particularly good one. For example,
one of the Events you imported earlier in this lesson is titled Beach. That title
won't be sufficient if you ever add photos to iPhoto from a different day at the
beach. We'll change it.

The steps you follow to give an untitled Event a title or to change an Event's
title are identical:

1   In the Source list, click Events.

2   Locate the Event titled Beach in the iPhoto viewing area.

3   Click the Event's title.

     The title changes to an editable field. For an untitled Event, the field is
     empty; for an Event that has a title, the title is selected in the field.

4 Type the new title, *Stinson Beach in November*, and then press Return.

The new title appears below the Event.

Adding Event Descriptions

Giving Events meaningful titles helps you quickly identify them when you view their key photos in the viewing area. Sometimes, though, a title doesn't provide enough information, especially when you make use of iPhoto's search abilities, which you'll learn about later. For example, "Stinson Beach in November" doesn't tell you what was notable about that day. That's where Event descriptions come in.

To provide a more detailed description of an Event, use the Information pane that optionally appears at the bottom of iPhoto's Source list.

1 If the Information pane isn't showing, in the row of buttons below the Source list, click the middle button.

2 Adjust the size of the pane by dragging the dimpled separator bar above the title Information up or down.

3 Click in the description area at the bottom of the pane.

4 Type a description: *Surfing, mud-packs, and a glorious sunset on a warm November day.*

5 Click anywhere outside the description area to apply your changes.

> **TIP** You can provide an Event with a title and a description at the time you import images from a camera or a card. Fill out the two fields that appear at the bottom of the viewing area before you click one of the Import buttons.

Changing an Event's Key Photo

Ordinarily, iPhoto uses the first photo in an Event as the Event's key photo. If the key photo is not a good representation of the Event's contents, however, you can change it to one that's more suitable.

1 Open the Rope Swing Event.

2 Click one of the Event's photos, such as one of a boy swinging on a rope.

3 Choose Events > Make Key Photo.

4 Click All Events. The Event in the viewing area now shows the photo you selected.

TIP ▶ When you skim an Event, press the spacebar to make the currently visible thumbnail the Key Photo.

Splitting Events

iPhoto automatically creates Events when you import photos, according to when the photos were created. Sometimes, though, you'll find that the photos in one iPhoto Event actually represent two or more real events. For example, if you take some photos at a birthday party in the morning and then take some photos at a softball game in the afternoon, iPhoto may put the photos in the same Event when you import them from your camera. If that happens, you need to split that one Event into two Events.

You may also wish to split an Event to organize the photos along thematic lines. For example, the Saint Martin Event contains two photos of parrots. We can separate those pictures out into their own Event.

1   Open the Saint Martin Event.

2   At the bottom right of the window, drag the size slider to the right so that you can see more detail in each of the Event's photos.

3   Click the first photo you find that contains a parrot.

4   Command-click the second photo of a parrot.

iPhoto adds the second photo to your selection.

5   At the bottom left of the viewing area, click Split.

iPhoto creates a new, untitled Event that contains the photos you selected, removing them from the other Event.

6   Drag the size slider to the left so that you can see both Events in the viewing area.

7   Double-click the untitled Event's title, type *Birds of Saint Martin,* and then press Return.

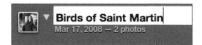

8   Click All Events.

The new Event appears in the viewing area.

Merging Events

Just as iPhoto may sometimes import photos that belong to two or more real events into one iPhoto Event, it may also break photos that belong to one real event into two or more iPhoto Events. For example, you may have taken photos on a two-day skiing trip that seem to belong to a single Event, but which iPhoto imports into two Events, one for each day of the trip. Or, you may have previously split an Event into several Events and have subsequently changed your mind. Fortunately, merging Events is even easier than splitting them.

Now that we've gone to all the trouble to split the Saint Martin Event in two, let's put those two Events back together again:

1   Click the Saint Martin Event.

2   Command-click the Birds of Saint Martin Event.

3   Choose Events > Merge Events.

A dialog appears asking you to confirm the merger.

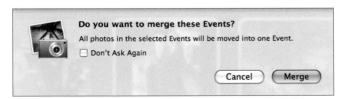

4   Click Merge.

The Events merge. The merged Event has the name of the first Event that you clicked.

TIP ▶ You can also merge Events by dragging one Event to another in the viewing area. The merged Event has the name of the Event on which you dropped the other one.

Reordering Events

iPhoto displays Events in iPhoto's viewing area in the order in which you imported them, but you can change the order. Changing the order is useful when you need to work with two or more Events that are widely separated in the viewing area, or if you want to see them organized by their titles or their dates.

Here's how to rearrange the display order of one or more Events manually:

1   Click an Event.

2   Optionally, Command-click one or more other Events.

3   Drag one of the selected Events to where you want them displayed.

As you drag, the other Events in the viewing area move out of the way to make room for the Events you're dragging.

4   Release the mouse button when the Events are positioned where you want them.

TIP ▶ Make sure not to drop the Events on another Event, because that will merge them rather than move them.

TIP ▶ You can also arrange the order in which Events are displayed by choosing an option from the View > Sort Events submenu.

Moving Photos Between Events

You may find occasions when you have two or more Events but one Event contains some photos that really belong in another Event. Here's one way to rearrange your pictures:

1   Click an Event.

2   Command-click another Event.

3   Double-click one of the Events you selected.

   Both Events open in the viewing area.

4   Drag the photos you want to move from one Event to the other.

5   Click All Events.

   iPhoto shows all of the Events in the viewing area.

   TIP▶ You can also move photos between Events using the standard Cut and Paste commands on the Edit menu or their keyboard equivalents.

Creating a New Event

When you have a number of photos scattered among your Events that really belong in an Event of their own, you can create a new Event and then move the photos to it.

1   In the Source list, click Events.

2   If an Event is selected, choose Edit > Select None.

3   Choose Events > Create Event.

A new, untitled Event is created, ready for you to put photos in it.

Identifying Photos with Faces

When you imported the photo files earlier in this lesson, you may have noticed the little spinning gear icon in the iPhoto Source list whirring away for a minute or two after the import finished. iPhoto displayed this icon to let you know that it was scanning all of the imported photos, looking for faces in each of them.

That's right: Whenever you import photos into iPhoto, it performs this quick facial recognition scan so that it's ready to help you associate each face in your photos with a name. And once you've associated a few faces with a name, iPhoto can find other photos that have the same face in them.

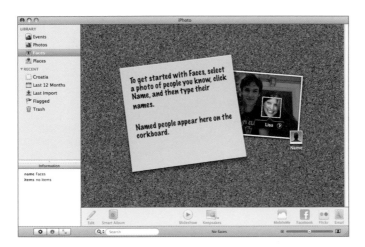

Manually Identifying Faces

Although iPhoto can usually recognize where a face appears in a photo, it can't tell you who that person is without some help. However, iPhoto is smart enough to find the same face in several photos once you've given it a little training.

So let's get started telling iPhoto who's who. You'll use the Croatia Event for this exercise.

1   Open the Croatia Event, and then choose View > Titles.

The photo titles supplied by the camera appear below each photo in the Event. You don't need to see photo titles to identify faces, but you will need to see the titles to do this exercise.

2 Click the photo titled DSC_2967 and then, at the bottom of the iPhoto window, click Name.

The viewing area displays the image with a box around the face of the boy. The label on the box says that it's an unknown face.

3 Click the label on the box and type *Aaron*, and then press Return.

The face in the picture is now associated with Aaron.

4 At the bottom of the viewing area, click Done.

You now see all of the Event photos again.

5 Click the photo titled DSC_3652, and then click Name.

6 In the unknown face label, type the letter *a*.

iPhoto presents the name Aaron as a possible label and displays a thumb-nail of the first Aaron photo.

7   Press Return to accept the proposed label, click Done, and then click the photo titled DSC_3688 in the Event.

8   Click Name, click the unknown face label for the boy in the photo, type *a*, and then press Return.

You have labeled this face as Aaron's as well.

9   Click Done.

You've now labeled three faces as being Aaron's face. Next you'll see how iPhoto uses these labeled faces to find other photos of Aaron.

Automatically Identifying Faces

iPhoto never automatically associates a name with a face on its own. What it does do is find photos that contain possible matches for faces that you've previously identified, and then it lets you decide if each possible match is correct. Here's how that works.

1   In the Source list, click Faces.

iPhoto displays the Faces corkboard, which shows all of the faces that you've previously identified.

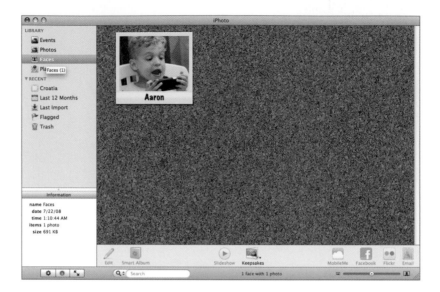

TIP ▶ You can skim each face thumbnail on the corkboard to see all of the faces associated with that name. Also, when your pointer is over a face thumbnail, you can click the circled "i" that appears at the bottom right of the thumbnail to bring up a dialog in which you can enter the full name and the email address of that person.

2   On the corkboard, double-click the Aaron thumbnail.

In the top half of the viewing area, iPhoto displays thumbnails of the photos in which you've identified Aaron's face, and it provides some photos that might also contain Aaron's face in the bottom half. However, the thumbnails show the full photo, which may make it hard to identify the faces shown.

3   In the row of buttons below the viewing area, at the left, click the right side of the View button.

The thumbnails now show just the faces that are in the photos.

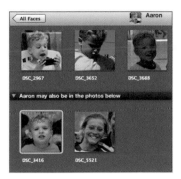

4   In the row of buttons below the viewing area, click Confirm Name.

Each thumbnail in the bottom half of the viewing area is labeled "click to confirm."

5   Click the thumbnail titled DSC_3416.

The label changes to show that the face is now identified as Aaron.

6   Hold down Option and click the thumbnail labeled DSC_5521.

When you hold down Option, the label under the thumbnail changes to "click to reject," and when you click the thumbnail, the label changes to Not Aaron.

7   Click Done.

iPhoto moves the confirmed thumbnail into the top half of the viewing area.

8   Click Done, and then click All Faces.

iPhoto displays the Faces corkboard again.

Next, you'll deal with faces that iPhoto doesn't recognize as faces.

Identifying Missing Faces

Regardless of how it's portrayed in the movies, facial recognition technology is not foolproof. Sometimes, iPhoto may not recognize that a face is in a photo, and sometimes it can mistake something else in a photo for a face. You can easily overcome these problems.

1   In the Source list, click Events, and then open the Croatia Event again.

2   Click the photo titled DSC_2629, and then click Name.

    For some reason, iPhoto didn't recognize that this picture contained a face.

3   At the bottom left of the viewing area, click Add Missing Face.

A box appears on the photo that you can move over the face that iPhoto didn't recognize. You can click anywhere inside the box to drag it, and you can use the handles at the corners of the box to expand or shrink the box.

4   Drag the box over the face, adjust its size so that it just covers the face, and then, in the label under the box, click Done.

    The box label is selected, ready for you to type a name.

5   Type the letter *a*, and when Aaron's name appears as a suggestion, press Return.

    The missing face is now labeled as Aaron.

NOTE ▸ iPhoto won't use missing faces that you've placed and labeled to help train it to recognize the same face in other photos. It only uses faces that it's recognized as faces.

Next you'll deal with an erroneously recognized face.

6   Click Done, then click the photo titled DSC_3130 and click Name.

It's not surprising that iPhoto identified this statue as having a face, but you can tell iPhoto to ignore it.

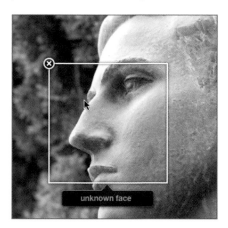

7   Move your pointer over the face box, click the close button that appears in the upper-left corner of the box, and then click Done.

The box disappears. iPhoto will no longer attempt to match this face to any of the faces that you've identified.

For practice, you may want to go through the other photos in this Event and label all the pictures of Aaron you can find. If you like, you can assign names to other faces, too, and you can eliminate face boxes for any erroneously identified faces.

Identifying Photos with Places

As you've seen, Events handles the *when* and the *what* of your photos, and Faces handles the *who*. The Places feature in iPhoto handles the *where*.

Some of the photos you imported into iPhoto already have geographic locations associated with them. iPhoto can show you on a map where these photos were shot.

1   In the Source list, click Places.

iPhoto displays a map of the world, with red pins indicating the places where geographically tagged photos in the iPhoto library have been shot.

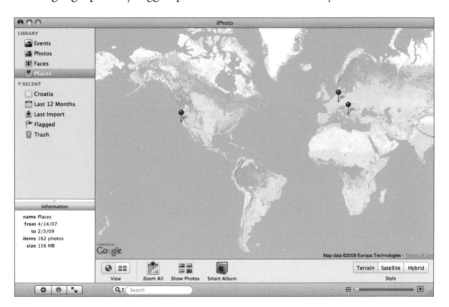

2   Click the pin on the west coast of North America.

A label appears above the pin describing its location.

3   Double-click the pin a few times.

Each time you double-click the pin, the map magnifies the pin's location so you can see more geographic detail.

4   Click once on the pin, and then on the right side of the label, click the round arrow button.

iPhoto displays all of the pictures taken at the pin's geographic location.

5   In the upper-left corner of the viewing area, click Map.

The map reappears.

TIP ▶ The Zoom All button below the map adjusts the map to show all the locations to which you have assigned pictures. The Show Photos button shows all of the photos associated with the pins that are currently displayed on the map.

6 In the lower-left corner of the viewing area, click the Column Browser View button.

At the top of the window is the Column Browser, which displays geographic categories, ranging from the most general on the left to the most specific on the right. The viewing area displays the photos associated with the category that is currently selected.

7 In the third column of geographic categories, click Ragusa.

iPhoto now shows a single photo taken in Ragusa.

In fact, there are several more photos from Ragusa among those you imported, but they haven't been geographically tagged. You'll do that next.

Placing Photos

iPhoto can use the Internet to look up the locations of thousands of places for you. If you know where a photo has been taken, you can look up the location and assign it to the photo.

1   Click Events, open the Croatia Event, and click the picture titled DSC_2629.

This photo was shot in Ragusa, Croatia, but has no location assigned to it in iPhoto.

2   Click the Info button on the lower-right corner of the photo thumbnail. A dialog appears.

3   Click the "Enter photo location" field, and then type *Ragusa*.

Two choices appear.

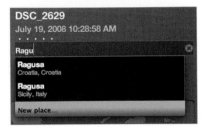

4   Click the location in Croatia, and then click Done.

The photo is assigned to that location. However, there are other photos in the Croatia Event that also can be assigned to that location. Fortunately, you don't have to do them one at a time.

5   Command-click the next three thumbnails (DSC_2674, DSC_2731 (1), and DSC_2787), and then click the Info button on the first thumbnail.

6   In the dialog, select the "Enter location of photos" checkbox, enter the same location information that you did for the first photo, and then click Done.

All three photos are assigned to Ragusa, Croatia.

You can also assign an entire Event to a location.

7 Above the viewing area, click All Events, and then click the Info button on the Soccer Event.

8 In the dialog, type *Roswell*, and in the list that appears, click Roswell, Georgia, United States.

The entire Event is assigned to that location.

9 Click Done.

Feel free to explore the Places map to see where Roswell, Georgia, is located.

Creating a Place

Occasionally, iPhoto is unable to find a location that you enter in the dialog for your photos. When that happens, you can create a new place and assign the photo to that place.

1 Click Events, and then click the Info button on the Saint Martin Event.

2 In the Location field of the information dialog, type *Saint Martin*, but don't press Return.

Notice that the Caribbean island does not show up in the list that appears as you type.

3 At the bottom of the list of proposed locations, click "New place."

An Edit My Places dialog appears with *Saint Martin* in the Google Search field. You can enter the Dutch name of the island in that field.

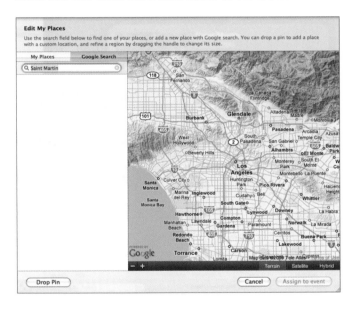

4 Type *Sint Maarten* in the search field and press Return.

The location appears in the search list on the left. The map on the right shows where it is.

TIP ▸ If the map doesn't seem to show anything, it may be zoomed in too much. Click the zoom out (–) button in the lower-left corner of the map to zoom the map out until you can see the location.

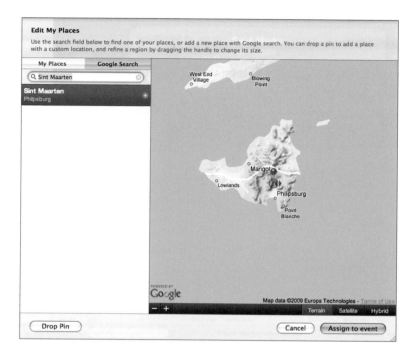

5   On the circle surrounding the map pin, drag the triangle handles away
from the pin until the circle surrounding the pin covers the whole island.

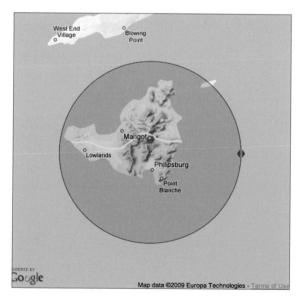

6   In the search list, click the Add (+) button to the right of the island's name, and then click Assign to Event.

The Add button beside the name in the search list adds that place to your list of custom places.

7   Click Done.

Now that you've assigned the right location, you can change its spelling to the English equivalent.

8   Choose Window > Manage My Places.

9   In the Edit My Places dialog, in the list on the left, click Sint Maarten.

The location appears in the map on the right and the name becomes editable in the list.

10   Type *Saint Martin*, press Return, and then click Done.

Now that you've imported photos, viewed and organized Events, located and labeled some faces, and assigned and added some places, you can take a break. You've earned it.

Lesson Review

1.   What is the rule of thirds and how will adhering to it improve your pictures?

2.   What is GPS?

3.   How can you control whether iPhoto opens automatically when you attach a camera to your Mac?

4. How can you tell if an item to be imported from your camera is a video rather than a still image?

5. How can you import image files into iPhoto?

6. What is an Event?

7. How can you see the faces that iPhoto has recognized in a photo?

8. How can you change the name of a place?

Answers

1. The rule of thirds helps improve a photo's composition by positioning the photo's subject a third of the way from the sides, top, or bottom of the photo rather than in the direct center.

2. GPS is the Global Positioning System, consisting of a group of satellites that transmit signals that terrestrial receivers can use to pinpoint locations. Some cameras contain GPS receivers.

3. Open iPhoto's preferences and choose iPhoto from the "Connecting camera opens" menu in General preferences.

4. Video thumbnails have a small white video camera icon in their lower-left corners.

5. You can import image files either by dragging them to the iPhoto icon in the Dock, or by dragging them to the iPhoto window.

6. A collection of pictures taken around the same time.

7. Select the photo and then click the Names button.

8. Choose Window > Manage My Places, and then edit the name in the Edit My Places list.

2

Lesson Files | No additional files

Time | This lesson takes approximately 60 minutes to complete.

Goals | Compare and rate photos

Give your photos keywords

Search for photos by name, keyword, or rating

Make quick fixes to photos

Retouch and color-correct photos

Use special effects

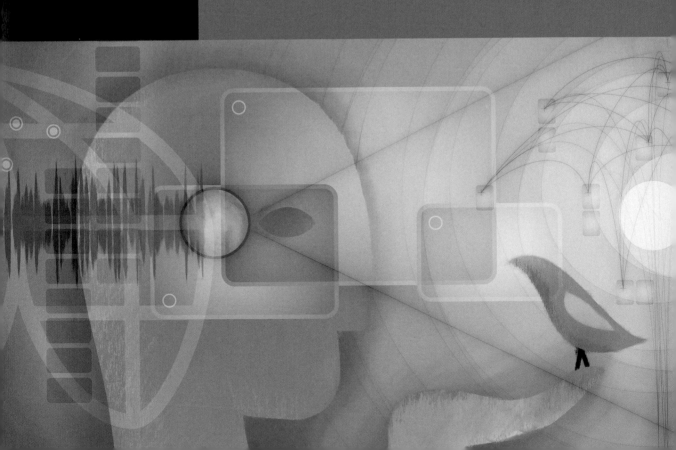

Reviewing and Improving Your Photos

When you have a digital camera, you can snap away to your heart's content and never spend a penny on film or developing costs. But unless you're an incorrigible pack rat, you eventually have to spend something.

That something is your time, as you go through the myriad free photos you blithely shot and divide them into the ones that make you say, "Yay!" "Okay," "Meh," or "Ow! My eyes! They burn!" (Yes, even the best photographers shoot pictures that fall into that last category.)

Good photos are never a problem. But what about the rest?

In this lesson you'll see how you can find your good photos quickly, improve your good-enough photos, salvage your marginal shots, and dispatch your failures to a well-deserved and quiet oblivion.

Comparing Photos

In the previous lesson you saw how you can zoom in to a photo in the iPhoto window to examine it more closely. In this exercise you'll compare two or more photos in detail using iPhoto's full-screen view.

1   Open the Saint Martin Event, and then select the two orange butterfly photos, DSC_0983 and DSC_0994.

2   Below the Source list, click the Full Screen button, the rightmost of the three buttons.

iPhoto blacks out everything else on your screen and displays the selected photos side by side in full-screen view.

3   Move your pointer to the top of the screen.

iPhoto displays the menu bar and a photo browser at the top of the screen.

4 In the photo browser, click the photo of the black-and-red butterfly.

The photo of the black-and-red butterfly replaces the photo with the white border.

5 In the photo browser, Command-click the photo of the blue butterfly.

The photo you clicked joins the two other photos on the screen.

6 Move your pointer to the bottom of the screen.

iPhoto displays the full-screen view toolbar.

7 In the toolbar, near its right side, drag the size slider to the right.

A small Navigation window appears beside the blue butterfly photo, and the photo is magnified.

TIP ▶ You can click in the Navigation window to change what part of the magnified image is displayed.

8   Click the black-and-red butterfly photo, and then click the close button at the top left of the white border surrounding the photo.

Only two photos are displayed.

NOTE ▶ When you view two or more images in full-screen view, the selected image is always surrounded by a white border that has a close button. If only one image is displayed, there is no border.

9   Press Escape.

The full-screen view is replaced with the normal view.

TIP ▶ You can also click the close button at the right side of the full-screen toolbar to dismiss the full-screen view.

As you can see, the full-screen view can give you a very close look at your photos without any distractions.

Rating Your Photos

You can assign star ratings to your pictures so you can see at a glance which ones are your really exceptional pictures and which are your not-so-exceptional pictures. Ratings help you find the best (or worst) pictures in your library more quickly.

Let's assign star ratings to a few of the pictures in the Saint Martin Event:

1   Choose View > Rating or press Command-Shift-R.

Nothing much changes if you haven't rated any pictures yet. However, if your pointer is over a photo, or if a photo is selected, you'll see five dots below the photo, indicating that the photo has no stars.

2   In the Saint Martin Event, under photo DSC_1055, on the row of dots, click the fourth dot from the left.

Four stars appear beneath the photo.

3   Select DSC_0965, DSC_0894, and DSC_0994, and then choose a five-star rating from the Photos > My Rating submenu.

The selected pictures all display a five-star rating.

TIP   To sort the pictures by ratings, choose View > Sort Photos > By Rating.

Assigning Keywords to Your Photos

A common way to categorize items in a large collection, such as a picture library, is to assign *keywords* to them. Keywords are simple tags consisting of a word or two, such as *vacation* or *night shot*. You can assign several keywords to the same picture, allowing the picture to belong to several categories simultaneously.

Try this technique on pictures in the Soccer Event:

1   Open the Soccer Event, and then choose View > Keywords or press Command-Shift-K.

An area for keywords now appears below each photo.

2 Choose Window > Show Keywords.

A Keywords window appears above the iPhoto window. It already has several keywords available, but you're going to add one that it doesn't have.

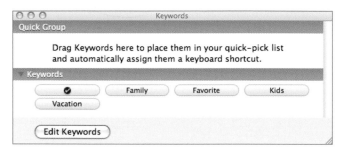

3 At the lower left of the Keywords window, click Edit Keywords.

The window changes appearance to provide a scrolling list of keywords that you can edit.

4 At the lower left of the window, click the Add (+) button.

A new entry appears near the bottom of the keywords list, with the keyword selected, ready for you to edit.

5 Type *Action* and then click OK.

The new keyword appears in the Quick Group area of the window. Notice that it has an "a" associated with it. iPhoto has assigned that letter as a shortcut so you can quickly assign that keyword to a photo selection by typing that letter when the Keywords window is open.

6   In the iPhoto window, select photos DSC_6105, DSC_9002, DSC_9009, and DSC_9032, and then click the Action button in the Quick Group area of the Keywords window.

The pictures all have the Action keyword assigned to them. You could, of course, have simply typed *a* to assign the keyword to the photos.

TIP ▶ You can remove a keyword from a photo by clicking its button in the Keywords window, or typing its shortcut, a second time.

Searching Your iPhoto Library

There's not much point to describing your photos, rating them, and attaching keywords to them unless you can use those descriptions, ratings, or keywords to find the photos you want. But of course you can; iPhoto offers a number of ways to search your photo collection.

Searching with Text

You can search your photo collection for the text in any title, keyword, or description. For example, in Lesson 1 you used the word "mud-pack" in your description of an Event. iPhoto can find the photos in that Event instantly:

1 Click Events in the Source list so that all the Events appear in the viewing area, and then choose Edit > Select None.

2 Click in the search field at the bottom of the iPhoto window.

3 Type the word *mud*.

As you type, the viewing area shows the photos that match what you're typing. By the time you finish typing the word, only the photos from that Event remain in the viewing area.

NOTE ▶ You can use the same techniques to describe an individual picture that you used to describe the Event in Lesson 1.

Searching by Date

But you aren't just limited to text searches. The simple-looking search field can search for other things as well. When you click the magnifying glass icon to the left of the field, a pop-up menu appears from which you can select other ways to search your photo library.

Let's try searching for photos by date:

1   Choose Date from the search field's pop-up menu.

The Calendar pane appears. The highlighted months are those that match pictures in the library.

2   If the year displayed is not 2008, in the upper right of the Calendar pane, click the left arrow until 2008 appears.

3   Click March.

The search field contains the range of dates in March, and the photos that match those dates appear in the viewing area.

4   In the Calendar pane's upper-left corner, click the small triangle.

The Calendar pane now shows the days in March 2008. The highlighted days are those that have matching photos.

5   Click one of the highlighted days to see the photos that match that date.

Searching by Keyword

Now try searching for photos that have particular keywords associated
with them.

1   Choose Keyword from the search field's pop-up menu.

The Keywords pane appears.

2   In the Keywords pane, click Action.

The photos to which you applied the Action keyword appear in the
viewing area.

Searching by Rating

You can also search the photo library by the ratings you've given to photos.

1   Choose Rating from the search field's pop-up menu.

The search field contains five small dots.

2   Click the second dot from the right.

Four stars appear in the field, and the photos that have ratings of four or
more stars appear in the viewing area.

Hiding Unwanted Photos

Not every photo is a gem, nor even a presentable pebble. When you import
the photos you've shot, it's common to end up with some that you don't want.
They may be too blurry, or obscured by your hand or a passerby who stepped

into the frame at exactly the wrong moment. You can, of course, discard the photo, but iPhoto also has several features you can use to protect your eyes from an unattractive or unusable image without deleting it.

The easiest way to preserve your aesthetic vision without deleting these photos permanently is to conceal them from view. For example, the Rope Swing Event contains several pictures of boys swinging on a rope swing. One of those pictures, though an otherwise fine action shot, is blurry and not framed very well. Although you could discard the photo (as you'll see how to do later in this lesson), you might not be ready to take that step, so you can hide the photo instead:

1   In the search field, click the x to clear the field, and then type *8722*.

The blurry photo is titled DSC_8722; iPhoto's search feature takes you right to it.

2   Click the photo to select it.

3   At the left side of the toolbar at the bottom of the viewing area, click Hide.

The photo disappears and the viewing area is empty. However, a message has appeared in the upper right of the viewing area. This message, though it doesn't look like it, is actually a button. When an Event or a search result contains some hidden photos, iPhoto lets you know about it with a message button in the upper right of the viewing area.

Show 1 hidden photo   Hide 1 hidden photo

4   Click the hidden photo message.

The photo reappears, and the text of the message button changes. Notice that the photo has a bright orange X to indicate that, although you can see it, it is still "hidden."

Unhiding Photos

If you can hide photos, it stands to reason that you can unhide them. Here's how:

1   Click the hidden photo that you've made visible.

The Hide button on the toolbar changes.

2   Click Unhide.

The hidden photo marker goes away, and the Unhide button again becomes a Hide button.

Throwing Photos Away

If you really don't want the photo hanging around anymore, hidden or not, you can discard it. Here's one way to do that:

1   Drag the photo to the Trash in the Source list.

2   When the Trash is framed by a line, release the mouse button.

> **TIP** ▶ Another way to put a photo in the Trash is to select the photo in the viewing area and press Delete.

Restoring a Photo from the Trash

Putting a photo in the iPhoto Trash from an Event, a search result, or the Photos collection removes it from your iPhoto library. As with your Mac's own Trash, however, you have to empty the iPhoto Trash to completely discard the photo. Until you empty the iPhoto Trash, you can always restore the photo to your library by doing the following:

1   In the Source list, click Trash.

    The photos in the Trash appear in the viewing area.

2   Click the photo you want to restore.

3   Choose Photos > Restore to Photo Library.

NOTE ▶ To actually empty the iPhoto Trash and discard unwanted photos forever, choose iPhoto > Empty iPhoto Trash. But remember, once you do that, they're gone for good.

Cropping Photos

Cropping is the act of trimming the edges of a photo. You may want to crop a photo for several reasons:

▶   To improve the photo's composition

▶   To change the photo's shape

▶   To remove unwanted elements from the photo

▶   To highlight an important detail in the photo

In this exercise, you're going to crop a photo for all of these reasons.

1   In the search field, type *9009*, and then click photo DSC_9009 in the viewing area.

This photo, displaying a young athlete in flight, should be the only photo in the viewing area.

2   In the toolbar below the viewing area, click the Edit button.

The iPhoto edit view appears. The photo expands to fill the viewing area, a collection of editing tools appears in the toolbar below the photo, and thumbnails of the photos returned by the search appear in a browser above the photo—because only one photo matches the search term, only one photo thumbnail appears. You'll crop the photo to highlight the young athlete.

3   Click the Crop button in the edit view toolbar.

A frame is superimposed on the photo, and a small, semitransparent cropping box appears. A pop-up menu in the Crop tool is labeled with the photo's current dimensions. You can drag the cropping box to move it anywhere you like on your screen.

4 Click the pop-up menu in the Crop tool, choose 4 x 3 (Book), and then click the pop-up menu again and choose "Constrain as portrait."

```
    1920 × 1200  (Display)
    3008 × 2000  (Original)
    2 × 3  (iPhone)
    3 × 5
    4 × 3  (DVD)
✓   4 × 3  (Book)
    4 × 6  (Postcard)
    5 × 7  (L, 2L)
    8 × 10
    16 × 9  (HD)
    16 × 20
    20 × 30  (Poster)
    Square
    Custom…

    Constrain as landscape
✓   Constrain as portrait
```

The Crop tool's pop-up menu offers several choices for the cropping box's aspect ratio; that is, the ratio between the box's horizontal and vertical dimensions. Choosing the 4 x 3 aspect ratio produces a box that is four units along one dimension and three units along the other. Choosing "Constrain as portrait" makes the longer dimension of the rectangle the vertical one.

5 In the Crop tool, select the Constrain checkbox if necessary.

When you select Constrain, changing the size of the cropping box maintains the aspect ratio you selected. When the picture's original dimensions are selected in the Crop tool's menu and Constrain is selected as well, cropping the picture changes the picture's size but retains its shape.

6 Click somewhere in the middle of the box and drag it to the right until the athlete is centered in the frame.

When your pointer is inside the cropping box, dragging slides the box over the picture. It also displays thin guidelines that divide the box into thirds both horizontally and vertically. These lines help you compose your cropped picture using the "rule of thirds" described in Lesson 1.

7 If necessary, drag the cropping box by one of its corners to adjust its size so that the athlete fits snugly in the box.

8 In the Crop tool, click Apply.

The Crop tool and the cropping box go away and the cropped picture fills the viewing area.

9 In the edit view toolbar, click Done to save your changes and to see the iPhoto viewing area again.

> **TIP** If the iPhoto window seems too cramped for you when you edit photos, you can use the editing tools available in the full-screen view, described earlier in this lesson. The tools are the same as those available in the iPhoto edit view.

Straightening Photos

An otherwise good-looking photo may not be quite on the level. It's easy to take a crooked photo: When you press your camera's shutter button, for example, you may unconsciously tilt the camera slightly in the direction that you press. The result is a photo that is slightly tilted. Many otherwise-perfect photos suffer from this flaw.

You can straighten out such photos with iPhoto's Straighten tool.

1 In the search field, type *5521*, and then click photo DSC_5521 in the viewing area.

This photo, displaying a group photo of a soccer team posing with their mascot, should be the only photo in the viewing area.

2 Click the Edit button in the toolbar.

3 In the edit view toolbar, click the Straighten button.

The Straighten tool's slider appears in the viewing area, and a grid of yellow lines is superimposed on the photo.

4   Drag the slider to the left.

As you drag the slider, the photo begins to tilt in the direction that you're dragging.

5   Continue dragging until the grandstand seats in the background align with the horizontal grid lines.

6   Click the close button at the left side of the Straighten tool.

The grid lines and the tool disappear.

7   In the edit view toolbar, click Done.

> **NOTE** ▶ When you straighten a photo, iPhoto must trim the photo's top, bottom, and sides in order to keep them straight as well. Take a close look at the photo you just straightened: The white heel on a player's shoe near the bottom left has been cropped, and the right and the left of the photo have been lopped off as well. The more severely you tilt a photo to straighten it, the more you'll lose from its edges.

TIP ▶ You can also rotate photos in 90° increments to the left or right. Although some cameras, such as the iPhone, can detect camera orientation, others don't, and when you turn such a camera sideways to take a portrait-style photo, iPhoto imports the photo sideways. To rotate a photo 90°, simply select it and click the Rotate button on the iPhoto toolbar. Hold down Option when you click Rotate to reverse the direction that iPhoto rotates the photo.

Touching Up Photos

Cameras can be cruel. Not only can they reveal, in all-too-visible detail, every blemish, wrinkle, or scar on your face; they can even add new flaws—especially when the camera's automatic exposure or flash is involved.

In this part of the lesson, you're going to undo some of the flaws that either nature or the camera has imposed.

Enhancing Photos

Your eye doesn't see what the camera does: Your brain processes what you look at, compensating for things like poor illumination, tinted light, and obscuring haze. As the eye and brain work together, you end up seeing a much richer image than the one your eye started out with.

Your poor camera, on the other hand, doesn't have the power of your brain to adjust its photos with the same subtlety or dexterity—the photos it produces may not match in color or clarity what you remember seeing when you took them. The Enhance tool in iPhoto can help align your brain-eye combination with your camera's more limited abilities.

1   In the search field, type *6761*, click photo DSC_6761 in the viewing area, and then click the Edit button.

This photo, displaying a runner, is slightly underexposed and dull-looking. This can be fixed with a single click.

2 In the edit view toolbar, click the Enhance button.

The Enhance tool uses predefined operations that can adjust a photo's exposure and colors. Often, this tool is all you need to improve a drab-looking photo.

3 Click Done to close edit view.

TIP ▶ If you want to see the technical details of what the Enhance tool has done to a photo, take a look at the Adjust pane in the iPhoto edit view. It displays the precise adjustments that the Enhance tool has made. Later in this lesson you'll use the Adjust pane to make more detailed changes to a photo's color, brightness, and contrast.

Removing Red-Eye from Photos

A very common photographic problem is the phenomenon known as *red-eye*. When you take a photo using a flash attachment mounted directly on the camera, the light from the flash can travel into your subject's eyes, brightly illuminating the blood vessels at the back of the subject's eyeballs. The iPhoto Red-Eye tool can get the red out.

1   In the search field, type *6014*, and then click photo DSC_6014 in the viewing area.

   Each of the three soccer players in this photo has minor red-eye issues.

2   In the edit view toolbar, click Edit.

3   Slide the size slider at the bottom of the iPhoto window far enough to the right to allow you to see one of the pair of eyes in the photo in detail, using the Navigation window that appears as needed to keep the eyes in view.

   TIP ▶ Pressing the spacebar turns your pointer into a hand when it's over the viewing area. While the spacebar is down, you can drag the image around the viewing area to position it instead of using the Navigation window.

4   Click the Red-Eye button in the edit view toolbar.

   A Red-Eye tool appears over the viewing area, and your pointer becomes a large circle.

5   On the Red-Eye tool, use the size slider to shrink the circle to the size of one of the pupils.

6   Position the circle over one of the eyes and click.

The part of the eye inside the circle loses its red.

Next, you'll use the Auto function of the Red-Eye tool. This function uses the face recognition information that iPhoto has about a photo to find the eyes in each face and to remove the red from them.

7   Slide the size slider at the bottom of the iPhoto window far enough to the left so that you can see the eyes of each person in the photo.

8   On the Red-Eye tool, click Auto.

All of the eyes lose their red cast.

9   In the edit view toolbar, click Done.

> **NOTE ▶** The Red-Eye tool eliminates the red component of any area that you click in a photo, whether it is an eye or not. If you're curious, try clicking the red parts of any photo to see what it does.

Retouching Your Photos

Next, you'll engage in a different kind of touchup: removing a stray hair from a close-up portrait using iPhoto's Retouch tool.

1   Open the Katie Event, click the photo Katie 57, and then click Edit in the toolbar.

This photo is actually a detail cropped from a larger photo, and it lacks some resolution, which should present the Retouch tool with a worthy challenge.

2   Drag the iPhoto window's size slider all the way to the right so you can see the child's face magnified in the viewing area.

Notice the long black strand of hair across her face that stretches from her left eye down to her mouth.

3   Click the Retouch button in the toolbar.

The Retouch tool appears and your pointer becomes an open circle.

4   Adjust the Retouch size slider so that the pointer becomes about twice as wide as the strand of hair.

5   Starting just below her eye, drag the pointer along the strand, then release the mouse button.

As you drag, the pointer paints a light color over the strand. When you release the mouse button, the light color and the strand both vanish.

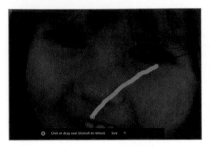 

6 Optionally, retouch the hair strand above her eye.

7 Click Done, and then, above the viewing area, click All Events.

> **NOTE ▶** The Retouch tool continuously calculates an average of the color and texture of the area surrounding the pointer as you drag, and it applies that average to the area under the pointer. The result is usually a smooth blend that eliminates small flaws and blemishes. However, when you drag the tool over the edge of an object, you'll often see strange smears and similar artifacts appear. Experiment with this tool on various parts of an image to see what it can and can't smooth.

Applying Adjustments to Improve a Photo

Among the editing tools that iPhoto provides, the Adjust pane may be the most powerful: It gives you individual control over brightness, exposure, contrast, color saturation and vibrancy, definition, highlights and shadows, sharpness, noise, color temperature and tint, and more. What's more, the changes you make are nondestructive. iPhoto remembers your changes and reapplies them to the original when you view the photo, so that the photo's quality doesn't degrade because of successive changes. And to top it all off, you can copy the settings you make in one photo and apply them to another.

Adjusting Exposure and Levels

Let's start with exposure—the lightness or darkness of the whole photo—and the range between the lightest and darkest levels of that photo. You'll use these controls to shed a little light on an underexposed photo.

1   Type *7540* into the search field, click photo PA147540.jpg, and then click Edit.

2   Click Adjust.

The Adjust pane opens. At its top is the Levels histogram, which displays the brightness range of the photo's colors. Below it are sliders that let you set the darkest value, the lightest value, and the midpoint value of that brightness range. Below that is the Exposure slider, which adjusts the total brightness level of the photo. As you move these, or any other sliders on the pane, the histogram changes to show you the current brightness distribution in the photo. Notice how the darkness of the photo is reflected by the color curves in the histogram, which are all bunched up at the left.

3   Drag the Exposure slider to the right until the value on the right reads about 2.55.

The photo brightens, and the histogram spreads the colors out along the entire range displayed.

4   Under the histogram, drag the rightmost slider left until its value reads 90%, drag the leftmost slider right until it's set at 5%, and then drag the midpoint slider about a third of the way to the left.

The brighter parts of the image get brighter and the darker parts get darker.

5 Press Shift and then release it.

The original photo appears when you press the key and the modified photo reappears when you release it. The Shift key allows you to compare your changes with the original photo quickly.

Adjusting Contrast and Definition

Contrast describes the difference between the light and the dark parts of a photo. The Level sliders adjust the range between brightness and darkness in a photo, whereas the Contrast slider adjusts the distribution within that range.

The Definition tool adjusts the contrasts between adjacent areas within a photo. Increasing the definition can make small details more visible.

1 Magnify the view so you can see details in the photo more clearly.

2 Drag the Contrast slider to the left until its value is –25.

The photo brightens slightly and the histogram shows the redistribution of the light and dark values in the photo. Reducing the contrast makes the distribution of light and dark values less evenly spread across the histogram.

3   Drag the Definition slider to the right until its value is 50.

The photo looks more vivid as the difference between adjacent bright and dark areas increases. The histogram reflects this change by making each of its color graphs more jagged.

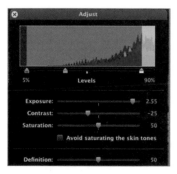

4   Click Done.

You'll adjust a different picture in the next exercise.

Adjusting Highlights and Shadows

When you take a photo in bright light, exposure settings that capture details in the most brightly lit part of the photo make details in the shadows hard to see. Similarly, exposing a photo to reveal details in the shadows can make the brightest parts of the photo wash out.

The Shadows control holds the brightest parts of the photo steady while increasing the exposure of the dark areas. Similarly, the Highlights control keeps the photo's dark areas constant while reducing the exposure in the brighter parts.

Two photos in the Stinson Beach in November Event demonstrate how these controls can reveal subtle details otherwise lost in the glare or the darkness.

1   Open the Stinson Beach in November Event, click the photo Summer_in_ November 013, click Edit, and then click Adjust.

2   Drag the Shadows slider to the right until its value is 50.

As you drag, notice how the dark-green translucency in the curling wave to the left of the surfer lightens, while the brighter areas of the photo remain unchanged. Watch what happens in the Levels histogram as well.

3   Click Done, click the photo Summer_in_November 006, click Edit, and then click Adjust.

4   Drag the Highlights slider to the right until its value is 50.

As you drag, you can see more details in the bright white sea foam appear, while the darker areas of the photo stay the same. Again, see how the curves in the histogram change: the rightmost part alters while the left remains almost untouched.

PHOTO: BT FOX

5   Click Done.

Adjusting Saturation

The Saturation slider controls how intense the colors are in a photo. You can use it to drain the colors from a photo, or to make the photo's colors glow garishly. Selecting the "Avoid saturating the skin tones" checkbox below the slider changes the control's behavior so that its effect is more muted and less apt to make any people in the photo look wildly painted or ghostly gray.

> **NOTE** ▶ Some image editing programs refer to saturation controls that leave skin tones and neutral colors untouched as *vibrancy controls*.

You'll use a photo from the Rope Swing Event to experiment with the Saturation control.

1   Open the Rope Swing Event, click the photo DSC_8718, click Edit, and then click Adjust.

2   If "Avoid saturating the skin tones" is selected, deselect it, and then drag
    the Saturation slider all the way to the the right.

    As you drag, you can see the colors in the photo intensify dramatically.

3   Drag the Saturation slider all the way to the left.

    The photo loses color, and the three separate color curves in the histogram
    line up as one.

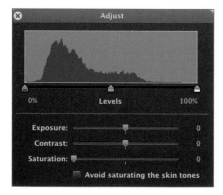

4   Select "Avoid saturating the skin tones."

    Color returns to the boy's face, but the greenery behind him
    remains colorless.

5   At the bottom of the Adjust pane, click Reset.

The settings in the pane all return to their default values, and the photo returns to its original appearance.

You'll use the same photo in the next exercise.

Adjusting Temperature and Tint

Your brain is pretty good at compensating for the color of the light that illuminates what you see; put on a pair of sunglasses, for example, and in just a few minutes you adjust to the color shifts that the glasses impose.

Modern automatic cameras try to do the same thing, eliminating slight color variations in lighting to produce photos with more accurate colors, but sometimes they just don't quite get it right. When that happens, a photo ends up with a color cast that is bluer, or greener, or redder, than it should be. The effect is most apparent in the white or gray areas of the photo, but it affects the entire image.

You can drag the Temperature and Tint sliders to adjust the color cast of a photo. The Temperature slider controls how warm/orange or cool/blue the photo looks. The Tint slider controls the balance between green and red in the photo.

However, there's an easier way to adjust these sliders: the White Point eyedropper tool. When you click an area in the photo that should be a neutral white or gray, iPhoto adjusts both sliders to make the place that you clicked colorless. As a result, the color cast of the entire photo changes.

You'll use the White Point eyedropper tool in this exercise to remove the slightly orange cast from the photo.

1   Near the bottom left of the Adjust pane, click the Eyedropper button.

Your cursor becomes a crosshair, and the White Point eyedropper tool appears at the bottom of the viewing area.

Now you need to find a neutral gray area in the photo. There's a small shiny area in the boy's wet hair above his right eye that will do.

2   In the toolbar, drag the size slider to the right, and then use the Navigation window to position the view so that you can see the boy's hair above his right eye.

3   Click the shiny area.

The Temperature and Tint sliders move, and the photo becomes less orange.

NOTE ▶ If you can't find the small shiny area in the boy's hair, you can manually adjust the Temperature slider to –21, and the Tint slider to –4.

4   Click the close button on the White Point eyedropper tool, and then drag the size slider all the way to the left.

Next, you'll apply these settings to another photo in the Event.

5   At the bottom of the Adjust pane, click Copy, and then, in the toolbar at the bottom-right of the viewing area, click the left arrow.

A photo of a different boy appears.

6   At the bottom of the Adjust pane, click Paste.

The Temperature and Tint sliders take on the values that you copied, and the photo becomes less orange.

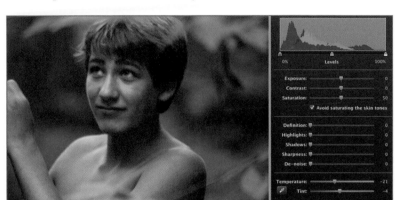

7   In the toolbar at the bottom right of the viewing area, click the right arrow.

You'll use photo DSC_8718 again for the final exercise with the Adjust pane.

Adjusting Sharpness and Noise

Even a modern digital camera with sophisticated state-of-the-art autofocus technology can produce a blurry photo if you move the camera slightly when you snap the shutter. And photos taken in low light can show digital noise when you pump up their exposure using the Adjust pane's Exposure or Shadows sliders.

You can't completely eliminate these problems with photo editing tools, but you can mitigate them with the Sharpness and De-noise sliders.

The Sharpness tool analyzes the color and brightness values of pixels near each other in a photo, and when there is a substantial difference, it emphasizes them. The result is that the edges in a photo appear sharper. The De-noise tool analyzes the color and brightness values of neighboring pixels and reduces the differences between them. The result is that noisy speckles in a photo appear blurred, becoming less obvious.

Rather than attempt to improve a photo with these tools, the effects of which are subtle, you'll take a close look at a highly textured portion of photo DSC_8718, which should still be open in the viewing area, to see how these tools work.

1   In the toolbar, drag the size slider all the way to the right, and then use the Navigation window to position the view so that you can see the sawed-off edge of the board nailed to the tree.

You'll adjust the sliders to control the appearance of the wood grain in the board.

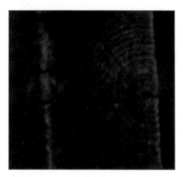

2   Drag the Sharpness slider all the way to the right.

The grain in the wood becomes more pronounced as the Sharpness tool amplifies the differences between nearby pixels.

3   Drag the Sharpness slider all the way back to the left, and then drag the De-noise slider all the way to the right.

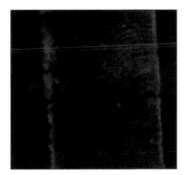

The grain in the wood almost completely vanishes as the De-noise tool smoothes the sharp gradations between nearby pixels.

4   Drag the De-noise slider all the way back to the left, and then click Done.

This concludes your work with the Adjust pane. Now it's time to play.

Using Effects

iPhoto includes an Effects pane that presents a number of interesting and amusing visual effects you can apply to photos. Some effects can be applied multiple times to intensify what they do. Other effects act like switches: They're either on or off. You might want to apply effects, for example, to photos that you plan to use for cards, or books, or calendars (you'll find out how to make these things with iPhoto in Lesson 4).

Rather than work through an exercise, you should simply pick a photo or two and try some effects out. Below you can see a few different effects that have been applied to a photo of the young child from the Katie Event, Katie 48. Have fun!

Black-and-white child   Antique child   Child with color boosted four times

Child with edges blurred seven times   Child with matte applied five times

Lesson Review

1. What does *cropping* mean?
2. Give a reason for cropping a picture.
3. What is *red-eye*?
4. What is a common cause for crooked pictures?
5. What is *color cast*?
6. Which iPhoto tool is used to correct color cast problems?
7. Where in a picture might the Retouch tool produce odd results?
8. Describe a side effect of using the Straighten tool.

Answers

1. Cropping is the act of trimming the edges from a picture.
2. There are several reasons to crop a picture: To improve the composition, to remove unwanted elements from the picture, to highlight a specific detail in the picture, and to change the picture's shape.
3. Red-eye is the glowing-eye effect created when the light from the camera's flash illuminates the blood vessels at the back of the photographic subject's eyes.
4. Crooked pictures are often caused by inadvertently tilting the camera when pressing the shutter button.
5. A color cast is a tinting of the picture created when the camera unsuccessfully compensates for the color of the light present when the picture is taken.
6. The White Point eyedropper tool in the Adjust pane is used to correct color cast problems.
7. Using the Retouch tool along the edge of an object in a picture can cause odd artifacts and smears to appear.
8. The Straighten tool has the side effect of slightly cropping the picture.

3

Lesson Files No additional files

Time This lesson takes approximately 60 minutes to complete.

Goals Create albums and Smart Albums

Share your photos on a network

Sync photos to an iPod or iPhone

Display your photos in a screen saver

Build a photo slideshow

Put your photos online with MobileMe, Flickr, and Facebook

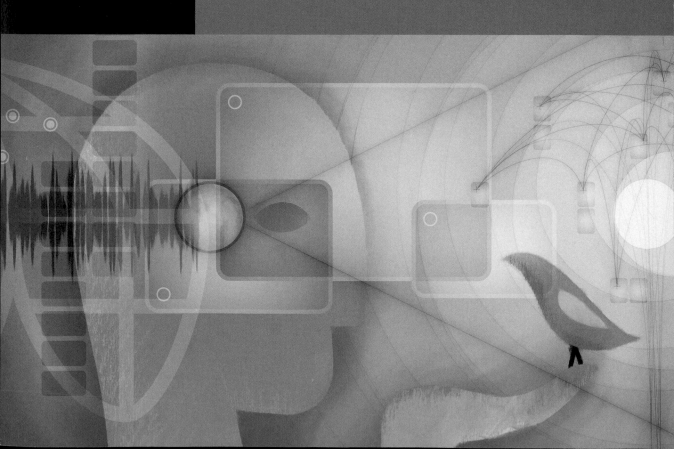

Sharing Your Photos

The seagulls in the film *Finding Nemo* know only one word, which they repeat endlessly to great comic effect: "Mine!"

But the more highly evolved among us learn the pleasures of sharing even as early as preschool.

In this lesson, you'll take the photos that you've collected, labeled, cropped, enhanced, retouched, color-corrected, and stylized and share them with your family, your friends, and the rest of the world—or at least that part of the rest of the world that has a network connection.

Making a Photo Album

Events are a great way of sorting the photos in your iPhoto library into manageable and useful containers, but they have one important limitation: A photo can be stored in only one Event at a time.

However, iPhoto offers you another, more flexible, organizing feature: *albums*.

Albums are similar to playlists in iTunes. Just as you can put the same song into as many iTunes playlists as you like, so you can put the same photo into as many iPhoto albums as you like. And, just as removing a song from an iTunes playlist doesn't remove the song from your iTunes music library, removing a photo from an iPhoto album doesn't remove it from your iPhoto library.

To see how this works, you'll make an album from some of the photos in the Soccer Event.

1   Open the Soccer Event and, if necessary, use the size slider at the bottom of the window to see picture details more clearly.

2   Click the first picture you see that has soccer action in it.

     In the previous lesson, you added the Action keyword to those photos. If keywords are not visible, you can choose View > Keywords or press Command-Shift-K.

3   Command-click two more photos that depict soccer action.

     You don't have to select all the photos that depict soccer action right now.

4   Choose File > New Album From Selection.

A dialog appears that offers to create a new album containing the selected photos for you and gives you the option of giving the album a name.

5 Type *Soccer action* in the Name field and click Create.

An Albums heading appears in the Source list, and under it is the new Soccer action album.

6 Click the album to see its contents in the viewing area.

7 In the Source list, under the Recent heading, click Soccer to see the Event and to verify that the photos placed in the new album haven't been removed from the Event.

Changing an Album's Contents

Once you've created an album, you can freely add photos to it and remove photos from it, because any changes you make to the album won't affect the contents of your iPhoto library.

Let's add the remaining soccer action photos to the Soccer action album:

1 Scroll through the Soccer Event until you find another action photo, and then click it.

2 Find another soccer action photo in the Event and Command-click it.

3 Drag one of the selected photos toward the Soccer action album in the Source list.

As you drag, a translucent image of the photo follows your pointer with a number on the image telling you how many photos you're dragging. All of the selected photos are included in the drag. A blue border frames the album when the pointer is over it.

4   Drop the photos on the album.

5   Click the album to see its contents in the viewing area.

It's even easier to remove photos from an album.

6   In the Soccer action album, click a photo to select it.

7   Press Delete.

If you prefer to use menus, you can choose Photos > Delete From Album instead.

TIP If you change your mind, or if you delete the wrong pictures, you can choose Edit > Undo Delete Photo From Album before you make any other changes.

Arranging an Album's Photos

You can arrange the order in which the photos in an album appear. Albums, as you'll discover later, can serve as the basis for several types of projects, such as slideshows and photo books, so being able to put an album's photos in an appropriate order is essential.

For example, inspired by Benjamin Button, you might want to arrange the photos in the Soccer action album in reverse chronological order. iPhoto provides menu commands to do just that.

1   In the Source list, click the Soccer action album.

2 Choose View > Sort Photos > By Date, and then choose View > Sort Photos > Descending.

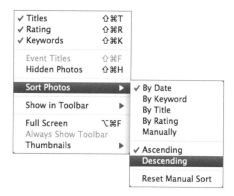

On the other hand, you may want to highlight the soccer photo that you cropped in Lesson 2 by making it be the first photo in the album. You can do that with a simple drag.

3 Click photo DSC_9009 and drag it to the left of the first picture in the album.

4 Release the mouse button.

The cropped photo appears in its new position in the album.

Creating Empty Albums

Often, you may want to make one or more albums before you actually choose the photos to put into them. For example, the Soccer Event contains photos taken of the team and of runners as well as soccer action photos.

You can make albums for each of these types of photos before you pick out the individual photos from the Event themselves. Here's how:

1 Click a gray area of the viewing area to make sure that nothing is selected.

2 In the lower left of the window, below the Source list, click the Add (+) button.

The same sheet appears that you previously saw when you made an album from selected photos.

3 Type *Runners* in the Name field, and then click Create.

The Runners album appears in the Source list.

4 Repeat steps 2 and 3, this time naming the new album *Team*.

You now have two new albums into which you can put photos.

Organizing Your Albums with Folders

As your collection of albums grows, you'll find you'll want to organize them. One way to do that is to put related albums into folders.

1 Choose File > New Folder.

An untitled folder appears in the Source list. The name of the new folder is conveniently selected so that you can rename it.

2   Type *Soccer Albums* and press Return.

3   Click the Soccer action album, and then Command-click both the Runners album and the Team album.

4   Drag the albums over the Soccer Albums folder and then release the mouse button.

The albums are now in the folder.

Changing the Order of Albums

You can rearrange the order of albums in the Source list and in a folder, too. For example, the Soccer action album should come before the Team album if you want the albums in the folder arranged alphabetically. A quick drag takes care of that.

1   Click the Soccer Albums folder to deselect the albums, then drag the Soccer action album to just above the Team album.

As you drag, a horizontal line appears to show you where the album ends up when you release the mouse button.

2 Release the mouse button.

TIP ▶ For extra credit, go ahead and look through the Soccer Event and put any running photos and team photos that you see into their respective albums.

Making a Smart Album

As you've just seen, when you create an album you manually put the photos that you want into the album. iPhoto's Smart Albums, on the other hand, fill themselves automatically according to the criteria you specify.

A Smart Album, in essence, is a way to save a search in the form of an album. A Smart Album contains the photos that match your search conditions. The most important thing to remember about Smart Albums is that their contents can change dynamically as the contents of your iPhoto library change.

In the last lesson you gave several photos ratings. Let's create a Smart Album that contains photos with ratings of at least four stars.

1 Choose File > New Smart Album.

A dialog appears in which you can name the Smart Album and specify its search conditions.

2 Type *Good and Great* in the "Smart Album name" field at the top of the dialog.

3   In the condition area, choose My Rating from the leftmost pop-up menu, choose "is greater than" from the second pop-up menu, and then, in the field on the right, click the third dot from the left.

When you finish, the dialog should look like the one below.

4   Click OK.

A new Smart Album appears in the Source list. Select it, and the viewing area shows the photos that match the condition you specified.

If, at any time, you assign four stars or more to any other photo in the library, that photo will appear in the Smart Album automatically.

Setting a Date Range for a Smart Album

When you import photos from a camera, as you learned back in Lesson 1, iPhoto arranges the photos into Events based on when they were taken. You may also have noticed that the iPhoto Source list has a special photo collection called Last 12 Months under its Recent heading. This collection always shows your photos taken within the last year.

But what about photos that might span several Events? Or photos taken years ago? For those, you can use a Smart Album to create a photo collection that uses date criteria that you choose. Such a Smart Album won't disturb existing Events, and it can cover dates other than the preset Last 12 Months collection.

1   Choose File > New Smart Album, and then type *January-June 2008*.

2   In the condition area, choose Date from the leftmost pop-up menu and "is in the range" from the second pop-up menu, and then fill out the remaining two fields to specify a start date of *1/1/2008* and an end date of *6/30/2008*.

You can click each number in each date to type your replacements, or click a number and use the arrow buttons to the right of the field to change it. You can also press Tab to move from one part of a date to the next. When you finish, the dialog should look like the one below:

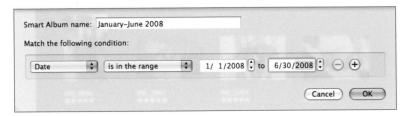

3   Click OK.

4   In the Source list, click the Smart Album you created, and then , if necessary, click the Info button below the Source list to see information about the Smart Album.

The album contains the photos in the library that fall within the dates you specified.

Putting People in Their Place with a Smart Album

A Smart Album's search conditions can be considerably more complex than the searches you can perform with iPhoto's search field. You can have several search conditions, and you can specify whether the Smart Album's contents can match any of the conditions, or whether the contents must match all of them.

For example, you can create a Smart Album that collects photos of several different people, such as members of a family, using the names of people whose faces you've identified. Or you can create a Smart Album that collects photos from several different locations to which you've assigned map locations with Places.

Or you can combine criteria and match people with places, as you'll do next.

1   Choose File > New Smart Album, and then type *Aaron in Ragusa* in the "Smart Album name" field.

2   In the condition area, choose Name from the leftmost pop-up menu and "contains" from the second pop-up menu, and then type *Aaron* in the field on the right.

3   To the right of the condition, click the Add (+) button.

A new condition row appears in the condition area, and the header to the condition area has reworded itself and gained a pop-up menu. You can add multiple conditions to a Smart Album.

TIP ▶ You can click the Subtract (–) button to the right of a condition to remove it from the list of conditions.

4   In the second condition, choose Place from the leftmost menu, choose "contains" from the second menu, and then type *Ragusa* in the field on the right.

The dialog should look like the one here:

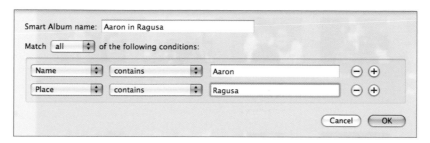

5   Click OK.

The Smart Album now contains photos of Aaron that were taken in Ragusa. Next, you'll change the condition-matching criteria so that the album contains all of the photos of Aaron as well as all of the photos that have Ragusa as their map location.

6 In the Source list, click the Aaron in Ragusa Smart Album, and then choose File > Edit Smart Album.

7 In the dialog that appears, in the header above the condition area, click the pop-up menu and choose "any" so that the header reads "Match any of the following conditions."

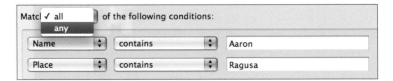

8 Click OK.

The Smart Album now displays the photos that match either condition. You might want to change the album name to *Aaron and Ragusa* to reflect that.

Displaying Photos as a Screen Saver

When you step away from your Mac (I know—why on earth would you ever want to?), after a few minutes a screen saver kicks in to provide an animated display on the screen. One way you can share your photos is to use them as raw material for your Mac's screen saver.

In this exercise you'll use your Mac's System Preferences to decorate your idle Mac's screen with photos from your iPhoto library.

1 Choose System Preferences from the Apple () menu.

2 In the System Preferences window, click Desktop & Screen Saver.

3 Near the top of the Desktop & Screen Saver window, click the Screen Saver tab.

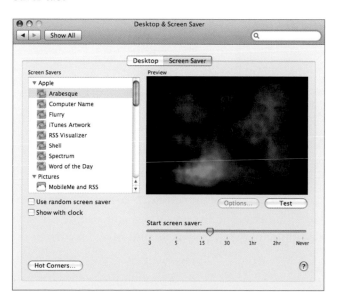

4   In the Screen Savers list, scroll down until the Stinson Beach in November Event is visible, and then click the Event.

You may need to click the triangle to the left of the Pictures heading in the list to reveal its contents. When you click the Event, a photo from the Event appears in the window's Preview pane and animates using the selected display style.

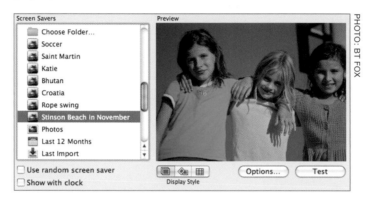

5   At the bottom left of the Preview pane, click the middle part of the Display Style button.

The screen saver's display style changes in the Preview pane.

If you like, you can click Test to see the screen saver on your entire screen. You can move your pointer to end the test. You might also want to check out the rightmost option in the Display Style button and see if you can figure out what it does.

6   Close the Desktop & Screen Saver window.

The Stinson Beach in November photo collection is now your screen saver.

Sharing Photos on Your Local Network

Macs love to network, and chances are your Mac is connected to a local net-work of some sort—maybe a home network, an office network, a classroom network, or one in your favorite coffee shop. It's simple and safe to share your photos over such a network. It's simple because it takes just a few clicks. It's safe because when you share your photos over a local network, they are avail-able for viewing only.

Let's try local network photo sharing with one of your albums.

1   Choose iPhoto > Preferences, and then, in the window's toolbar, click Sharing.

The iPhoto Preferences window displays its Sharing pane.

2   Select the "Share my photos" checkbox.

You can share all the photos in your library, or just the photos in albums that you select. In this context, the term *album* includes albums, folders,

Smart Albums, keepsakes like slideshows or books, and the items that appear under the Recent heading in your iPhoto Source list, such as flagged photos, or the photos that you most recently imported.

3   Select "Share selected albums," and then scroll down the album list and click the Soccer Albums folder.

4   Type a name for your shared photos in the "Shared name" field.

This name identifies the pictures you share from your iPhoto library on the local network. Providing a name is important because more than one Mac at a time can share pictures on the same network, and the name you specify helps other iPhoto users tell which sets of shared pictures are which.

5   Select "Require password," and then enter a password.

When you assign a password to your shared photos, other iPhoto users on the network can see that you have shared photos, but they won't be able to view the photos unless they enter the password. Requiring a password is, of course optional; you may not want to bother with one on a home network, but you might when you share photos on an office or a school network.

When you finish, the Sharing pane of the iPhoto preferences should look something like this:

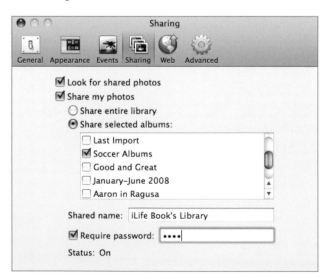

6 Close the Preferences window.

Notice, by the way, that there is no OK button that you have to click. From the moment that you select the "Share my photos" checkbox, iPhoto begins sharing your photos. As long as iPhoto is open, your photos continue to be shared.

The next two steps are optional: If you have another Mac on your network, you can use it to view your shared photos.

7 Go to another Mac on the network, open iPhoto, and choose iPhoto > Preferences.

8 Click the Sharing button in the Preferences window, and then, if the "Look for shared photos" checkbox is not selected, select it.

When the "Look for shared photos" option is selected, iPhoto looks for shared photos from other Macs on the network and displays those shared collections in the Source list.

9 Close the Preferences window.

That's it; no other steps are required. Whenever someone shares iPhoto photos on your network, a Shares heading appears in your iPhoto Source list, and below it are the names of the shared photo collections.

To see the shared photos, click the name of the shared collection in the Source list. The shared photos appear in your iPhoto viewing area. You may have to enter a password first if the shared photos require one.

NOTE ▸ Your photos are shared "live"—that is, any changes you make, such as adding, deleting, or modifying the shared photos in your copy of iPhoto, are immediately visible to anyone on the network who is viewing your shared photos.

TIP ▸ Create a special album just for network photo-sharing purposes. Keep this album shared, and update it whenever you have any photos you want to make available to others.

Emailing Photos

Probably the most common way folks share digital photos is by attaching them to an email message. iPhoto makes this sharing method very easy to do.

1 Open the Soccer Event and then click DSC_9009.

You can email any selected photo or groups of photos. You can even select an Event and email all of the photos it contains.

TIP ▸ Don't overload someone's mailbox with a message containing dozens or hundreds of photos. It doesn't take long to select just the best photos and to send those, and the recipient will appreciate your consideration.

2 At the bottom right of the iPhoto window, click Email.

Email

3 In the dialog that appears, select the Include checkboxes for the information you want to accompany each photo.

4 In the Size menu, choose a size.

You can send photos at their original sizes, or have iPhoto scale them. Remember that the larger the photo, the longer it takes to upload and to download. Choose a size suitable for the recipient. For example, if your recipient has a dial-up Internet connection, choosing Small is a much kinder choice than Actual Size.

5 Click Compose Message.

iPhoto sends the photo to your default mail program, which creates a message with the photo attached.

6   In the mail message, specify a recipient, modify the subject if necessary, optionally add a personal message, and then send the message.

> **TIP** If your mail program is Apple's Mail, you don't even have to open iPhoto to send mail with photos from your iPhoto library. You can use the Photo Browser button on the email window to view and select photos you want to attach to a message.

Syncing Photos to an Apple Device

Whether you're on the go or relaxing like a well-stuffed couch potato, you don't need to leave your favorite photos behind. You can sync photos from your iPhoto library to your Apple TV, iPhone, and all current iPods (except, for obvious reasons, the iPod shuffle). No need to burden your wallet with a few favorite photos when you can store hundreds on your iPhone or iPod, and no need to gather round the computer when you can show your photos in widescreen loveliness in the comfort of your living room.

If you have one or more of these devices, here's how to sync your photos to them. (If you don't, just read this exercise or skip ahead.)

1   Open iTunes, and then connect your iPod or iPhone to your Mac.

The iPod, iPhone, and Apple TV all use iTunes to sync with your Mac. By default, iTunes begins syncing your devices the moment you connect them, unless you've changed the default iTunes settings. There's usually no need to connect your Apple TV: if you've set it up on your local network and paired it with iTunes, iTunes automatically connects and syncs with it over your network.

2   In the iTunes Source list on the left, click your device, and then, at the top of the iTunes list pane on the right, click the Photos tab.

When you select a device in the iTunes Source list, the large list pane on the right of the iTunes window shows a row of tabs along the top for each of the kinds of items you can sync with that device. The Photos tab displays the photo syncing options, such as those for an iPhone, shown here:

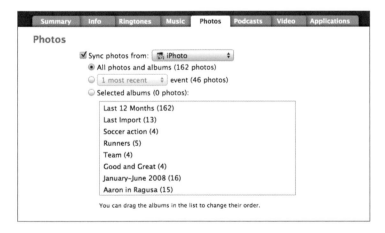

3   If necessary, select "Sync photos from" and then choose iPhoto from the pop-up menu.

You can sync photos from other sources instead, such as your Aperture library or a folder of pictures.

4 Select "Selected albums" and then, in the list of albums, select "Soccer action."

You can select multiple albums to sync, or you can sync Events, choosing all of them or just one or more recent Events. You can also drag albums in the album list to rearrange their order: iTunes syncs albums in top-to-bottom order, and if your device is almost full, you can put the most important albums first to make sure that they sync before you run out of room.

TIP ▶ Apple TV has an additional checkbox: "Sync photos before other media." iTunes ordinarily syncs other media, such as videos, before it gets around to syncing photos with Apple TV, and if you have a lot of video to sync, the photos may never end up on the Apple TV. This checkbox lets you specify that your photos get onto your Apple TV before anything else has a chance to crowd them out.

5 Near the bottom right of the iTunes window, click Apply.

The album syncs to your device. iTunes converts the photos to a resolution suitable for the device as it syncs, so that you don't have multimegabyte high-resolution photos, for example, taking up room on an iPod nano.

6 If necessary, eject the device from your Mac.

The photos are now on your device.

Making a Slideshow

If you hear the word *slideshow* and think of your mother's cousin Ernie hauling out his projector, screen, and the 200 faded slides that show every mile of his road trip in 1982 to see the Giant Lady's Leg Sundial in Lake Village, Indiana, then you've never seen an iPhoto slideshow. Unlike Ernie's version of after-dinner entertainment, iPhoto slideshows can both dance and sing, and they are *much* more fun to set up and view.

To see how to make an iPhoto slideshow from your own pictures, you'll use the Stinson Beach in November Event.

1   In the Source list, click Events, and then click Stinson Beach in November.

2   Below the Source list, on the left, click Add (+).

You can use this button to create a variety of items, as noted by the help tag that appears when you rest your pointer over the button.

3   In the dialog that appears, click Slideshow, and then click Create.

A Slideshows heading appears in the Source list, and the slideshow view opens in the iPhoto window.

TIP   To create a slideshow from an existing album, select the album in the Source list, and then click the Add (+) button.

PHOTO: BT FOX

4 In the toolbar at the bottom of the slideshow viewing area, click Play.

The slideshow occupies the whole screen and begins to play, accompanied by music. If you move your pointer, a controller appears over the slideshow. You can use the controller to pause the show, move manually among the slides, and adjust the slideshow settings. If you move the pointer to the bottom of the screen, a row of thumbnails of all of the photos in the slideshow appears. You can click any thumbnail to display the photo in the slideshow.

5 Press Esc.

The slideshow ends. You can also click the close button on the controller to end the slideshow.

Customizing a Slideshow

The music and visual style of the slideshow you just created are dictated by iPhoto's default slideshow theme, music, and slide settings. You don't, however, have to accept the creative choices that iPhoto has made. You can modify any of them for your slideshow.

In this exercise, you'll change the theme, music, and slide display settings for the Stinson Beach in November Slideshow.

1   In the toolbar at the bottom of the slideshow viewing area, click Themes.

PHOTO: BT FOX

Previews of the available themes appear. A slideshow's theme controls the basic visual style of the slideshow, the transitions between slides, and the default music that accompanies the slideshow. After you choose a theme, you can further customize the slideshow.

TIP ▶ Hold your pointer over a theme thumbnail to see a brief animation of the theme in action.

2   Click Sliding Panels, and then click Choose.

The appearance of the slideshow in the viewing area changes.

3   In the toolbar, click Music.

The Music Settings window appears with a list of songs from which you can choose to give your slideshow a musical accompaniment. iPhoto provides a selection of music samples you can use, but you can also choose music from your iTunes library or from any GarageBand compositions you may have. You can use the search field at the bottom to find songs i n your music collection, and you can click the window's Play button to hear the music.

4 Select Endless Summer, and then click Apply.

5 In the toolbar, click Settings.

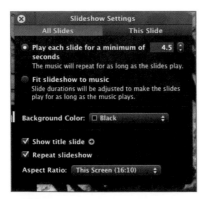

The Slideshow Settings window appears. It has display and playback settings that apply to the entire slideshow. You can click This Slide at the top of the window to see and change settings that apply to the currently selected slide in the photo browser at the top of the viewing area. The settings you can change for either a single slide or for the whole slideshow vary depending upon the theme you have chosen.

6   Deselect "Repeat slideshow," and then close the settings window.

Closing the window applies the changes you have made.

7   In the photo browser, find the thumbnail that is framed diagonally, and drag it so that appears before the first slide in the show.

As you drag, the other thumbnails move aside to give you room to drop the thumbnail you're dragging.

Notice in the main viewing area that the slideshow title doesn't fit. That's an easy fix.

8   In the Source list, click the slideshow's name and delete the word *Slideshow*.

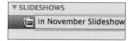

The title now fits in the slideshow viewing area.

9   In the toolbar, click Play.

The slideshow plays using the settings you've applied. When the last slide is shown, the music fades out and the slideshow ends.

Exporting a Slideshow

Once you've made your slideshow, you can export it as movie that you can play in iTunes or in QuickTime Player. And once it's in iTunes, you can put it on your iPod or your iPhone or your Apple TV. All it takes is a few quick clicks.

1   In the toolbar on the right, click Export.

The "Export your slideshow" dialog appears. You can save your slideshow as an MP4 video file in multiple sizes, suitable for different devices and uses, or you can click Custom Export to specify advanced QuickTime export options.

By default, the "Automatically send slideshow to iTunes" option is selected. This option places a copy of the slideshow movie in your iTunes library, ready to be synced to any of your Apple devices.

NOTE ▶ iPhoto does not put a copy of the slideshow in your iTunes library if you choose more than one size when you export it.

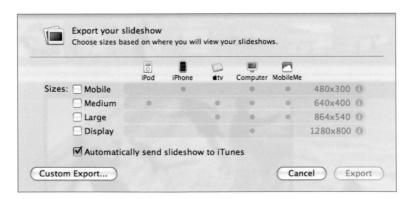

TIP ▶ Put your pointer over the information icon at the right of each size that's offered to see technical details about the video file that the export creates for that size.

2   In the dialog, select Medium, and then click Export.

iPhoto presents a standard file-saving dialog so you can pick the folder where the movie is to be saved. The default is the iPhoto Slideshows folder in the Pictures folder in your home folder.

3   Click OK.

The export begins. A progress indicator (a moving bar) shows the status of the export. How long the export takes depends on the size of the slide-show and how many sizes you have chosen to export. A one-minute slideshow in a single size typically takes just a couple of minutes.

When the export is complete, a Finder window opens to show you where the slideshow movie has been saved. If you've also chosen to send the slideshow to iTunes, iTunes opens up instead and shows you the movie listed in the iTunes window.

Sharing Photos in MobileMe Gallery

Sharing photos on a local network, as you saw earlier, is easy, but the world is much larger than your local network. If you want to share your photos with a bigger audience, iPhoto and a MobileMe account can make your pictures available worldwide.

NOTE ▶ A MobileMe account costs $99 a year, and in addition to iPhoto MobileMe Gallery albums, it provides you with 20 gigabytes of online storage, email, software, and a bunch of other features. Most iLife applications can make use of a MobileMe account. If you don't have a MobileMe account and want to try it out, you can sign up for a free 60-day trial account. Otherwise, just read through this exercise to see how MobileMe Gallery works.

For this trip into the world of MobileMe Gallery, you'll share your Soccer action album.

1 In the Source list, open the Soccer Albums folder, click the Soccer action album, and then click the MobileMe button in the iPhoto viewing area's toolbar.

TIP ▶ You can also create a MobileMe Gallery by choosing Share > MobileMe Gallery, or by choosing File > New Album from Selection and then clicking MobileMe in the dialog that appears. It's good to have choices.

NOTE ▶ If you don't have a MobileMe account, or haven't signed into it on your Mac, iPhoto gives you a chance to rectify that problem.

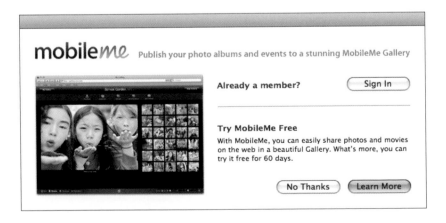

When you create a MobileMe Gallery, a dialog appears with options you can select to control who has access to the MobileMe Gallery, how it appears, and what visitors to it can do. For example, by making a choice from the "Album Viewable by" pop-up menu, you can make the Gallery's photos available to yourself only, to everyone, or to one or more specific individuals. In this exercise, you'll share the photos with the world.

Would you like to publish "Soccer action" to your MobileMe Gallery?

This will create an album in Apple Training Series's MobileMe Gallery. The album can be viewed with Safari or any modern web browser. The title of this album will be visible to everyone viewing your Gallery.

Album Viewable by: | Everyone |

Allow: ☐ Downloading of photos or entire album
☐ Uploading of photos via web browser
☐ Adding of photos via email

Show: ☑ Photo titles
☐ Email address for uploading photos

(Show Advanced)   (Cancel) (Publish)

2   In the dialog, click to select all of the checkboxes and then click Publish.

When you select "Adding of photos via email," the final checkbox, "Email address for uploading photos," becomes available, so be sure to click it, too.

NOTE ▶ If you have an iPhone, be sure to select "Adding of photos via email." This option allows you to send photos to the Gallery directly from your iPhone with a single tap. If you don't have an iPhone, you can add photos to your Gallery from any computer just by emailing the photo to your Gallery's email address.

As soon as you click Publish, the photos that belong to your new MobileMe Gallery appear in the viewing area, and iPhoto begins uploading them to your MobileMe account. A progress indicator appears in the viewing area's title bar. Also, a MobileMe Gallery heading appears in the iPhoto Source list with the name of the new Gallery album beneath it. A circular progress gauge appears beside the album's name in the Source list, so you can switch to some other activity in iPhoto and still keep tabs on the upload's progress.

When the upload is done, the MobileMe Gallery's title bar changes. At the left is the address of the new Gallery album followed by a circular arrow link icon that you can click to view the Gallery in your web browser. If you have chosen to allow email uploads to the Gallery, the email address of the Gallery appears at the right side of the title bar.

3   Click the circular link icon to the right of the album's web address in the title bar.

Your web browser (typically Safari unless you've chosen a different default browser on your Mac) opens and displays the album.

NOTE ▶ Like a locally shared album, a Gallery album is live; any changes you make to it are uploaded to the Gallery. In addition, any pictures added to the Gallery by other users (if you've allowed them to do so) are downloaded to your Gallery in iPhoto. This means, for example, that you can post pictures to your MobileMe Gallery with your iPhone while on a trip or while visiting friends, and have the pictures arrive on your Mac the next time you open iPhoto.

Sharing Photos with Flickr

Although MobileMe offers fantastic photo-hosting and display capabilities, it's not the only online photo-hosting service you can use with iPhoto. Take Flickr, one of the world's most popular online photo-hosting services, with more than three billion photos stored and shared from its servers. If you have a Flickr account (they're free, and setting one up takes just a few minutes), you can post photos to it right from the comfort of iPhoto.

NOTE ▶ This exercise assumes you already have a Flickr account. If you don't, just read on or skip ahead.

1 In the Source list, select the Soccer action album, and then, near the right side of the toolbar, click Flickr.

The first time you use iPhoto's Flickr posting feature, you need to authorize iPhoto to open the lines of communication with the Flickr service. You'll need to do this only once.

2   In the dialog that appears, click Set Up.

iPhoto opens your web browser to the Flickr sign-in page.

3   Sign in to Flickr, and then, in the iPhoto Uploader authorization page that appears, click OK, I'LL ALLOW IT.

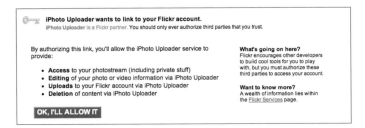

Flickr uses the iPhoto Uploader program from one of its partners to manage the communication between iPhoto and Flickr.

4   When you see the Flickr confirmation message in the browser window, close the window.

A dialog appears in the iPhoto window containing posting options for the photos you've selected to share. The default options are fine, but feel free to examine the choices iPhoto offers.

5   Click Publish.

iPhoto uploads the selected photos to Flickr. As it did with MobileMe, iPhoto shows you the progress of the upload, and creates a new item in the Source list.

When the upload finishes, the address of your uploaded photo set appears above the set in the iPhoto window's main viewing area.

6 Click the circular link icon to the right of the photo set's web address in the title bar.

Your web browser displays the new photo set in Flickr. Next, you'll add a photo to the set.

7 In iPhoto, find the photo DSC_6761, and then drag the photo to the Flickr set in the iPhoto Source list.

iPhoto uploads the photo to the set.

8 Select the Flickr photo set in the Source list again, and then click the circular link icon to the right of the photo set's web address.

Your browser displays the updated photo set on Flickr.

NOTE ▶ Just as with MobileMe, changes you make to a Flickr photo set on the Flickr site are reflected in the linked photo set in iPhoto.

9   Close your web browser.

Now you're ready to try the same thing again with another popular web service.

Sharing Photos with Facebook

If Flickr is not your social-networking cup of java, you might want to try Facebook, as like 175 million people around the world do. iPhoto makes photo sharing with Facebook as easy as it does with Flickr. Plus, you can share your Faces tags between Facebook and iPhoto.

NOTE ▶ This exercise assumes you already have a Facebook account. If you don't, just read on.

1   In the Source list, select the Soccer action album, and then, near the right side of the toolbar, click Facebook.

The first time you use iPhoto's Facebook publishing feature, you need to authorize iPhoto and Facebook to communicate with each other. You'll need to do this only once.

2   In the dialog that appears, click Set Up.

iPhoto presents a Facebook sign-in dialog.

3   Enter the email address you use when you log in to Facebook, enter your Facebook password, select "Keep me logged in to iPhoto Uploader," and then click Login.

The dialog now asks you to allow access to the iPhoto Uploader.

4   Click Allow, and then, when the dialog prompts you, click Close.

Another dialog appears in the iPhoto window with publishing options for the photos you've selected to share.

5   In the "Photos Viewable by" menu, choose Only Friends, and then click Publish.

iPhoto uploads the selected photos to Facebook. iPhoto shows you the progress of the upload and creates a new item in the Source list under a new Facebook heading. When the upload finishes, the address of your published album appears above the iPhoto window's main viewing area.

6   Click the circular link icon to the right of the album's web address in the title bar.

Your web browser displays the photos you published to Facebook.

Sharing Facebook Tags with Faces

Now let's pass some Faces information between Facebook and iPhoto. You should already have your newly published Facebook album open in your web browser, so let's start.

1   In the web browser, click photo DSC_9009.

You can see the photo names in Facebook by holding the mouse pointer over each photo. When you click, the photo expands, and, below it to the right, Facebook offers several options.

2   Click Tag This Photo, and then, in the photo, click the soccer player's face.

A frame appears around the face, and a panel appears beside it with a space to enter a name tag.

3 In the "Type any name or tag" field, type *D. Beckham*, and then click Tag.

A confirmation message appears in the yellow area above the picture.

4 In the area above the picture, to the right, click Done Tagging.

5 In the iPhoto Source list, beneath the Facebook heading, to the right of the Soccer action album label, click the small Publish icon.

iPhoto retrieves the tag information from the Facebook album. When you click the Publish icon, Facebook and iPhoto sync their shared information.

6 In the iPhoto viewing area, click the photo that you tagged in Facebook, and then, in the toolbar, click Name.

The player's face is labeled with the name you entered in Facebook, along with a Facebook icon. The icon indicates that you must confirm the name for iPhoto's Faces collection.

7 Click the Facebook icon beside the name tag, and then press Return.

This confirms the name.

8 In the Source list, click Faces.

The face now appears in the Faces collection with the name that you gave it in Facebook.

TIP ▶ When you publish pictures to Facebook that you've tagged with face information in iPhoto, the iPhoto names appear as Facebook tags in Facebook. If the people in the pictures are Facebook friends of yours, and the names and email addresses you tagged them with match their Facebook information, Facebook notifies them that you've tagged them in a Facebook picture.

In this lesson you've made albums, Smart Albums, slideshows, MobileMe Gallery albums, Flickr photo sets, and Facebook albums. Now it's time to make yourself some refreshments and take a break. You're entitled.

Lesson Review

1. What is an album?
2. Describe two ways to rearrange the order of photos in an album.
3. What is a Smart Album?
4. How can you create an album that contains photos of your family?
5. How can you email photos from your iPhoto library without opening iPhoto?

6. Why would you want to rearrange the order of your photo albums in the iTunes Photo syncing tab?

7. What is a slideshow theme?

8. How can you add photos to MobileMe Gallery without using iPhoto?

9. How do you sync pictures between iPhoto and Flickr or Facebook?

Answers

1. A collection of photos from one or more Events; the iPhoto equivalent of an iTunes playlist.

2. Drag the photos into the order you want, or choose a sorting order from the View > Sort Photos submenu.

3. A Smart Album is an album that contains just the photos matching the conditions that you've specified and that dynamically changes its contents as necessary.

4. Use Faces to identify photos of each family member, and then make a Smart Album with multiple conditions, one for each family member's name.

5. In Apple's Mail application, click the iPhoto Browser button that appears at the top of each mail message you create and select the photos from the iPhoto Browser window that appears.

6. iTunes syncs photo albums in top-to-bottom list order; if the device to which you are syncing photos is almost full, the albums at the top of the list are more likely to sync to the device before it completely fills up.

7. A slideshow's theme controls the basic visual style of the slideshow, the transitions between slides, and the default music that accompanies the slideshow.

8. Make sure that the Gallery is configured to allow photo uploads from a web browser and from email. Then go to the Gallery in your web browser and use the Upload button, or email the photo to the Gallery's email address.

9. In the Source list, to the right of the published album's name, click the small Publish icon.

4

Lesson Files No additional files

Time This lesson takes approximately 45 minutes to complete.

Goals Print photos

Order prints

Make a photo book

Make and order a greeting card

Back up photos

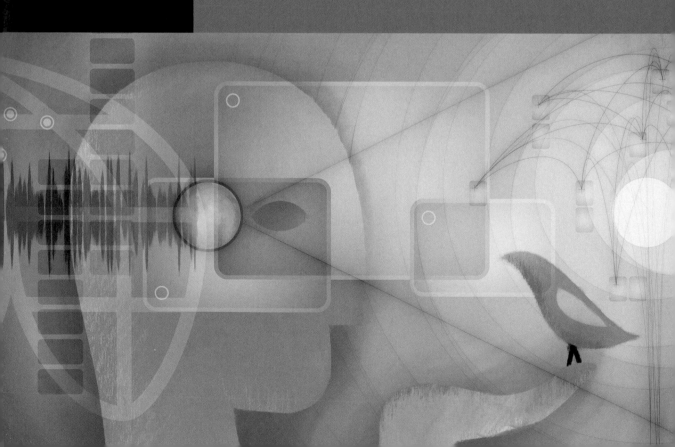

Publishing Your Photos

In the previous lesson you learned several ways to share your photos digitally. But, as much fun as that can be, there's something undeniably satisfying about physical keepsakes that you can hold in your hand, hang on your wall, stick on your refrigerator, or proudly display on your coffee table.

This lesson is all about the good old-fashioned analog objects that you can make with iPhoto.

Printing Photos

Whether it's a photo of loved ones that you tack to the bland fabric of your work cube's walls or a finely framed print gracing the hallway of your home, you need pigment on paper, not pixels on a screen. iPhoto works with your color printer to deliver the goods.

To learn how iPhoto's printing feature works, you'll print a picture from the Katie Event.

1   Open the Katie Event and click the photo Katie 35.

2   Choose File > Print.

The print settings view appears with various printing layout controls and options. Along the left side are several printing *themes*. Themes provide different layouts for printing; for example, the Contact Sheet theme is good for printing thumbnail photos for an entire Event, so that you have a printed record of its contents. For this picture, the default choice, the Standard theme, is fine.

3   From the Printer pop-up menu, choose the printer you want to use, and from the Paper Size pop-up menu, choose the size of the paper on which you want to print the photo.

The available paper size choices vary depending on the printer you choose. For this photo, we chose an inkjet printer and a 4 x 6 inch paper size.

NOTE ▶ If necessary, iPhoto crops the photo to fit the aspect ratio of the paper size that you've chosen.

4   From the Presets pop-up menu, choose a preset appropriate for the kind of printer and paper you're using.

Different types of printers offer different presets. For example, a laser printer might offer only a single preset, whereas a color inkjet printer might offer several presets for printing on different kinds of paper.

At this point, you could simply click the Print button and let iPhoto and your printer do their work. Or you could customize the print, which is what you'll do next.

Customizing a Printed Photo

You can fine-tune the photo layout—for example, by adjusting its magnification or adding a caption—before you print it.

1   In the print settings view, click Customize.

The viewing area is replaced by the print layout area. In the photo browser are thumbnails of the photos you've selected to print (in this case, there's only one). Across the bottom is a toolbar with layout tools.

2 Click the Layout button.

A pop-up menu appears, with a single choice: One. Different themes offer different choices on this menu.

3 In the Layout pop-up menu, choose One > 2.

This choice lays the photo out in a landscape view with a caption below the photo.

4 In the layout area, click the photo's caption and type *Pumpkin Girl.*

When you click the caption that iPhoto provides, it's automatically selected so you can quickly change it.

> **TIP** ▶ Click the Settings button in the toolbar to see a dialog in which you can choose a font, style, and size for the caption.

5 Click the photo in the layout area.

A size slider and the Hand tool appear above the photo, which you can use to adjust the photo's size and position.

TIP ▶ If iPhoto has cropped the photo to match the aspect ratio of the paper size you've chosen for printing, you can restore the full photo in the layout area. Control-click or right-click the picture and choose Fit Photo to Frame Size.

6   Drag the size slider to magnify the photo slightly, and drag the photo so that the girl is roughly a third of the way from the left of the frame. (In other words, apply the "rule of thirds" from Lesson 1.)

Try to adjust the photo layout so that it looks like the one here.

Pumpkin Girl

TIP ▶ Click the Adjust button in the toolbar to open a pane with a combination of adjustment and effects controls similar to the ones in the iPhoto viewing area's Adjust and Effects panes. Use this pane, for example, if you need to make any temporary color or exposure setting changes before you print.

7   In the toolbar, click the Print button.

A Print dialog appears with standard printing controls.

8   If you want to print the image now, in the Print dialog, click Print.

The photo prints on the printer you've chosen. When the printing finishes, the print layout area is still present, so you can print again.

NOTE ▶ When you customize printing, a Printing project appears under the Recent heading in the Source list. Until you choose something else to print, or click Cancel in the print layout area, you can click the Printing project to return to the print layout area and print more copies using that layout and to make additional layout changes.

Ordering Prints

You don't need a color printer, or even a printer at all, to get high-quality color prints. You can order professionally produced color prints of your photos right from within iPhoto.

Here's how it works—but don't worry, this exercise won't cost you any money; you'll cancel before you order anything!

1   Open the Katie Event, and then click the photo Katie 35.

2   Choose File > Order Prints.

An Order Prints dialog appears. If you haven't previously ordered prints with your copy of iPhoto, the ordering options are unavailable until you sign in.

At this point, instead of signing in or creating an account right now, click Cancel, and then read the following description of how the ordering and the account creation processes work.

If no one has ever ordered prints from your copy of iPhoto, the Order Prints dialog offers a Set Up Account button. Click this button to either sign in to your existing account or to create a new account. A Set Up Account dialog appears that provides for both possibilities.

If you already have an Apple account, you enter your Apple ID and your password in the Set Up Account dialog to sign in.

Otherwise, click Create Account at the left of the Set Up Account dialog. A dialog appears. Follow the instructions in this dialog to create an account. Among other things, you'll need to supply your email address (this becomes the Apple ID that you use when you sign in to the account), your credit card number, its expiration date, and a shipping address. Once Apple has verified the credit card information you've supplied, your account is ready for you to use.

NOTE ▸ The Apple Account creation process uses a secure Internet connection to protect your personal information.

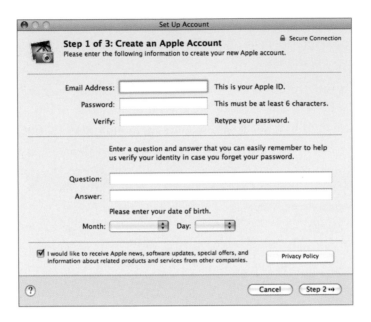

Once you've signed in to your Apple account, you use the Order Prints dialog to specify the number and sizes of the prints you want. You can also choose where to have the prints sent and how to have them shipped. When you finish specifying your order, click Buy Now. iPhoto uses your Internet connection to transfer the photos to the print service, and within a few days, your prints arrive in the mail.

NOTE ▶ The Order Prints dialog places a yellow warning icon by any print sizes that may not look good at the photo's resolution—for example, a 2-megapixel photo can't produce a good-quality print in sizes larger than 8 x 10 inch.

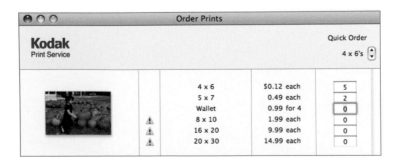

Assembling a Photo Book

If a picture is worth a thousand words, how many words is a book of photos worth? Here's your chance to find out: iPhoto gives you the opportunity to use your photos to make professionally printed photo books in a variety of sizes and designs.

The book you create can be made from any selection of photos you like. You'll start with the photos in the Bhutan Event. You'll construct the book in stages, setting up the book's basic layout, adding the photos to the book, customizing a map, and finally previewing the book for printing.

1   Open the Bhutan Event, and then click the Book button on the viewing area's toolbar.

>   **NOTE ▶** If your iPhoto window is not wide enough to display all of the toolbar buttons, you see a Keepsakes button instead of a Book button. Click the Keepsakes button and then choose Book from the menu.

The book themes view appears. The themes appear in a list on the left, and an illustration appears on the right showing a book made using the currently selected theme. Above the theme list is the Book Type pop-up menu. The list of available themes depends on the type of book you select.

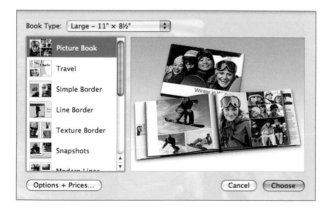

2   From the Book Type pop-up menu, in the Softcover section of the menu, choose Medium – 8" x 6".

You can create a hardcover book, a softcover book, or a wire-bound soft-cover book. Both kinds of softcover books are available in several sizes.

3   In the themes list, click Travel and then click Choose.

The viewing area becomes a book layout area, and a message appears explaining how to add photos to the book. Also, your book project appears in the Source list under the Keepsakes heading. You can return to your book project at any time by clicking it in the Source list.

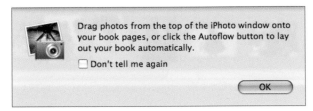

Drag photos from the top of the iPhoto window onto your book pages, or click the Autoflow button to lay out your book automatically.

☐ Don't tell me again

OK

4   Click OK.

The message goes away, and your book is ready to be laid out.

Laying Out Your Book

The main part of the layout area displays the current page of the book on which you're working. The photos that you can add to the book appear in the scrolling photo browser along the top of the layout area. You use the buttons at the left side of the browser to switch between the photo browser and the page browser. The toolbar at the bottom of the layout area has layout and photo adjustment tools.

Let's start putting your book together.

1 On the cover image, in the layout area, click the book title placeholder and type a title, and then click the subtitle placeholder and type a subtitle.

When you click the title and subtitle placeholders, the text is selected so that what you type immediately replaces it.

2 Drag a photo from the photo browser to one of the photo placeholders on the book's cover in the layout area, and then drag another photo to the other placeholder.

When you place a photo in the book, a checkmark appears under it in the photo browser to indicate that you've used it so you can see which photos you've used and which photos you haven't. Of course, you can use the same photo more than once in the book if you want.

3 Click the Page button at the top left of the photo browser.

The photo browser becomes a page browser. You can scroll through the browser to see how your book lays out. Beneath each item in the page browser is a page number or page name.

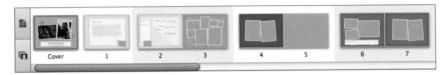

4 Click page 1 in the browser to show it in the main layout area, and then click and type to replace the placeholder text on the page.

Although this page is intended to contain a title and some introductory text, you can type whatever you want, or even delete the text and leave the page blank if you prefer. It's your book!

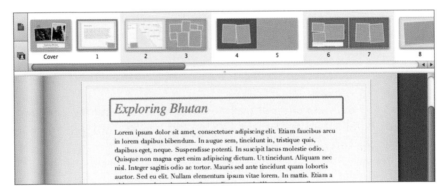

5 In the toolbar, click the right side of the two-part View button.

The page browser and book layout area now show the pages individually. The View button lets you switch the page browser between two-page spreads and individual page views. You can still tell which pages are included in each spread by the browser's background shading, which groups the pages by spread.

Next, you'll change the layouts of the pages in the book. A photo book must have at least 20 pages for it to be professionally printed by the service iPhoto uses. However, there aren't enough photos in the Bhutan Event to fill out the book right now because many of the pages require multiple photos—some pages require as many as seven photos! You'll change all of the multiple-photo pages to single-photo pages.

6   Click page 3, and then, in the toolbar, choose Layout > One.

Page 3 currently requires seven photos. The One submenu shows you all of the page layout choices that require only one photo.

> **TIP** Many of the page layout choices have caption areas in which you can enter descriptive information about the photos. You can adjust the caption fonts and sizes by clicking the Settings button on the toolbar. If you've entered descriptions of your photos in iPhoto's Information pane, those descriptions will be used for the photo captions in the book when you select the Settings dialog's "Automatically enter photo information" checkbox.

7   Choose a one-photo layout from the One submenu, and then proceed through the rest of book's pages, changing all of the multiple-photo page layouts to single-photo page layouts.

> **TIP** You can change the background color of a selected page by clicking Background in the toolbar and choosing a background from the menu that appears.

8   In the toolbar, click the Autoflow button.

The pages shown in the page browser are now filled with pictures rather than placeholders. Autoflow places unused photos in photo placeholders until it runs out of photos to place.

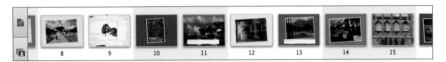

9   In the page browser, drag a page to a new location.

As you drag, the pages in the browser move aside to make way for the page you're dragging. When you drop the page, the browser adjusts to show the new arrangement.

10 In the browser, click a page, and then click the photo on that page in the main layout area.

A magnification and positioning pane appears, like the ones you've seen for customized printing. You can use the slider to zoom in on the picture, and the Hand tool to adjust what part of the magnified picture is seen on the page.

NOTE ▶ iPhoto picture books are designed to use pictures that have a 4:3 aspect ratio, which is the most common aspect ratio for digital cameras. If your pictures have a different aspect ratio, you may want to crop them before using them in a book.

Customizing a Map in Your Book

One of the page layout choices you have in the Travel book theme is a map layout, such as the one on page 2. You can set a map to show any location in

Customizing a Map in Your Book   **147**

the world. In this exercise, you'll set the map on page 2 to show Thimphu in
Bhutan.

1 In the page browser, click page 2, and then, in the layout area, click the map.

A pane appears beside the map. You use this pane to mark locations on the
map and to give the map a title.

2 At the bottom of the pane, click the Add (+) button.

"New Place" appears in the Places field of the pane. The text is selected.

3 Type *Thimphu*, and then, below what you've just typed, click the "New
place" button that appears.

The Edit My Places dialog appears with the Google Search option chosen
and *Thimphu* entered in the search box.

4 Press Return, and then, when the location of Thimphu appears on the
map in the layout area, click Done.

The map on page 2 now shows Thimphu in Bhutan. The name of the country is covered by the Thimphu label, however, so you need to add a title to the map.

5   In the pane, in the Title field, type *Bhutan*, and then press Return.

A label appears in the map's lower right.

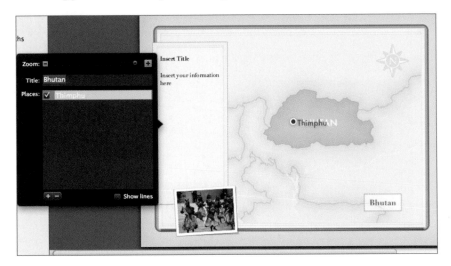

TIP ▶ You can use the size slider at the top of the pane to change the magnification of the map. You can also drag in the map to reposition the geographic area displayed.

Previewing Your Book

Although the Bhutan book in these exercises would require more work before you'd want to print it, it's never too early to preview it. In fact, you should always preview a book as you work on it, and certainly before you print it, to make sure it is laid out properly. iPhoto provides two ways to preview your book: a slideshow, so you can see how the sequence of pictures in the book works; and a print preview, so you can get an idea of how it will look when printed.

You'll use both options to preview the Bhutan book.

1 In the toolbar, click Slideshow.

The screen goes black and a "Preparing Slideshow" message appears. After a few seconds, the slideshow begins to play. It uses the Classic slideshow template and, by default, plays the template's associated music.

2 Press the Spacebar.

The slideshow pauses and the slideshow controller appears. You can use the Music and Settings buttons on the controller to change the behavior of the slideshow, but you can't change the theme. You can also click the arrow buttons, or use the Left Arrow and Right Arrow keys on your keyboard, to page through the slideshow.

3 Page through the slideshow using the arrow keys on your keyboard, and then press Escape.

The iPhoto window appears. Next you'll create a print preview.

4 In the layout area, in the gray region beside the page that is showing, Control-click or right-click, and then, on the shortcut menu that appears, choose Preview Book.

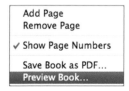

An Assembling Book progress indicator appears that shows you the status of the preview assembly.

When the book preview is assembled, the Preview window opens with your book's preview. The first page shows the book's front and back cover.

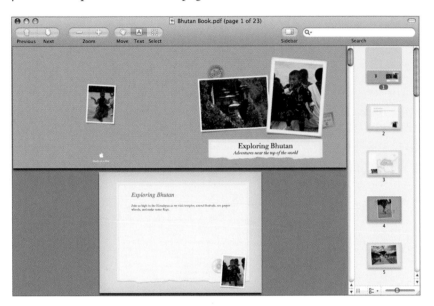

5   Use the Up Arrow and Down Arrow keys to look through your book, and then choose Preview > Quit Preview.

All that's left to do now is to finish the book, and then buy it. The purchase process is similar to the way you buy prints: Click the Buy Book button in the toolbar and complete your order in an Order Book dialog that looks much like the Order Prints dialog that you've already seen.

Of course, this is just an exercise, so you're not going to do that now—unless the book you've just made has really struck your fancy!

Making a Greeting Card

Suppose you have a photo that would be perfect for a holiday card or a party invitation. You can use iPhoto to create such cards and have them professionally printed, just as you can with photo prints and books.

To learn how to make a card, you'll use one of the photos from the Bhutan Event.

1   Open the Bhutan Event and click photo PA137456.jpg.

2   In the toolbar, click Card.

> **NOTE ►** If your iPhoto window is not wide enough to display all of the toolbar buttons, you see a Keepsakes button instead of a Card button. Click the Keepsakes button and then choose Card from the menu.

Previews of various card themes appear. From the pop-up menu at the top left you can choose whether to create a greeting card or a postcard. A Greeting Card layout has the picture on the front and opens to reveal a message inside. A Postcard layout has the picture on the front and the message on the back. You'll use a greeting card for the invitation.

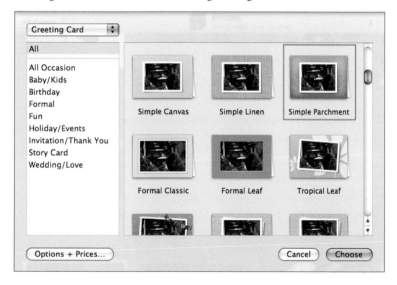

3   At the top of the category list on the left, click All, and then, in the thumbnails on the right, click Simple Parchment.

4   Click Choose.

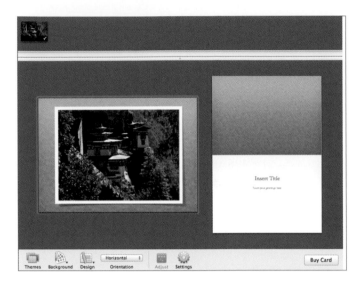

The viewing area becomes a card layout area, with the outside and the inside of the card displayed, and a toolbar beneath it with tools similar to those in the book layout area's toolbar. Also, under the Keepsakes heading in the Source list, an "untitled card" project appears

5 In the Source list, rename the card project *We're moving card*.

6 In the toolbar, choose Vertical from the Orientation menu, and then click Background and choose a green background.

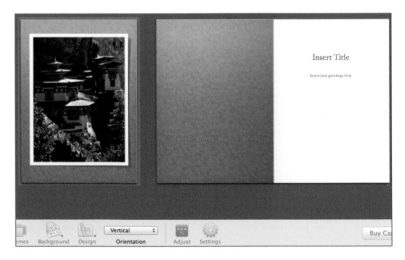

7   In the card's interior, click Insert Title and type a new title, then click "Insert your greetings here" and type the invitation's details.

You can type multiple lines of text by pressing Return in both the card's title and its information. You can see what we typed for the invitation here.

NOTE ► You can also adjust the font family, size, and typeface of the card's interior text by choosing Edit > Font > Show Fonts (or by pressing Command-T) and then selecting different settings in the standard Font window that appears.

That's all there is to making a card. You can click Buy Card to see what the prices and options are, if you so desire.

Making Backups of Your Photos

The last way you'll learn to publish your photos is to backup media: You're going to back up your iPhoto library.

iPhoto is completely integrated with Time Machine. If you have Time Machine running, your library is already backed up.

If you are not using Time Machine, you can still back up your iPhoto library. iPhoto can easily and quickly burn your iPhoto library to a recordable CD or

DVD. This is something you should consider doing regularly. Recordable discs are cheap, but the time you've spent creating, arranging, and cleaning up your photos isn't.

You'll look at both backup options.

Backing Up to a Recordable Disc

When you burn your library to a disc, iPhoto puts an iPhoto library on the disc that contains the albums, Events, and folders from your Mac's iPhoto library. What you're doing is taking a snapshot of your library at the moment you burn the disc.

You can use this snapshot to recover from mistakes—such as accidentally deleting the wrong Event—or to store photos and albums that you don't want to throw away but no longer want cluttering up your iPhoto library.

Pull out a blank recordable disc and let's get started.

1   Open iPhoto and make sure that all the Events are showing.

     When iPhoto burns a library to disc, it copies only the items that are selected. In this activity, you're going to back up your entire iPhoto library.

2   When all the Events are visible, choose Edit > Select None to make sure that nothing is selected.

     TIP When you don't have anything selected, iPhoto's burn feature copies your entire library—but if you do have something selected, the burn feature copies only the items you have selected. You can use this behavior to your advantage. For example, if you're working with other people on a photo project, you can burn just the albums needed for the project, and then give the disc to your collaborators. They can use this disc with iPhoto on their own Macs; the pictures will be conveniently titled, rated, and arranged exactly as they were on your Mac.

3   Choose Share > Burn.

A dialog appears instructing you to insert a blank disc in your Mac.

4   Insert the recordable disc in your disc drive and click OK.

iPhoto takes a few moments inspecting the disc to make sure that it's recordable. Then the disc burning pane appears at the bottom of the iPhoto viewing area. The pane tells you how many items and how much data will be burned to the disc (in megabytes, abbreviated as MB); provides a graphical representation of how much of the disc's capacity the library will use; and presents a field in which you can give the disc a name other than the one iPhoto suggests. The suggested name is useful if the disc is going to be part of a series of regular backups, because it includes the date when you made the backup.

5   In the burning pane, click Burn.

The Burn Disc dialog appears, confirming what iPhoto is about to burn, and giving you another opportunity to cancel the burning process.

6   In the dialog, click Burn.

A progress indicator appears, and iPhoto begins burning the library to the disc. Depending on the size of the library and the speed of the disc burner, burning the disc could take anywhere from a few minutes to half an hour. After iPhoto finishes burning the disc, iPhoto verifies it, which takes additional time—though not, usually, as long as it takes to burn the disc.

When iPhoto finishes burning and verifying the disc, a Shares heading appears in the Source list, with the disc that you just burned below it.

NOTE ► Your Mac may eject the disc when it finishes the burn. If it does, reinsert the disc before the next step.

7   In the Source list, click the newly burned disc's disclosure triangle to see its contents.

The disc contains a copy of your library's Events, along with copies of any albums and folders that the library includes. Although you can't change any of the disc's contents, you can use them for projects, export them, and even copy them back to your current iPhoto library.

8   Click the Eject button beside the disc's name in the Source list.

iPhoto ejects your disc from the drive.

9   Label the disc and put it in a safe place.

Restoring Photos with Time Machine

There's nothing to backing up with Time Machine—literally. If Time Machine is on, changes to your iPhoto library are backed up along with everything else that Time Machine backs up automatically. The only time you need to bother with Time Machine is when you want to restore something from a backup:

1   Choose File > Browse Backups.

Time Machine opens and displays the iPhoto window for each of the backups it has.

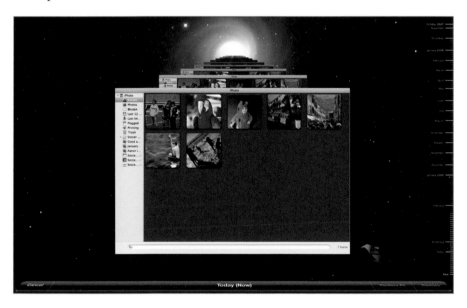

2   Click an iPhoto window from some previous date.

3   Select a photo, and then, in the lower right of Time Machine, click Restore.

iPhoto will import any photo no longer in the library into iPhoto. If the photo is still in the library, iPhoto gives you a chance to decide whether to import the duplicate or not. If you've restored multiple photos, you can also apply your decision to any other duplicates iPhoto encounters.

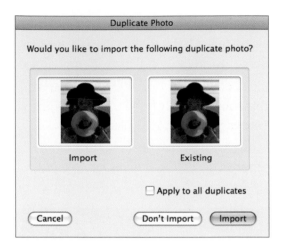

So now, with your library backed up safe and secure, you can quit iPhoto and relax. Or you can keep playing around with iPhoto to discover some of the other things it can do. After all, you can always use your backups to recover from any missteps.

Lesson Review

1. How can you save a snapshot of your iPhoto library?
2. What do you have to do to back up your iPhoto library with Time Machine?
3. What is a theme?
4. What is a layout?
5. What do you need an Apple account for?
6. What does a yellow warning icon mean when you see it on a picture in a card, calendar page, or book page, or by a print size on a print order form?
7. What aspect ratio should pictures have in a book?
8. How can you preview how your picture book will look when printed, without ordering it?

Answers

1. Record a copy of it on a recordable CD or DVD by using the Burn command.

2. Make sure that Time Machine is turned on and backing up your Mac to a backup drive. Time Machine automatically backs up your library along with other changes you make on your Mac, at regular intervals.

3. A theme is a collection of visually related layouts for printing or display. When you create a greeting card, picture book, or calendar project, you begin by choosing a theme. You can change a project's theme at any time.

4. A layout is a particular arrangement of items on a page. For example, one page in a picture book may use a single-picture layout, and the next page may use a four-picture layout.

5. You need an Apple account to buy professionally printed copies of picture prints, books, greeting cards, and calendars using iPhoto.

6. The yellow warning icon appears when a picture's resolution is too low for it to look good when it's printed professionally.

7. Picture books are designed to use pictures that have a 4:3 aspect ratio.

8. Control-click or right-click in the gray region beside a page in the book's layout area and then choose Preview Book. You can also click Slideshow to preview the book as a full-screen slideshow.

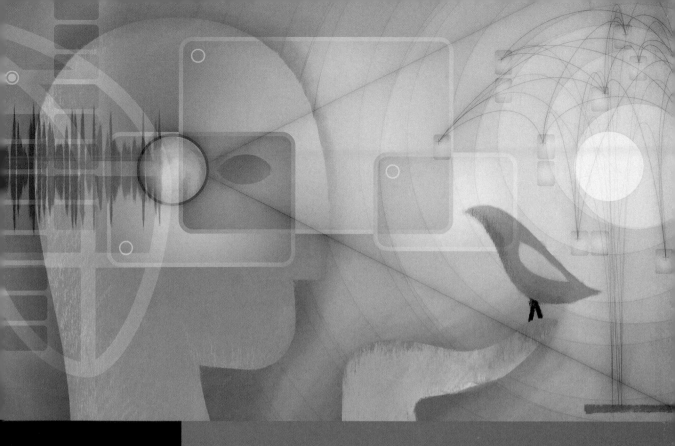

iMovie: Making Great Movies

Michael Wohl is an award-winning filmmaker who has written, directed, and edited independent films for more than fifteen years. He was part of the original team that designed Final Cut Pro's award-winning workflow and interface. Currently teaching at UCLA film school, Michael's other books include *Apple Pro Training Series: Final Cut Pro 6 Beyond the Basics* and *Apple Pro Training Series: Final Cut Pro 6: The Craft of Editing*.

5

Lesson Files   After installation:

~/Movies/iMovie Projects/Christmas Morning - Finished

Time   This lesson takes approximately 30 minutes to complete.

Goals   Create a new iMovie project

Organize Events in the Event Library

Understand the video skimming, playback, and selection tools

Assemble, adjust, and reorder clips in your project

Learn how to add transitions to your movie

Add background audio

Apply a theme to your movie

Customize the theme transitions

Do it all in 30 minutes or less

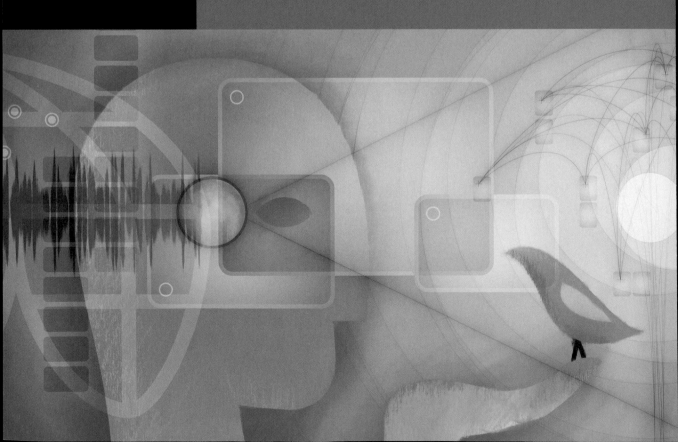

Instant Moviemaking: Creating Your First iMovie

Video has become ubiquitous. Most of us have many hours of video, recorded on special occasions like weddings, births, vacations, or sometimes just fooling around at home. Your video probably came from a camcorder, but these days, it's almost as likely it came from your still camera, a Flip camera, your phone, or from your computer's built-in camera.

iMovie '09 provides everything you need to organize, streamline, and edit those precious memories to capture the highlights, eliminate the junk, and effortlessly share your edited movies with the world.

iMovie '09 is remarkably simple to use and will feel very familiar to iPhoto users. In iMovie, your video is automatically organized into Events and individual shots, just like your photos in iPhoto. If all you want to do is hide the bad parts and catalog the good stuff, you'll be finished in no time—and you'll likely find the process fun and instantly rewarding. But iMovie can also do so much more.

From constructing sequences and fine-tuning edit points, to adding titles and transitions, to once-complicated special effects like green screen, color correction, and image stabilization, iMovie allows you to make your movies look indistinguishable from those cut with the most advanced tools available today.

Opening iMovie

iMovie is designed to streamline and simplify the video editing process. It works very differently from other video editors, so if you have some experience with similar tools, there might be a slight adjustment required. Fortunately, iMovie is quite intuitive and flexible. Regardless of your experience level, you'll likely find yourself comfortable with it very quickly.

> **NOTE** ▶ If you have a camcorder, make sure it's unplugged from your Mac before launching iMovie. When you connect a camera to your Mac (as we'll do in Lesson 7), iMovie will automatically recognize it and open the Import Video window. But for this exercise, we'll use the movie files on the DVD, so we don't want iMovie to see your camera just yet. For now, keep the camera disconnected.

1   Open iMovie by clicking its icon in the Dock or double-clicking its icon in your Applications folder.

The application window opens.

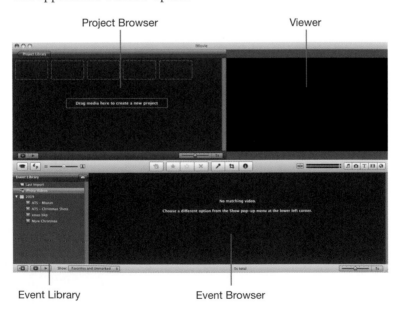

The window is divided into four main areas, with a toolbar in the middle. The upper-left area is the Project Browser. The dotted rectangles will be replaced by the clips of your movie when you start assembling it shortly.

The upper-right area is the Viewer, where clips will play.

The lower-left area is the Event Library, which works exactly like iPhoto's, displaying your footage organized by date or by Event.

The lower-right area is the Event Browser, where you view all of the clips stored in each Event.

The toolbar runs through the middle of the window. It contains buttons to perform the most commonly used functions and to access additional media types such as music and still images, as well as transitions, titles, and other useful things.

Managing Events

Before you get carried away making your movie, you'll need to get familiar with the way the raw footage is organized and managed in the Event Library.

> **NOTE ▶** There are many additional ways to get footage into iMovie, which will be covered in Lesson 7, but for this lesson, you'll use the footage provided on the DVD.

1   If you did not already do so, double-click the installer on the enclosed iLife09 DVD and restart iMovie to get access to the project files.

2   In the Event Library in the lower-left portion of the screen, expand the 2009 folder to reveal the individual Events.

In addition to any Events of your own, you should see several events that were added when you installed the book files.

3   Select ATS - Christmas Shots.

The clips from the Event fill the Event Browser.

Viewing Clips

The Event Browser shows you thumbnails of the clips within the Event. The clips can be any length; the number of frames that a thumbnail represents is determined by the setting on your zoom slider, in the lower-right corner of the Event Browser.

Moving your pointer across items in the Event Browser automatically displays that clip in the Viewer. This is called *skimming*.

1   Drag the zoom slider in the lower-right corner to 10s.

This sets each thumbnail to represent up to 10 seconds and allows you to view the entire Event in the Event Browser.

2   Skim across the clips to review the footage.

NOTE ▶ Skimming shows you exactly what's at the point of the playhead. Because you can move your pointer quickly or slowly, you can skim through your footage at whatever speed and in whatever direction you prefer.

TIP ▶ As you begin to skim through the video, you'll notice that the audio is skimming, too. This can be distracting to people around you, or even to your own train of thought. To turn off the audio while you're skimming, click the Audio Skimming toggle button on the center toolbar.

Audio Skimming button

Although skimming is very helpful for getting a quick overview of the footage in your Event, there is no substitute for simply watching the footage play.

3 Skim back to the beginning of the first clip, then press the spacebar to play the footage.

Playhead

The playhead moves across the clips, beginning wherever your pointer is and moving directly from one clip to the next until all the footage has been played. If you started in the middle, it will loop back to the first clip at the end.

Rejecting Footage

Even if you never intend to edit your clips into a slick finished movie, it's a great idea to at least eliminate the junk so next time you watch it, you won't have to sit through the bits that are boring or out of focus, or that time when you forgot the camera was on.

Just like hiding the bad photos in an iPhoto event, you can quickly and easily hide selected parts of your footage by using the Reject feature, either hiding them without deleting them permanently or flushing them to save disk space.

1 Skim the first clip.

The first half of the shot has a nice moment where the blond girl walks off, revealing the crawling baby behind her, but a moment later, a man walks in front of the baby and there's a good five or six seconds of "junk" before another clear shot of the girl emerges.

2   Click just after the man picks up the trash and drag the pointer to the right until the shot comes back into focus (about 5–6 seconds).

A yellow highlight appears on the selected region.

3   Click the Reject button in the toolbar or press R.

That section of the clip is removed from the project. The area before it and the area after it become two separate clips.

The Event Browser is set by default to hide rejected clips, but if you ever want to see them again (just to make sure they're complete junk), you can set the Browser to several different view modes.

4   Set the Show menu in the Event Browser to Rejected Only.

5   Set the Show menu to All Clips.

The rejected area is marked with a red bar.

TIP ▶ You can also reject a selection by pressing Delete. This doesn't remove the footage from your hard disk, just adds it to the rejected clips list.

6   Set the Show menu back to "Favorites and Unmarked" or press Command-L.

You haven't yet marked any favorites, but the "Favorites and Unmarked" setting allows you to see everything except what you've rejected.

NOTE ▶ For the sake of this lesson, most of these clips have been pre-trimmed to include only the best moments. In your own footage, you will likely reject huge swaths of your footage. If you do, you're in good company. Most Hollywood feature films only use 1 to 5 percent of the footage they shoot. Documentaries use even less than that! Trust me: The shorter your movie is, the better.

Marking Favorites

The opposite of rejecting clips is marking your favorites. This gives you another opportunity to review your footage and identify all the best parts.

1   Position your pointer over the beginning of the third clip and press the spacebar to play it.

The shot shows the two girls running into the room to get their presents.

2   Press the spacebar to stop playback. Find the frame just before the first girl enters and drag to the right, all the way to the end of the clip.

The selected area is bordered in yellow.

3 Click the "Mark as Favorite" button or press F.

A green bar appears at the top of that section of the clip.

4 Click anywhere in the gray background area to deselect the clip.

The yellow selection goes away, but the green bar remains.

Your finished movie may not include all of your favorite bits, but marking them is a great way to refine your selections before adding anything to your sequence.

Building a Project

For some Events, just rejecting the junk and highlighting your favorites may be all you need to do. At any point you can come back and review the Event, just as you would look at an Event in your iPhoto library.

But for some other Events, you may want to string a bunch of clips together to create a polished movie. You may have deliberately shot your footage to be edited, with multiple angles, and lots of coverage and carefully planned shots, or you may be trying to construct a finished-looking movie from footage that was haphazardly shot, such as the Christmas footage used in this lesson.

In either case, iMovie can help. However, if you want to learn some great shooting tips that will make your editing job easier, check out Lesson 7.

Creating a New Project

You can create new projects in a number of ways, including just dragging a clip into the Project Browser. For this lesson you'll create a project before adding any clips to it.

1 Click the Project Library button in the upper-left corner of the window.

The Project Library opens. The Project Library is where you can see all of the projects saved on your disk.

2 Click the Add (+) button in the lower right of the Project Library.

A dialog appears in which you can enter a name and select a theme for your project.

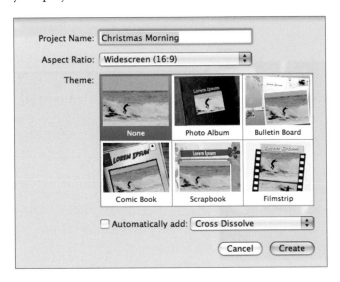

3 In the Name field, type *Christmas Morning*.

4 Leave the Aspect Ratio set to Widescreen (16:9).

iMovie has several great themes that add character and fun graphics to your project. Later in this lesson you'll add a theme to this project, but for now, start with a plain un-themed project.

5 Click the None box in the group of themes and then click the Create button.

A new project is created, and the Project Browser automatically reopens.

6 In the Event Browser, click the green Favorite bar you created in the previous exercise.

NOTE ▶ Be careful to click the green bar itself, not the clip. Your selection should look like the picture below.

The marked section of the clip is automatically selected.

7   Choose View > Play Selection or press the / (forward slash) key to watch just the selected area. It's always wise to check exactly what you've selected before you add it to your program.

8   Drag the selected clip to the Project Browser in the upper left.

The clip is added to the project.

The Project Browser works very much like the Event Browser. You can skim or play the clips, and there is a slider in the lower right to adjust the size of the clips in the window.

Adding More Clips

There are a variety of ways to add clips to your project. In the next few steps you'll add clips using different methods.

1   In the Event Browser, click the fifth clip, of the two girls unwrapping gifts.

When you click a clip, iMovie automatically selects a four-second section. This is Apple's polite way of encouraging you to keep your shots—and by extension your finished movies—short. Your audience will thank you.

However, for the sake of this lesson, you're going to override that good intention and add the whole clip.

2   Press Command-A to select the whole clip.

3   Click the "Add to Project" button in the toolbar.

The clip is added after the first clip. This is a good time to play your project to see how the two clips look together.

4   Position your pointer anywhere over the Project Browser and press \.

Pressing the spacebar plays the clip from the current pointer position, but pressing the \ (backslash) key always plays from the very beginning.

As you add clips to the project, they're marked with an orange bar at the bottom of the clip in the Event Browser.

5   Click anywhere on the next clip in the Event Browser (the sixth clip).

6   Shift-click the second-to-last clip to select all the clips between.

7   Press E to automatically edit the clips into the project.

NOTE ▸ When you add multiple clips to your project simultaneously, iMovie suggests adding clips individually. This is a great tip, but for this lesson, just click Continue.

The clips are added in the order they were selected.

8 Move your pointer over the Project Browser and press \ to watch your whole project. Then click the last clip in the Event Browser.

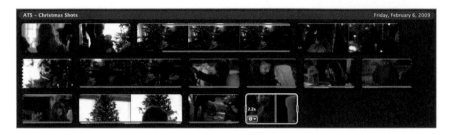

Because this clip is shorter than five seconds, the whole clip is automatically selected.

9 Drag the clip to the project, and drop it between the second and third clips.

A green bar appears to show you where the clip will be dropped. Be careful not to drop it on top of one of the existing clips.

By dragging to a specific location in the Project Browser, you can control exactly where in your movie the new shot will be added. By dragging to a space in between two clips, you can insert the new shot between those two shots.

If you drag onto an existing shot, a menu of choices will appear when you release the mouse button. To learn more about these options, see Lesson 8.

10 Click the first clip in the Event Browser. Then press Command-A to select the whole clip, and drag it into the project. Drop it just before the last clip.

Rearranging Clips

Now that your project is coming together, you can begin to finesse it by making changes in the Project Browser.

1 Play the project by pressing \.

   The show is coming together very well, but you may notice that there are two shots of the blond girl in a row, and then two shots of the dark-haired girl. It might feel more balanced to alternate between them.

2 Click the first shot of the blond-haired girl (the third clip in the project).

3 When the pointer turns into a hand, drag it between the two shots of the dark-haired girl (clips 5 and 6). When you see the green bar appear, release the mouse button.

The clips are rearranged.

4   Play the project again.

The rearrangement works, and the show is looking pretty good. But there are still a few improvements you can make.

Adjusting Clips

Although you already decided how long each clip should be when you added it to the project, it's very common to refine those choices once you watch the whole show.

Making small changes to individual clips in your project is easy, and there's more than one way to do it.

1   Position your pointer on the second-to-last clip and press the spacebar.

This clip shows the baby crawling toward the presents, but then that guy walks in front of the camera and ruins our shot.

2   Skim over the clip until you see the frame just before the man crosses into view.

3   Click there, and drag to the right to select the rest of the clip.

A yellow border appears around the selected region.

4 Press Delete to remove the frames, then move your pointer to the beginning of the clip and press the spacebar.

The beginning of the next clip also has a few frames that are out of focus. Now you'll use a different technique to shave off those few bad frames.

5 Position your pointer over the beginning of the last clip and hold down the Command and Option keys.

An orange border appears around the edge of the clip, and the adjacent clips temporarily scoot out of the way.

6 Click the orange handle, and while watching the Viewer, drag to the right until the shot comes into focus. Then release the mouse button.

The bad frames are removed.

Precision Editing

One of the best new features in iMovie '09 is the Precision Editor. You'll learn the ins and outs of this powerful tool in Lesson 8, but for now we'll open it briefly to make one additional edit.

1 Position your pointer over the fourth clip from the end, as pictured below, and press the spacebar.

Play this clip

This is a great moment, as the girl's face lights up when she realizes what the present is, and then she says, "That was just what I wanted!"

Unfortunately, the videographer was so taken by her cuteness that he stopped paying attention to the camera, leaving us with great sound but useless picture. (Thanks, Dad!)

You'll fix this by removing the boring video frames but leaving the audio to overlap the next shot.

2   Double-click the space after this shot ends and before the Christmas tree shot begins. (Click the gray area to the right of the clip.)

The Precision Editor opens, covering the Event Browser.

The Precision Editor is like a zoomed-in view of the edit point between the two clips, and it allows you to make fine adjustments to each of the clips.

3   Position your pointer over the end of the first (upper) clip and drag left, watching the Viewer.

4   Drag until just before the blond girl's face moves out of the frame (about 6 seconds).

Time Offset Indicator

When you release the mouse button, the clip is shortened.

Removed frames

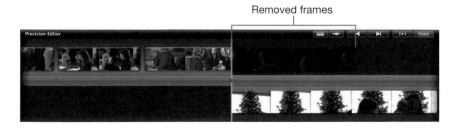

The edit point updates back to the center of the screen. The darkened thumbnails to the right show the frames you removed from the shot.

5   Move your pointer to the beginning of the left clip and press the spacebar to see the new edit.

The clip is shorter, which is great, but you also cut off the audio that was so cute. Next you'll add that audio back in, on top of the Christmas tree clip.

6   Click the Show Audio Tracks button.

Blue bars indicating the audio tracks appear above and below the video clips. The darkened portion to the right of the playhead contains the audio we want to hear, but currently it's turned off.

7   Position your pointer over the edit point on the upper audio clip and drag right until you reach the end of the clip.

The audio is added back to the project, overlapping the beginning of the Christmas tree shot.

8   Move your pointer to the left side of the screen and press the spacebar to play the project.

9   If you're satisfied with the edit, click Done in the upper-right corner of the Precision Editor.

    The window closes and your edits are incorporated into your movie.

Now, that's a pretty fancy edit!

Finishing Your Movie

Once you've gotten the edits the way you like, there are many additional bells and whistles you can add to create a professional, polished-looking finished piece. The first one you'll learn is how to reframe a clip.

Sometimes the framing of your shots may be less than ideal. The action may be off-center or the camera may be zoomed out too far. Fortunately, iMovie has a powerful cropping tool that allows you to zoom in on your clips and make them look their best.

1   Click the last clip in the project to select it.

2   Click the Crop, Rotate and Ken Burns button in the toolbar.

Crop, Rotate, and Ken Burns button

The Viewer updates to show a selection rectangle around the video. In this case, you'll zoom in to center the baby in the frame. You want to be sure the sequence looks great when the kid looks at the camera at the end of the shot.

3   Move your pointer over one of the last frames in the clip and click it to freeze the Viewer on the frame.

4   In the Viewer, grab the corner of the green selection rectangle and shrink it, then position it so the baby is well-framed within the shot.

5   When you're satisfied with your cropping, click Done in the upper-right corner of the Viewer.

The crop is applied and the Crop, Rotate and Ken Burns window closes.

NOTE ▶ By zooming in on this frame, we're changing the resolution of the clip. Because we're planning to post this on the Internet (and we started out with high-definition video), this resolution loss shouldn't affect the picture quality noticeably. But be aware that playing cropped footage on a TV or a large monitor may show a loss in quality.

To learn more about cropping and creating Ken Burns effects, see Lesson 9.

Improving Color

Another aspect of your project that could use some improvement is the picture quality. One shot might be too dark, or the camera's white balance might have been set incorrectly, and so on. iMovie has easy-to-use tools to hide such mistakes and make your movie look beautiful.

1   Position your pointer over the first clip and pause until a small blue menu appears.

Action pop-up menu

2   Click the menu and choose Video Adjustments.

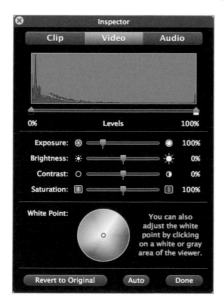

The Video Inspector opens. The controls here are very similar to the options available in iPhoto.

This shot is underexposed and will look a lot better if you brighten it up.

3 Increase the Exposure slider to about 160%.

This succeeds in brightening the image, but brightening it caused the color to seem a little drab.

4 Increase the Contrast to about 30% and increase the Saturation to about 160%.

5 When you're satisfied with the color settings, click Done.

TIP You may want to make similar adjustments to some of the other clips in this project.

Adding Transition Effects

Another way to make your movie look slick and professional is to add transition effects between clips. iMovie makes adding transitions easy and fun.

In this movie, the first two clips are making a jump cut, because the girls are in almost exactly the same place, but some frames have been removed. Such an edit feels abrupt and is a perfect place to add a transition effect.

1   Click the Show Transition Browser button in the toolbar.

Show Transition Browser button

The Transition Browser appears to the right of the Event Browser.

2   Position your pointer over the icons for the different transition effects to see a preview of each effect.

3   Drag the Wipe Right transition to the space in between the first two clips.

4   Press \ to play the project from the beginning and watch the transition effect.

The effect looks cool, but if you're not satisfied, you can easily preview how the other effects look on these two clips.

5 Double-click the transition icon in the Project Browser.

The Transition Inspector opens. Here you can type in a new duration to make the transition effect longer or shorter, and you can swap out a different transition effect.

6 Click the Transition button (which currently reads Wipe Right).

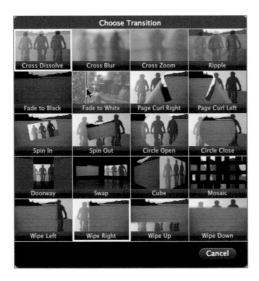

The Transition Browser appears.

7 Skim across the transition icons and watch the Viewer to see how the different effects look on your two clips.

8 Press the spacebar to begin preview playback.

The Viewer shows a loop of the transition effect. As you move your pointer over the different effects, you can see each of them play in real time.

9 Press the spacebar again to stop looping, and click the Circle Open effect to select it.

The Transition Browser closes.

10 Click Done to close the Transition inspector.

TIP ▶ Although the tasteful use of select transitions can make your show look more professional, overusing such effects or, worse, mixing many different types, tends to have the opposite effect.

Adding Audio

Music and sound effects are incredibly powerful tools for improving your movie. Simply putting the right song behind a collection of clips transforms it, uniting the shots and giving the whole movie a consistent tone. Of course, choosing the wrong music can do an equal amount of damage, so choose wisely.

In iMovie, you can access all the music in your iTunes library, as well as any music you may have created in GarageBand. Furthermore, iLife '09 comes with a large collection of music and sound effects ready to be added to your project quickly and easily. Adding sound effects can be your secret weapon to make your movies feel realistic and professional.

1   Click the Audio Browser button in the toolbar.

Show Audio Browser button

The Audio Browser appears. In the top half of the window you'll see the available libraries.

2   Poke around in the libraries to see the variety of sounds available to you. To sample any sound, select it in the list and click the Play button.

You can also search for specific sounds.

3   Select the iMovie Sound Effects folder in the top of the window, and in the search field in the bottom of the window, type *Sleigh Bell*.

A single file is listed in the bottom of the window.

4   Select Sleigh Bell Percussion.mp3 and click the Play button.

5   Drag the audio file into the Project Browser.

If you position your pointer over the gray background area, it lights up green.

6   Drop the audio in the gray area to add it as a background track.

The clip is added to the project, starting at the beginning of the movie.

NOTE ▶ Don't drop the music clip on any of the video clips themselves, or the music will attach to that clip. We'll get into iMovie's more advanced audio tools in Lesson 10.

Because the audio clip is short, it ends in the middle of the first clip. If you wanted the sleigh bell sound to loop, you could just drag additional copies of it into your project.

If the clip were longer, as a music track might be, it could extend all the way to the end of your video clips. If the clip were longer than your movie, iMovie would automatically fade it out as your last video clip ends.

For more on working with audio in iMovie, see Lesson 10.

Using Themes

iMovie '09 comes with a set of fun themes that apply customized titles and transition effects to your movie. Using a theme ensures that all the effects in your movie have a consistent, stylish look. Adding a theme will transform your movie from a group of clips into a finished movie with a single click.

1   Open the Transitions Browser, then click the Set Theme button.

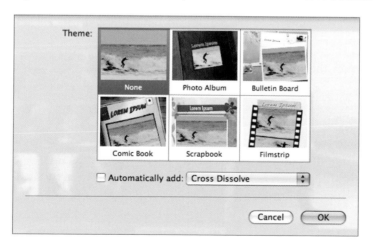

The Theme Selection window opens.

2 Skim across the theme icons to see a sample of each type of graphics the theme employs, and click the Scrapbook theme.

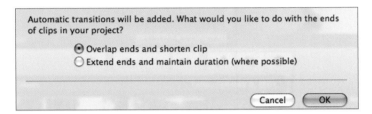

Additional settings appear.

3 Leave the other at their defaults and click OK.

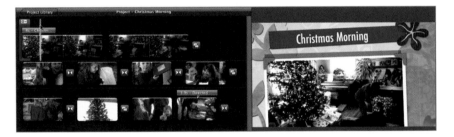

The theme is applied to your project.

The gold bars on top of the first and last clips are titles. iMovie '09 also adds transition effects between each of the clips.

4 Press \ to play the whole project from the beginning.

Customizing Your Theme

Each theme uses special, custom transitions that match the visual style of the titles, but applying these to every edit would get tedious. So iMovie automatically uses a mix of special transitions and simple cross-dissolves to create the perfect balance.

Of course, you might not agree with the default arrangement. In that case, you can rearrange the transition effects or set different effects for any individual edit, just as you did in the previous exercise.

When the theme is applied, four new transitions are added in the top row of the Transition Browser.

These transitions are unique to the active theme, and are not available to use unless the theme is applied.

Customizing Transitions

The theme transitions have another special element to them. They incorporate still images taken from clips in your movie.

iMovie selects a few frames at random, but you can customize which frames of your movie are used, ensuring that you get the very best images.

1   Select the custom transition between the second and third clips.

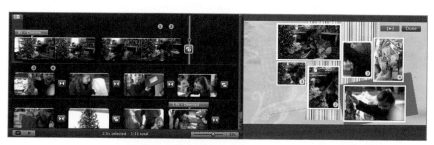

The transition is displayed in the Viewer, and four numbered markers appear in the Project Browser. The markers indicate which frames are being used for the still images in the transition effect.

2 Drag the #1 Marker to another frame in the movie. Watch the Viewer to see the new frame you're selecting.

3 Repeat step 2 with the other three markers, choosing your favorite frames from the movie.

4 When you're satisfied, click the Done button in the Viewer and play across the transition to see the results of your work.

Modifying Titles

Themes also add titles to your movie. Titles appear on top of clips, and those clips play inside the window of the title card. To change the video shown in the title card, drag the title to a new position, or even add a new clip just for the title.

1 In the Event Browser, click anywhere in the fourth clip, the close-up shots of the Christmas tree.

A four-second section of the clip is selected.

Earlier you learned to move the yellow handles to select different parts of a clip, but if you want to keep the four-second duration and change which four seconds to use, you can move the yellow boundary from side to side without resizing it.

2   Click the top or bottom of the yellow boundary and drag left or right to move the selection earlier or later in time.

TIP ▶ If you have a Multi-Touch trackpad, you can also use a two-finger swipe to move the selection left or right in the clip.

3   Press / (forward slash) to play the selected area. When you've found a good section, drag it to the project, dropping it before the first clip.

The title plays over the new clip, and the clip that used to begin the movie starts right after the title.

You can also change the text in the titles. By default, the opening title uses the name of the project, and the closing credit uses your system login name, but naturally you can change both to read whatever you like.

4   Click the gold title bar above the last clip in the project.

The title opens in the Viewer. The text boxes are editable.

5 Click the "Directed by" text and type *Delivered by.* Then press Enter. You can also change the name text if you like.

6 When you're satisfied, click Done in the Viewer.

> **NOTE** ▶ Most titles also allow you to modify the font and color of the text. These options are not available in Theme titles.

We'll go much deeper into adding and customizing titles in Lesson 9.

Adding a Map

Well, your movie is just about perfect now, but that doesn't mean you can't keep trying to improve it. Another one of the great new features in iMovie '09 is the ability to add fun animated maps to your movies. Most people use this to highlight their vacation and travel videos, but that's not all it's good for.

1 Click the Show Maps and Backgrounds button in the toolbar.

Show Maps and Backgrounds button

The Map Browser opens. In addition to a variety of maps, this window also has a variety of backgrounds you can use for titles and other effects.

2 Drag the Old World Globe map to the project and drop it between the first two clips.

The map is added to the project and the Map Inspector automatically opens.

Maps create magical little animations to show travel from the start location to the end location—or if you choose just one place, the map will perform a simple zoom in to the selected spot.

3   Click the Start Location button.

The window flips over, and a list of locations appears. iMovie has thousands of places to choose from.

4   In the search field, type *Barrow*.

Two choices should appear.

5   Select BRW – Wiley Post Will Rogers Mem.

6   In the "Name to display on map" field, type *North Pole* and click OK.

The map updates to show the selected city. Barrow is the northernmost spot available in the iMovie map, so it will have to stand in for the North Pole.

7   In the Map Inspector, click the End Location button.

The window flips over again.

8   Type *Atlanta* into the search field (or enter the city of your choice).

9   Select your city from the list, and In the "Name to display on map" field, type *Our House* and click OK.

10   Click Done to close the Map Inspector.

11   Press \ to play your whole movie from the very beginning.

Congratulations! You've completed your first iMovie!

In the next few lessons you'll learn how to share your project with the world, and we'll venture much deeper into all the powerful editing and effects tools that iMovie has to offer. If this lesson whetted your appetite, then get ready for a feast of fun and fascination ahead.

Lesson Review

1. Where do you view your raw footage?

2. Are rejected clips automatically deleted from the hard disk?

3. Name two ways to add clips to a project.

4. True or false: Once a clip is added to a project, its length can't be changed.

5. Where can you zoom in on a clip?

6. How do you change the exposure of a clip?

7. How do you preview different transition effects on the clips in your project?

8. Where do you drop an audio file to add it to the background?

9. How do you customize the still frames used in a theme transition?

10. Where do you set the name of the cities displayed on a map?

Answers

1. In the Event Browser.

2. No, they're just hidden in the default Event Browser view.

3. Drag to the Project Browser, click the "Add to Project" button, or press E.

4. False.

5. In the Crop, Rotate and Ken Burns window.

6. Click the Clip pop-up menu, choose Video Adjustments, and drag the Exposure slider.

7. In the Inspector, click the Transition button and skim or play over the different effects.

8. Drop it on the gray background in the Project Browser.

9. Double-click the transition and move the numbered markers in the Project Browser.

10. In the "Name to display on map" field of the Map Inspector.

6

Lesson Files   No additional files

Time   This lesson takes approximately 30 minutes to complete.

Goals   Play your movie and your source footage full screen

Learn how to share your movies in a variety of sizes and formats using iTunes

Understand how to send your movies to GarageBand, iDVD, and iWeb

Publish your movies to YouTube and your MobileMe Gallery

Prepare to burn a DVD of your movie

Export to QuickTime

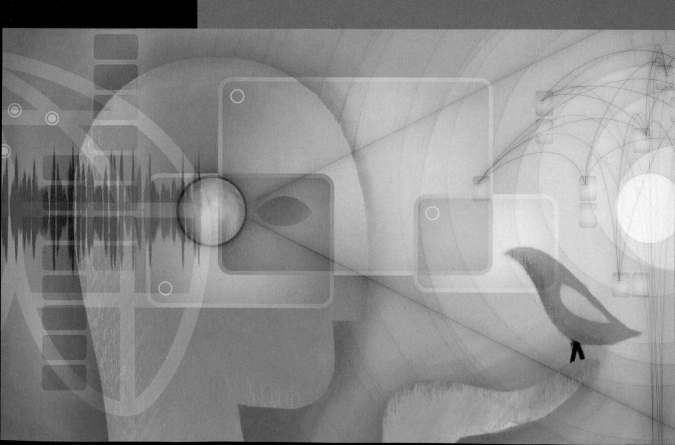

Lesson 6

Tell All the World: Sharing and Publishing Your Movie

It's satisfying to put the finishing touches on your movie, dust off your hands, and close the project, but that's nothing compared with the giddy enjoyment of sharing your work with friends, family, and strangers alike.

This lesson will describe the various ways iMovie makes it dangerously simple to publish your movies to a variety of formats and venues, often with nothing more than a single click.

Fortunately, if you decide to make changes to your movie after you've published it (and trust me, you will), iMovie keeps track of when and where you've sent your baby out into the world, so you can effortlessly update the public versions as soon as you declare your local copy *fin*.

Sharing Right Here, Right Now

The most immediate (and most fun) way to share your movie with others is to play it for them right on your computer, straight out of iMovie. No rendering time, no waiting by the phone for their feedback. This also has the added benefit that you can implement their suggestions in real time.

Playing Movies Full Screen

iMovie can play your project back full screen anytime, anywhere. In fact, you can watch your raw footage full screen too, selecting your Events using the Cover Flow interface.

1   If the Christmas Morning project isn't already open in your Project Browser, click the Project Library button in the upper-left corner of the iMovie window.

2   In the Project Library, double-click the Christmas Morning - (Lesson 6) project.

   The Project Browser will reopen with the Christmas Morning - (Lesson 6) project loaded.

3   Click the Play Project Full-screen button or press Command-G.

Play Project Full-screen button

Your display will fade to black, and your movie will begin to play full screen.

TIP There is a similar Play Full Screen button in the bottom-left corner of the Event Browser that will load your raw footage into the full-screen player.

4   Press the spacebar to start and stop playback.

5   Move your pointer to open the Full-screen Playback controls.

Play

"Show Projects or Events" button

Close Full-screen Viewer

Thumbstrip

Cover Flow View button

Automatically Hide Thumbstrip button

Although this view does make your picture a little smaller, these controls allow you to do much more than just watch your movie. You can skim the project, jump right to a particular section, or even access your library Events.

6   Move your pointer over the thumbstrip to skim across your project.

Switching Between Projects and Events

The Full-screen Viewer can display anything you normally view in the Viewer. That means not just projects, but Events, too.

1 Click the "Show Projects or Events" button in the lower left.

The thumbstrip updates to show all of the Events in your library in a Cover Flow view.

2 Click the Cover Flow button in the upper right.

The view updates to show a single thumbstrip for the current Event.

When you're ready to return to the regular iMovie interface, or if you want to switch to another program on your Mac, you must close the Full-screen Viewer.

3 Click the close button in the lower-left corner of the screen or press Escape.

The main iMovie window reappears.

Sharing at School

It's one thing to bring someone over and show your movie on your computer screen, but it's even more fun to whip out your iPhone and show it to the guy in line behind you at the campus bookstore … or more realistically, to share it with Aunt Cecily at the family reunion, or an agent during a big interview.

Sharing to iTunes

To create a movie that can be played on an iPod, iPhone, Apple TV, or any computer using iTunes, you use the Share to iTunes command.

1   Make sure the Christmas Morning project is open.

2   Choose Share > iTunes.

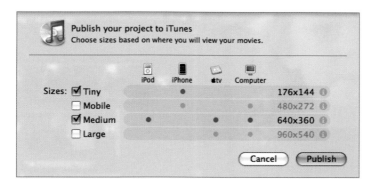

A dialog opens asking you which size you would like to publish to. The icons help you identify your target device (iPod, iPhone, Apple TV, or computer), and the dots beneath each icon indicate which sizes are suitable for which one. The numbers to the right indicate the video's dimensions (width x height) in pixels.

NOTE ▶ If your original media isn't large enough to render in any of these sizes, those options will be dimmed.

3   Select the Tiny and Medium options.

When you select these two options, your movie will be viewable on all three of the Apple devices, as well as on full-size computers.

4   Hold your pointer over the "i" at the far right of a size option, and information about that choice will pop up.

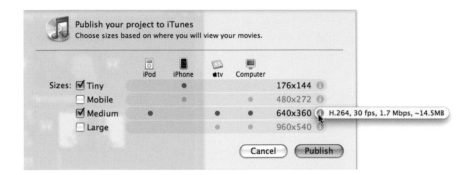

The pop-up shows you the compression format, frames per second, megabits per second, and the approximate size of the file you'll be creating.

TIP Pay close attention to the last number: the file size. Longer movies with larger file sizes, particularly those created with HD footage, can quickly chew up your iPod or iPhone disk space.

5   Click Publish.

When iMovie has finished publishing your movie in the sizes and formats you've selected, iTunes will open automatically.

Once your movie is in iTunes, you're ready to load it onto your iPod, iPhone, or Apple TV, and of course you can play it right there in iTunes.

NOTE ▶ When your files have been published to iTunes, the files can be found in the Movies section of your iTunes library.

Once your project has been shared, iMovie lets you know at a glance where your movie is, and in which sizes you've rendered it.

Movie sizes (white squares are already saved)

The four bars represent the four sizes: Tiny, Mobile, Medium, and Large. Because you chose Tiny and Medium, the first and third bars are highlighted. iMovie also notes where you've published your movie, adding a "Shared to" bar at the top of the Project Browser.

NOTE ▶ If you're not seeing the bars, open the "Finished" version of the project in the Project Library to show the bars.

6   Click the View button on the "Shared to" bar to open iTunes and watch your movie.

Sharing to the Whole World

The more confident you are with your movie, the more people you'll want to share it with, and if you want to share it with the whole world, you can post your movie on YouTube. It's free, and it's the most popular video sharing website in the galaxy.

Sharing to YouTube

iMovie will handle the whole process: rendering your movie, uploading it to YouTube's servers (provided you have a YouTube account), and even generating an email for you to send to your friends with a link to the movie.

TIP If you don't currently have a YouTube account, or you want to create a new one just for the movies you publish with iMovie, go to YouTube.com and click Sign Up.

1 Choose Share > YouTube.

The "Publish your project to YouTube" dialog appears.

If this is your first time sharing to YouTube, you need to add your account name to the Account pop-up menu.

2 Click Add.

3 Enter your YouTube username in the Add Account field and click Done.

4 Select the username from the Account pop-up menu.

5 Enter your YouTube password in the Password field.

6 Choose a category, type a description of the movie, and enter some tags that will help people find your movie when searching.

7   Select Medium as the "Size to publish."

Because you already created a Medium-sized movie when sharing to iTunes, selecting that option will be much quicker than selecting the Mobile size, which you haven't yet created.

8   Select the "Make this movie personal" checkbox. Your movie will be available only to people on your YouTube Friends & Contacts list.

> **TIP** ▶ If you want to make your video available to anyone in the whole YouTube community, deselect the "Make this movie personal" checkbox.

9   Click Next.

10 Read the YouTube terms of service (no, really, read them) and click Publish.

iMovie uploads the movie to YouTube.

> **NOTE** ▶ If iMovie has trouble connecting to YouTube, which might happen if you entered your password improperly, or your Internet connection isn't working, you will get an error message, requiring you to share to YouTube again. However, this second time, the process will go more quickly because the file to be uploaded will already have been created.

When it's finished, iMovie provides you with the direct link to the video and gives you the option to tell a friend, view the movie, or do neither of those things right now.

Your video has been uploaded to YouTube. It may be several minutes or hours before your video is processed and viewable, depending on YouTube's server load.

Your video can be viewed at: http://www.youtube.com/watch?v=pqmLlzlOHf4

[Tell a Friend]   [View]   [OK]

11 Click OK.

A new bar appears at the top of the Project Browser.

12 Click the "Tell a friend" button.

Your email program opens and loads a pre-written email message, directing the reader to a link for your YouTube movie.

13 Enter a name or two into the email To field and go shopping for your Oscar outift.

Sharing to the Whole World At Better Quality

So now you've shared your movie with the world on YouTube, and like many other aspiring filmmakers, you may be disappointed with the way your masterpiece looks on its site.

Sharing to Your MobileMe Gallery

Although YouTube makes videos that just about anyone with an Internet connection can watch, they're not exactly known for having the best image quality (although recent improvements have helped some).

If you want to publish your movie at the highest possible quality and share it with friends, family, or clients, you can upload it to your personal MobileMe Gallery (account required). It may not be seen by quite as many people as the YouTube version, but you can be sure of the quality, and your viewers can download the movie to their own computers and watch it at their leisure.

1 Choose Share > MobileMe Gallery.

If you're not currently signed in to your MobileMe account, a Sign In dialog appears.

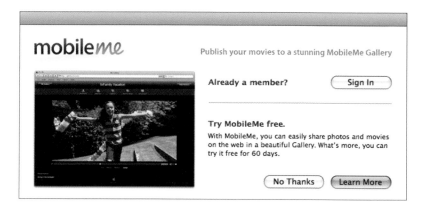

If you are already signed in, you can skip to step 4.

2   Click Sign In and follow the instructions, or click Learn More to sign up
for a new account.

3   When you have finished signing in, return to iMovie and choose Share >
MobileMe Gallery again.

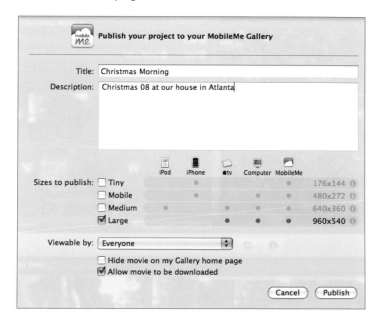

The "Publish your project to your MobileMe Gallery" dialog appears.

4   Enter a description for your movie and choose the Large size.

5   Choose who can view the movie in the "Viewable by" pop-up menu.

Selecting the "Hide movie on my Gallery home page" checkbox will
still publish the movie to your site, but viewers will need to know the
exact web address to find it. Otherwise, iMovie will add a link on your
MobileMe homepage that anyone can follow.

Selecting the "Allow movie to be downloaded" checkbox means a download link will be added to the MobileMe Gallery page. Otherwise, viewers
will have to watch the video play on your webpage.

6   Click Publish.

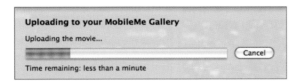

iMovie will create the new (large) version of the movie, then upload it to
your MobileMe page.

NOTE ▶ Because this file is so much bigger than the others, uploading it
may take significantly more time, depending on the speed of your Internet
connection.

When it's finished, iMovie will provide you with a direct link to the movie
as well as the Tell a Friend option.

7   Click OK.

Sharing with Your Collaborators

So now you know how to share your movie with the world, but what if you're
not quite finished with your movie yet? Maybe you need to polish the soundtrack in GarageBand, or prepare the movie for iDVD.

Sharing to the Media Browser

To share your movies seamlessly between programs, publish them to the iLife
Media Browser.

1   Choose Share > Media Browser.

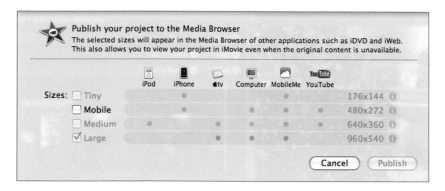

2   Select the size(s) you want, and click Publish.

> **NOTE** ▸ If you've already shared a particular file size to iTunes, that option
> won't be available here. (And if you've shared all the file sizes to iTunes,
> the Share > Media Browser command won't even be available.) That's
> because everything in iTunes is accessible through the Media Browser. The
> opposite is not true, however—files published to the Media Browser are
> not accessible through iTunes.

Finding Movies in the Media Browser

When you open GarageBand, iDVD, or iWeb, you'll find a small button near
the lower-right corner of the screen that opens the iLife Media Browser.

1   Open GarageBand, iDVD, or iWeb.

2   From within the application, open the iLife Media Browser.

In GarageBand

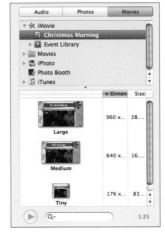

In iDVD

In iWeb

3   Click the Movies button, expand the iMovie section, and select the project name (in this case, Christmas Morning).

The various sizes you've published to the Media Browser or to iTunes are available for you to use.

Making Changes After Publishing

If you attempt to make changes to your project after you've already shared it, iMovie will try to stop you.

If you ignore the warning and make changes anyway, iMovie adds an "out of date" warning on the "Published to" bars at the top of the Project Browser.

At this point you have two options: Re-publish the movie or remove it from the published site.

Choosing "Remove from iTunes" will remove the movies from your iTunes playlist, delete the files from your disk, and remove the "Shared to" bar from the Project Browser. Choosing "Remove from MobileMe Gallery" will remove the movie from that site, and so on.

Choosing one of the Re-publish commands will reopen the pertinent "Publish your project to" dialog, and when you click Publish, the old movie files will be overwritten with the new ones.

Sharing in the Living Room

Yet another way you can output your finished movie is by sending it to iDVD to publish a disc that can be watched in any DVD player.

Adding Chapter Markers

When making DVDs, you can create chapter markers so your viewers can skip right to the best parts with their remote control. Having chapter markers in your movie will also allow iDVD to create a useful Chapters menu, just like the ones you see on commercial DVDs.

1   Choose iMovie > Preferences and click the General button.

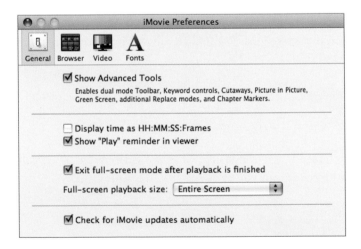

2   Select the Show Advanced Tools checkbox.

This adds a selection of new controls to the iMovie interface, allowing you to perform a variety of advanced techniques.

3   Close the Preferences window.

Chapter Marker button
Comment Marker button

Among other changes, two new controls appear in the upper-right corner of the Project Browser: the brown Comment Marker and the orange Chapter Marker buttons.

Adding comment markers to your program is a great way to add notes to yourself or to a potential collaborator (markers are always visible when a movie is opened in another program from the Media Browser).

Chapter markers are specifically used for chapter breaks on DVDs.

4   Drag an orange chapter marker from the icon in the upper-right corner to your video, and drop it just after the globe shot.

The marker is added as an orange flag above the video track. By default, the markers are numbered, but you can type anything you want.

5   Click the marker label and type *Girls Enter*.

6 Drag another marker to the shot where the Christmas tree is visible, and name it *Christmas Tree*.

7 Click the small pop-up triangle to the right of the marker buttons in the upper-right corner of the Project Browser.

This menu lists all the markers in your project. Choosing an item from the menu will take your playhead right to that spot.

Once you've added your chapter markers, you're ready to create a DVD version of your movie.

8 Choose Share > iDVD.

iMovie converts your movie to the format necessary for iDVD, and opens that application. A new DVD project is automatically created, and your movie is loaded.

Simply choose a theme and use iDVD to burn your disc.

Exporting a QuickTime Movie

When you need to share your movie with the other programs in the iLife suite, you'll use the Media Browser. But to share a high-quality copy of your movie with other people, the format of choice is QuickTime.

QuickTime has long been one of the most popular video formats on the Internet because of its impressive quality-to-compression ratio and because of the enormous flexibility of your export options. You can choose precise picture quality, compression rates, screen dimensions, sound-quality options, and more to suit your exact needs and file-size requirements.

Suppose you're creating an iWeb video blog, and you need your movie to be exactly 320 pixels wide. You can easily export a QuickTime movie to fit.

1   Choose Share > "Export using QuickTime."

2   Give your movie a filename, such as *Christmas Morning*, and choose where to save it.

For our purposes, save it to the desktop. That way it won't get lost.

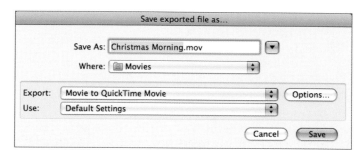

3   Click Options.

The Movie Settings dialog opens, enabling you to change Video and Sound settings (compression rates, size and scale, audio rates, and so on).

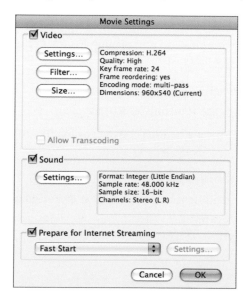

4   Click Size, choose Custom from the Dimensions menu, and enter *320* and *175* into the dimension boxes.

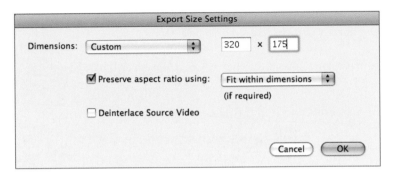

5   Select the "Preserve aspect ratio using" checkbox and choose "Fit within dimensions" from the pop-up menu.

6   Click OK, and then OK again on the Movie Settings dialog.

7   Click Save.

This will save a QuickTime copy of your file with the custom settings you selected to the destination you chose in step 2.

Lesson Review

1.   How do you switch between playing projects and playing Events in the Full Screen Viewer?

2.   How many file sizes can you publish to iTunes?

3.   When published to iTunes, where are your movies stored?

4.   Do you have to choose between sharing to YouTube or Sharing to MobileMe?

5.   How do you share movie files between iMovie and GarageBand?

6.   If the Share to Media Browser menu item is dimmed, what does that indicate?

7. How do you make the Comment Marker and Chapter Marker buttons available?

8. How do you add a chapter marker to your video?

Answers

1. Click the "Show Projects or Events" button in the lower-left corner.

2. iMovie has four file-size options: Tiny, Mobile, Medium, and Large.

3. They can be found in the Movies folder within your iTunes Music folder.

4. No. You can share your video to both YouTube and your MobileMe Gallery.

5. Publish to the iLife Media Browser, which exports a rendered movie that is easily available within GarageBand.

6. All four sizes have already been shared to the Media Browser or to iTunes (which makes them accessible to the Media Browser).

7. Select Advanced Tools in the iMovie General preferences.

8. Drag the Add Chapter Marker button directly to your video in the Project Browser.

7

Lesson Files

After installation:

iLife09_Book_Files > Lesson_07 > Unlikely Hero.mov

iLife09_Book_Files > Lesson_07 > Flying Background.mov

Time

This lesson takes approximately 45 minutes to complete.

Goals

Learn to shoot for the edit

Master the three rules of camera movement

Import footage footage into iMovie from a variety of camera types

Import video files already on your disk

Organize your footage with keywords

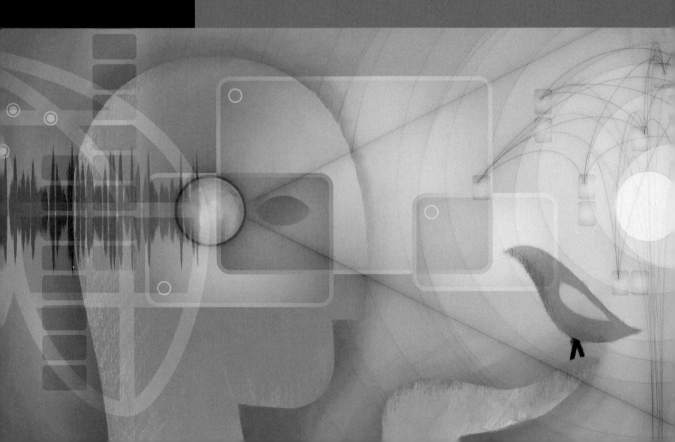

Making Your Masterpiece: Shooting and Importing Video

In Lesson 5, you learned that not everything you shoot needs to be edited into a finished movie. You can happily enjoy a collection of raw video clips right in your Event Brower—just as you do with your still photo collection in iPhoto.

But some events, such as graduations, weddings, or memorable trips, beg for special treatment. Some of you may also plan to use iMovie to create more familiar forms of filmed content, including documentaries, promotional videos for your business, music videos, or even narrative fiction. Such Events require editing to reach their full potential.

This lesson contains some shooting tricks that will help you get cool results when editing in iMovie. These tricks are not special effects, mind you, but rather they are simple concepts for gathering footage that will give your videos a more sophisticated style.

This lesson also covers the various ways of importing footage into iMovie, as well as preparing footage to make the editing process as smooth and quick as possible.

Shooting to Edit

At its heart, editing is about collecting the "good parts" and stringing them together in an engaging way. But in order to edit something, you need to have shots that will go well together, so moving from one to the next isn't jarring or confusing. Getting the right shots while you're shooting will make the time you spend editing much shorter and more enjoyable.

Over the past 100 years of film history, a film language has emerged. You may not know how to speak it fluently, but you certainly can understand it. Whenever you watch a movie or a television program, you follow intuitively what's going on, even though the content has been chopped up and recombined in all sorts of ways. Now that you're behind the camera, you can take advantage of the same techniques to help make your video easy to understand and fun to watch.

The most basic idea is that you want to get multiple shots of the same subject from different angles. If you're shooting a group of people playing pool, you want to get some shots that show the whole pool table, and some shots of individual players, and some shots of the balls on the table. The more shots you get, the more choices you have in the editing room, and the better you can make your movie. The combination of shots that cover a particular scene is called *coverage*.

Covering a Scene

Instead of collecting a series of random shots with your camcorder, shoot in pairs. Think of every shot as having some kind of relationship to at least one other shot. If you shoot someone from far off, your next shot should be the same person close up. If you show someone reading a book, show the audience what she's reading. Whatever you do, get a minimum of two shots of the same subject. You'll use these when you go to edit.

Then, after you've gotten a few pairs of shots, shoot a few short *cutaways*. A cutaway is a shot that's not part of your main action but is somehow related. If you're shooting a scene at the beach, get a few shots of seagulls or the waves. That way, if you can't find a smooth edit between any of your pairs of shots, you can *cut away* to the seagulls to cover the transition.

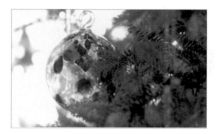

Ultimately, the whole trick to effective filmmaking is to choose each shot to answer a specific question: *Who* is this scene about? *What* are they doing? *Where* is it taking place?—and so on. If you don't know precisely what the subject of each shot is, chances are your viewers won't either, and that will leave them bored or confused.

Looking for Story Structure

Another important aspect of coverage is story structure—that is, finding shots that represent the *beginning, middle, and end* of the event you're shooting. Your video shouldn't be a random sequence of shots; it should be a short story. Fortunately, this is easier than it sounds. Sometimes all you need is a shot of people walking into the frame for a good beginning or people walking out of the frame for the ending.

It's also a good idea to shoot some kind of *establishing shot*: a shot that shows the location where the event takes place. This could be a shot from far away showing an entire room, or it could be the sign over the door. Establishing shots serve as natural beginnings or endings to most scenes.

Natural events also make near-perfect beginnings and endings. Someone walking off into the sunset is a classic (even clichéd) finale. A car pulling up and parking, someone opening a door to enter a house, or people walking into a room are all natural introductions to a scene.

> **TIP** ▶ One of the great things about digital video edited with an application such as iMovie is that you can cut together your shots in any sequence you want, regardless of when you shot them. For example, you might get your establishing shot last but use it at the beginning of the scene, or get your cutaways last but intersperse them with the main action.

Moving the Camera

In many ways, shooting with a camcorder is the same as shooting with a still camera. All the rules of exposure and lighting apply (keep light behind you, not behind your subject), as do the rules of composition (don't always center your subject; remember the rule of thirds). It's important to hold the camcorder steady (two hands, always) and frame any shot before pressing the Record button.

But a camcorder has the added feature of motion, and consequently it can do lots of things that a still camera can't. You can move the camera or zoom the lens during a shot, and the camera records all of it. So in addition to basic photography skills, you need to learn some rules about moving pictures and good video.

The Lingo of Motion

Before you start moving your camcorder around, familiarize yourself with the relevant vocabulary.

Pan A pan is a move from side to side, along an imaginary horizon.

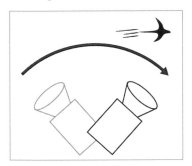

Tilt A tilt is similar to a pan but up and down, like scanning a tall building.

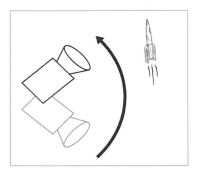

Track In a tracking shot you move the camera along with a moving object, such as shooting from one car to another. (The term *dolly* is also used when the camera is moving closer to, or farther away from, the subject.)

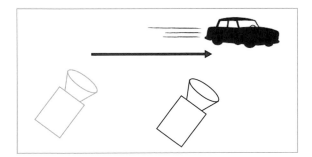

Zoom A zoom is a change in frame size that moves toward or away from an object, using the lens and without physically moving the camera.

Justify Any Movement

Your camcorder is small. It's light. It fits in your hand. It seems natural to walk around with the thing recording, shooting up and down, left and right, following people around, and so on. But effective camera technique is all about choosing a particular subject and filming that one thing.

To help you make the best use of the moving camera, learn and practice the following three rules of camera movement.

▶ **Rule 1:** The single most important rule about moving the camera is that you should **never move the camera without a reason**. Something must motivate the camera movement; otherwise the viewer doesn't know what to look at. Why are you moving the camera? If you can't answer that question, stay put! One common trick is to follow an object. A bird flying by might motivate a pan; so might a car going across a bridge.

▶ **Rule 2: Practice the move before you press Record.** If you know where you're going to start and stop the movement, you can move confidently and stop cleanly. If you're figuring it out as you go, your audience will feel your ambivalence, and they'll stop paying attention to the subject of the shot and start thinking about you shooting it.

▶ **Rule 3: Always let the camera run for a few seconds before you begin the camera move and for a few seconds after you stop.** This extra room around the edges of your camera move will be essential when you get to the editing room.

One more critical bit of advice: Always let people enter and exit the frame. We all have a natural tendency to follow people as they move around, but when you're editing, it's very difficult to make a smooth edit when the camera keeps following people. Rather than pan around to follow someone's movement, let them exit the frame in one shot, then frame up the next shot and let them walk into it. Presto! You'll have a beautiful seamless edit.

Think of moving the camera as a special effect—it's fun and can produce cool results, but it's also something you should reserve for when the moment is right.

Fix It Later

What you're about to read is considered heresy among traditional filmmaking instructors, but iMovie '09 is anything but traditional. As you'll learn in Lesson 9, iMovie '09 has a very powerful video stabilization feature. Your handheld shaky camerawork can be magically transformed into smooth-as-glass camera moves that will look as though used a $5,000 camera dolly.

Take advantage of this! Don't worry so much about using the tripod, and don't be afraid to walk around with your camera or shoot from a moving car (while following the rules above, of course). Sure, try to keep everything as smooth as possible—the video stabilizer has limits to what it can repair, and it can take a long time to work its magic. But thanks to advancing technology, a little bit of shakiness is now entirely fixable.

If you're going to follow this blasphemous advice, then a trick you can employ is to frame the shot a little bit wider than you actually plan to use. When a shot is stabilized, it will have to be digitally zoomed in a little bit. If you plan for this and leave a little extra space around the edges of the frame, it will help you get what you ultimately want. It also will help that the wider the framing, the less distracting the remaining shakiness will be.

Recording Sound

Unfortunately, sound can be difficult to manage on your camcorder if you try to do it while you're shooting video. The built-in microphone picks up sounds from everywhere around you while you record, resulting in a lot of unwanted noise. Also, because you shoot from a number of different positions—moving close to and far away from your subjects, starting and stopping the camera between shots—getting a consistent stream of audio is almost impossible.

Because it's so hard to get good-quality sound from the camera's microphone while you shoot video, the fastest way to get good sound in your finished project is to mute most of the audio from your shoot when you're working with the footage in iMovie and replace it with music from a professionally created CD.

If you want *production sound*—that is, the sound that's going on while you're shooting the video—it takes more effort. You need to use additional microphones and have someone carefully monitor how everything sounds while it's being recorded.

Alternatively, you can use your camcorder not only as a digital video recorder but also as a digital audio recorder. And your Mac itself has a built-in microphone. With these handy audio tools and a little basic information, you can add professional-quality sound to your videos.

> **TIP** To get the best possible sound from your camcorder's built-in microphone, try to film in quiet locations and avoid loud or disruptive background noises. If your subject says something important while a car horn blares in the background, ask your subject to repeat what they've said. And try to keep the area nearest to the camcorder's microphone quiet whenever you're recording sound from farther away.

Bringing It Home

Once your video is shot, you need to get it into iMovie before you can play with it. The process is different depending on where the footage came from.

There are an awful lot of different cameras out there, and it seems like each one records onto a different medium and in a different format. The good news is that iMovie can work with just about any format, and it will automatically convert the footage as it's captured to a format it can edit.

Understanding Video Formats

There's a lot of technical mumbo-jumbo about video formats, and it can be downright mind numbing: Which one is the best? Which one is the smallest? Which one can also be used as a hair tonic?—and so on. The fact is, there are only a few bits of information that you need to know.

Definition, Please

The most significant distinction in video formats is standard definition (SD) versus high definition (HD). Put simply, HD is higher resolution and, as with a higher-megapixel still image, you can zoom in and the image remains sharp.

You can also show it on a bigger TV set, just as you can print those higher-resolution stills at a larger size.

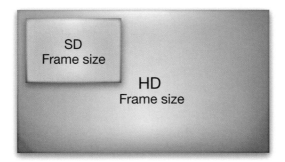

Clearly HD is superior, but SD is still pretty good. All of your regular DVDs are in SD, and they look perfectly good to most viewers (which is an excellent reminder that it's the content, not the format, that makes a movie good). Of course, iMovie can work with both HD and SD, and you can even mix and match the formats.

There are a lot of different names for the various ways to store video: HDV, AVCHD, MPEG-2, H.264, and so on. These are different types of video compression, and the bottom line is that they all work very well.

► **The Shape of Things: Frame Sizes**

HD and SD typically have different shapes. HD is widescreen (16:9), and SD is nearly square (4:3). When you're working in iMovie, you can choose whether you want your movie to be edited in 16:9 or 4:3.

If you put HD footage in a 4:3 project, the left and right sides of the image will be cut off. If you put 4:3 SD footage in a 16:9 project, it will automatically be scaled to fill the frame, and the top and bottom of the image will be cropped off.

Continues on next page

▶ **The Shape of Things: Frame Sizes** *(continued)*

A 4:3 SD clip placed in a widescreen project

A 16:9 widescreen clip placed in a 4:3 project

The precise position of the cropping can be changed using the Crop, Rotate, and Ken Burns tool.

NOTE ▶ In the Timing pane of the Project Properties (File > Project Properties, or press Command-J), you can choose "Fit in Frame" from the Initial Video Placement setting. This will create a black border around part of the clip (such as a *letterbox*) instead of cropping out the excess area.

Continues on next page

▶ **The Shape of Things: Frame Sizes** *(continued)*

Different cameras record HD in different sizes, but they will always be 16:9 widescreen. The different sizes include 1920 x 1080 (sometimes called *1080i*), 1440 x 1080, 1280 x 720 (sometimes called *720p*), and so on. iMovie always works at one of two sizes, 1920x1080 (Full) or 960 x 540 (Large).

When you import your footage, you have the opportunity to choose between these two sizes. The first time you import anything, iMovie will present you with an informative dialog.

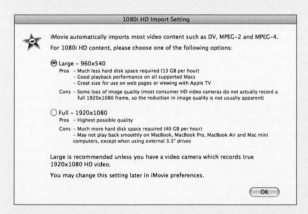

The truth is, unless you're going to be playing your movie back on a very large 1080 HD monitor or projecting it in a theater, there's no reason to choose Full.

NOTE ▶ Video can also be recorded at different rates, measured in frames per second (fps): 24 fps, 25 fps, 30 fps, and 60 fps. iMovie always edits at 30 fps except when using European PAL footage, which is edited at 25 fps. If you import footage shot at a different frame rate, iMovie will automatically convert it to 30 fps (or 25 fps).

Finding a Happy Medium

What's more important than the name of the compression format your camera uses is what medium it records to. Some formats record to tape, and others to flash memory, hard disk (HDD), or DVD.

To import footage from a tape-based camera, connect the camera to the computer using a FireWire cable (also known as i.Link, IEEE 1394, or just "DV").

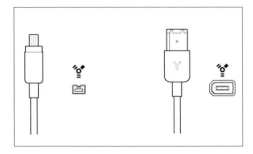

FireWire connectors: Connect to Camera (left), connect to computer (right)

NOTE ▸ Not all Mac computers have a FireWire port, and some only have a FireWire 800 port. Check your system configuration to confirm that your Mac includes FireWire support (and what connector type) before attempting to connect a DV or HDV camcorder.

To import footage from cameras that record to flash memory, DVD, or hard disk, use a USB connector.

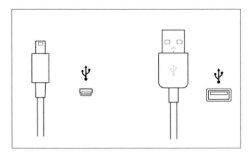

USB connectors: Connect to camera (left), connect to computer (right)

Whether you use FireWire or USB, iMovie automatically recognizes the connection type once you connect your camera and opens the Import From Camera window.

TIP ▸ You can also open the Import From Camera window manually by choosing File > "Import from Camera" or pressing Command-I.

NOTE ▸ A DVD application may open when you connect a DVD-based camera. If it does, just close it.

1   Select the footage you want to import.

Note that iMovie treats tape and non-tape devices differently:

▸   If you're importing from DV or HDV tape, you'll see the Viewer. The simplest way is to select Automatic and click Import. iMovie will rewind and capture the whole tape. Alternatively, you can switch to manual controls to queue up specific footage to import.

▸   If you're importing from a DVD, HDD, or flash-based (tapeless) device, you'll see a list of all the clips you've shot. Use the playback controls at the bottom of the Viewer to review the clips, and then decide which ones you want to import.

If you want everything, select the Automatic option. Or select the Manual option and deselect the clips you don't want to import.

2   Click Import, Import Checked, or Import All, depending on your system and what you've selected for import.

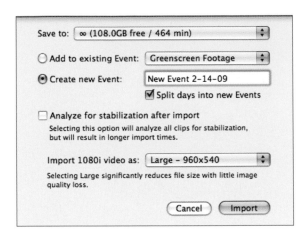

TIP ▶ Video files consume large amounts of space. If you're going to be working with a lot of video, an external hard drive can be enormously useful. Any footage that has been imported into iMovie and stored on an external drive will be instantly available through the Event Library as soon as you plug in your drive.

3   Select "Create new Event" to store your footage in a new empty Event.

4   Choose Large for the size for 1080i video and click Import.

It takes about 13 gigabytes (GB) to store an hour of DV video and 40 GB to store an hour of HD video, so make sure you have enough space on the disk you choose. The amount of free space on each available disk is shown in parentheses next to the disk's name in the pop-up menu.

iMovie then imports your footage and creates thumbnails for the library.

Importing Movie Files

Occasionally you may get a video file that didn't come straight from a camera. You may have downloaded it from the Internet, a friend may have given it to you, or you may have exported it out of another program. You can easily import nearly any video clip format into iMovie. However, iMovie will most likely convert it into an editable format.

1   In iMovie, choose File > Import > Movies.

> **NOTE ▶** If you've never imported anything before, the HD Format dialog opens. Choose Large and click OK.

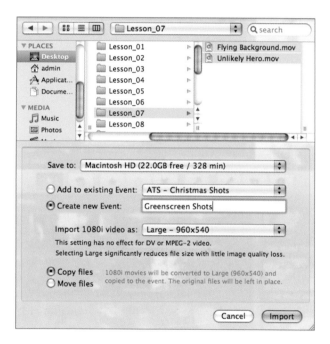

The Import window opens.

2   Navigate to the desktop and find the iLife09_Book_Files folder. Choose the Lesson_07 folder and Shift-click to select both **Flying Background.mov** and **Unlikely Hero.mov**.

3   Select "Create new Event" and name it *Greenscreen Shots*. Then Select "Copy files" and click Import.

The files are imported, copied to your Movies folder, converted to a proper format (when required), and a new Event is added to your Event Library.

NOTE ▶ You can ignore these files for now. But don't delete them. You'll be using them to learn how to do green-screen effects in Lesson 9.

Capturing from a Flip Camera

If you're one of the millions of happy Flip camera owners, you'll likely want to bring that video into iMovie and add it to your library. Importing footage from Flip cameras is easy, but it works differently if you're using the MinoHD or an older Flip model.

With a Flip MinoHD, you can import the files on the Flip camera the same way you imported the files in the previous exercise.

1   Connect the Flip MinoHD camera to your Mac using a USB cable.

2   In iMovie, choose File > Import > Movies.

The camera should appear in the list of disks.

3   Navigate to that disk, and choose DCIM > 100VIDEO (or similar).

All the video files on your Flip will be listed in that folder. Shift-click or Command-click to select the files you want to import.

4   Choose which Event to add the clips to (or create a new one) and click Import.

The files are added to your library.

Using Older Flip Models

Older Flip models require an additional step. Before you can import your video into iMovie, you must install two pieces of software. Fortunately, they come right on your Flip camera, so the software will be on the FLIPVIDEO volume once you connect the camera.

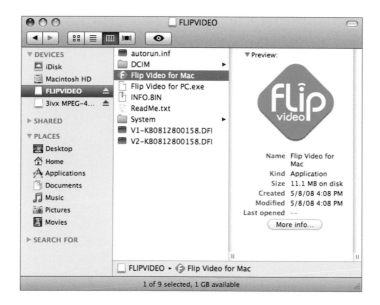

1   Double-click to install the Flip Video for Mac software.

2   Then install the 3ivx MPEG-4 Decoder, which will appear on a second volume.

At this point, you can follow the same instructions as listed for the MinoHD above.

Getting Footage from iPhoto

When you're working with a still camera that shoots video, you won't import directly into iMovie. Instead, you'll import your footage into iPhoto, as we did in Lesson 1.

The first time you open iMovie after importing video into iPhoto, iMovie asks if you want to generate thumbnails now or wait until later.

1   Click Now.

The filmstrips and thumbnails are automatically generated and placed into the Event Library.

2   Select iPhoto Videos in the Event Library.

If you named your Events in iPhoto, the Event names will be visible in the Event Browser.

Your iPhoto videos are now available to use alongside any other footage you've shot.

> **TIP** ▶ Any video that you capture with a cell phone that records video will be treated the same way as a still camera. In both cases, simply import the clips into iPhoto, and access it through the Event Library in iMovie.

Capturing from iSight

You can also record video live, straight to your computer, using your Mac's built-in iSight camera or any FireWire-enabled camera or camcorder.

1   Connect your camera if your computer doesn't have iSight built in.

2   To open the Import From Camera window, click the camcorder icon above the Event Library or choose File > Import from Camera (Command-I).

3   If Built-in iSight (or your connected FireWire camera) is not chosen from the Camera menu in the bottom left, choose it now.

4   Click Capture.

5   Choose the disk where you want to store the video.

> **TIP** Make sure your disk has enough available storage space for the video you're recording. The amount of free space on each available disk is shown in parentheses next to the disk's name in the pop-up menu.

6   To create a new Event, type a name for it in the "Create new Event" field. To add the recorded video to an existing Event, choose its name from the pop-up menu.

7   When you're ready to begin recording, click Capture.

The camera begins recording immediately.

8   When you want to stop recording, click Stop.

A new video clip is created and the thumbnail images are generated. You can start and stop as often as you like. Each time you start and stop the camera, you must click OK to add the next clip to the same Event, select a different Event, or type the name for a new Event.

9   When you're finished recording, click Done.

Preparing Your Footage

Once you've gotten your footage into iMovie, there's more you can do to help prepare it for editing.

In Lesson 5, you learned about rejecting clips as well as marking favorites. One thing you didn't learn is how to change the category of a marked shot.

1   Click the ATS – Bhutan event in the Event Library.

This is footage shot from a festive cultural event in the Himalayan country of Bhutan.

2   Skim through a few of the shots to get a sense of the footage from the Event.

3   Select the first few seconds of the first clip.

> **NOTE** ▶ If your selection doesn't start at the beginning of the shot, drag the yellow clip start handle all the way to the left.

This is obviously not very useful footage, so it's a good candidate to be rejected.

4   Click the Reject button or press R.

The section you marked is rejected, and because your Event Browser is set to show only favorites and unmarked, the clip is immediately hidden.

5   Click the Show menu and choose All Clips.

The rejected area reappears, but it is marked red.

Suppose that you change your mind and now you want to un-reject it.

6   Click the red area to select it again. Click the Unmark button or press U.

Unmark button

You can also unmark only part of a previously marked selection.

7   Skim the second clip and click just as you see the dancer about to jump.

The default four-second selection box appears on the clip.

8   Drag the clip end handle of the yellow selection bar to the end of the clip.

9   Click the "Mark as Favorite" button or press F.

The selected area is marked green. But again, imagine that later you change your mind and want only the middle of the clip marked as a favorite.

10   Click in the gray background area to deselect the clip, then click anywhere near the end of the clip to select the last four seconds.

11   Click the Unmark button or press U.

Now, only the middle area of the clip is marked as a favorite.

Adding Keywords

Although marking some areas of your footage green and other areas red goes a long way to organizing your shots, you're going to need more than "good, bad, or undecided" if you've got a large project.

iMovie allows you to add keywords to your shots, so you can identify whenever a certain person is in the shot, whether it's a wide angle or a close-up, and so on.

In order to access the Keywords window, you must have Advanced Tools selected in General preferences.

1   Choose iMovie > Preferences and click the General button.

2   Make sure that Show Advanced Tools is selected and close the Preferences window.

Additional buttons appear on the toolbar.

Keyword button

3 Click the Keyword button or press K to open the Keywords window.

4 Click the Auto-Apply button.

This puts you in the mode to begin marking clips with specific keywords. Although some of the keywords listed in the window may apply to this footage, it will usually be more practical to choose your own keywords.

5 Type *Dancers* in the New Keyword field at the bottom of the Keywords window and click Add.

6 Type *Crowd* in the New Keyword field and click Add.

The two keywords are added to the list. Because these are the two keywords you're going to use most, bring them to the top of the list.

7   Drag the Dancers and Crowd keywords to the top of the list.

8   Select the checkbox for Dancers.

9   In the Event Browser, drag across the second clip.

A blue highlight appears to indicate the area you've selected. When you let go, the highlight goes away, but a blue bar remains. The blue bar indicates that the footage has one or more keywords applied.

10   Drag across the next three shots to add the Dancers keyword to each of those shots.

You can add multiple keywords by selecting more checkboxes or selecting different checkboxes and dragging again over the same area.

11   Select the Wide Angle keyword (in addition to Dancers) and drag across the wide-angle shot of the dancers.

12 Deselect Dancers and select Crowds (keep Wide Angle selected).

13 Drag across the next shot (the wide-angle shot of the crowd) to mark it with both of those keywords.

Once you've added keywords, you can use the Inspector (the other button at the top of the Keywords window) to see which keywords are applied to the selected clip in the Event Browser and to remove keywords you no longer want.

Filtering Events

You can also filter the Event Browser so it shows only video with specific keywords.

Show/Hide Keyword Filtering Pane button

1 Click the Show Keyword Filtering Pane button at the bottom of the Event Browser.

Only keywords that have been used appear, and the list shows how many seconds of footage have been marked with each keyword. Additionally, it allows you to hide and show your shots based on which keywords are applied.

2 Click the green side of the pill-shaped button next to the Dancers keyword.

The Event Browser updates to show only the footage marked with that keyword. You can also omit other keywords.

3 Click the red side of the button next to the Wide Angle keyword.

The one shot marked with both Dancers and Wide Angle is removed from the list. This can very helpful if you're trying to find a specific shot and you don't remember where it is in your Event.

And never fear, you can easily show all your clips again.

4 Click the Hide Keyword Filtering Pane button.

Whenever you load new footage into iMovie, it's a good idea to go through this process of rejecting the junk, marking the highlights, and adding keywords.

Editing is an *iterative* process: a series of gradual refinements where you throw out some footage and keep other bits until your finished movie emerges from the raw footage as a sculpture emerges from a block of marble.

After the first pass, when you reject the outright junk, you leave behind just the average and good pieces.

The second pass is easier to watch, now that some of the unusable stuff has been weeded out. This time you mark your favorites and add keywords, helping to slim down the pile even further.

On the third pass, you select the bits that go into your project, choosing only the best few seconds of even those select shots.

You may even make a fourth pass, tightening the edits, and so on.

This may seem tedious, but the more time you spend with your footage, the more familiar with it you'll become. And that means you'll have a good idea of all your options when you're constructing your movie.

Lesson Review

1. What is *coverage*?
2. What is the single most important rule of camera movement?
3. If you know you're going to be relying on iMovie's video stabilizer, what can you do to improve your chances of getting a good shot?
4. When should you capture 1080i footage at the full setting?
5. How do you see movie clips shot with a still camera?
6. How do you unmark a clip that you already rejected?
7. What preference must be set to add keywords to your shots?
8. How do you filter the view of the Event Browser to show only footage with a certain keyword applied?

Answers

1. All the different shots photographed for a single event.
2. Never move the camera without a reason.
3. Hold the camera as steady as possible, and frame your subject with extra space around it.
4. When you're going to be projecting your movie on a very large HD screen.
5. Import them along with your still images into iPhoto, and they'll automatically appear in the iMovie Event Library in the iPhoto Videos category.
6. Set the Event Browser to Show All (or show Rejected Only), select the section you want to unmark, and click the Unmark button or press U.
7. Show Advanced Tools.
8. Show the Keyword Filtering Pane and click the green button next to the keyword in the list.

8

Lesson Files   After installation:

~/Movies/iMovie Projects/ATS-Bhutan - (Start)

Time   This lesson takes approximately 30 minutes to complete.

Goals   Learn some fundamental editing rules and guidelines

Use insert, replace, and other advanced editing techniques

Employ cutaways to create flexible edits

Use the Clip Trimmer and Precision Editor with confidence

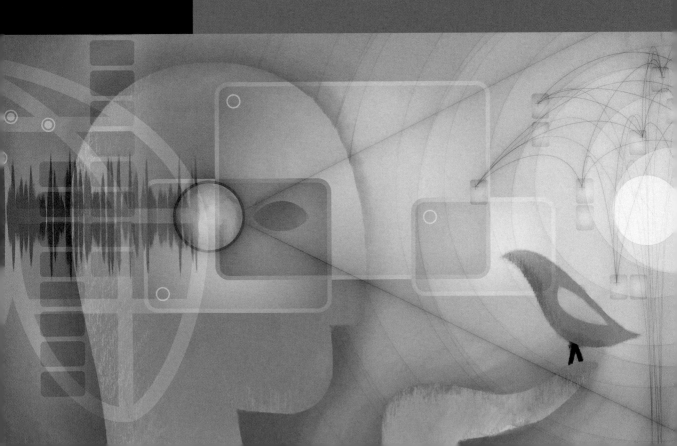

The Cutting Edge: Advanced Editing Techniques

Making a great movie has much more to do with your ability to tell an effective story than with which software you are using. By choosing shots that have a clear point of focus, avoiding redundancy, and keeping the story moving along, you can make a film that will impress anyone, regardless of your level of professional experience.

Still, editing is a craft as much as it is an art, and the more comfortable you are with the tools available to you, the easier it will be for you to follow your inspiration and realize onscreen what you envision in your head. iMovie has everything you need to make your movie feel as polished and professional as any other tool does, and you can master all of its bells and whistles with very little effort.

This lesson will introduce you to many of the powerful advanced tools at your disposal, as well as provide the context for when each of these tools is most appropriately employed. Lesson 5 covered the basic tasks needed to create and edit a project in iMovie. In this lesson, you'll pick up a partially completed project and finish it using these specialized features.

Editing Tips

It's not necessary for you to become a master editor in order to cut together some fun and satisfying videos, but there are a few tips that carry a lot of bang for the buck. Familiarizing yourself with this short list of handy editing guidelines can noticeably elevate the quality of your projects almost instantly.

Why Cut at All?

Probably the most fundamental question facing every editor is how to decide when and where to make edits. This is such a basic question that it's easily overlooked. But trust me, professional editors can spend hours agonizing over every single cut.

The easy answer is that each shot should convey a single, unambiguous piece of information: a wide vista showing the lake where you're going fishing; a medium shot of your uncle starting the motorboat engine; a close-up on the jar full of wriggling bait, and so on. Each shot must provide one clear piece of information that is a part of your story. If you can't easily say aloud what the subject of the shot is, don't use it. If you have a single shot that is trying to show too much, cut it into pieces or find a different piece of footage to use.

By collecting a series of shots that each have a clear point of focus, you'll make it possible for your viewers to understand exactly what's going on without getting bored or distracted.

Avoid Redundancy

Another great benefit of choosing shots that have a clear subject is that you can more easily recognize when the same information is overused. If, when cutting that fishing trip, you have three shots that all show your mother expertly baiting a hook, you'll probably realize that you need only to include one of them.

The most common error made by editors is to make their movies too long. You want to include *all* the highlights, *all* the beauty shots, *all* the funny moments. You want to convey the experience of what happened, and you think every detail is critical. Unfortunately, when you put all that together, your movie begins to feel too long and repetitive. Rather than strive to include everything, try instead to find one perfect example of each aspect.

Every movie is better when it's shorter. Two minutes of amazing footage is always going to be more fun to watch than five minutes of pretty good stuff. The easiest way to keep your movies as short as they can be is to look for repetition and redundancy. If your uncle has a funny habit of licking his finger before casting his line, you may be tempted to include three different occasions when he does this. Unless this is a movie specifically about your uncle's funny habits, one shot of this is enough.

If over the course of the day you caught ten fish, no one wants to watch ten shots of a fish being pulled off the line and thrown into the bucket. Instead, show the first one, and then later, show the ninth or tenth fish being added to the now-full bucket. Everyone will understand, and they will thank you for sparing them the extra five minutes of screen time.

Cut on Action

Ideally, every shot should feel inevitable based on the shot that precedes it, and should compel the shot that follows. If you have a shot of the fishing line being cast, it begs to be followed by a shot of the hook landing in the water, and then of the fisherman holding the rod. If you have a shot of someone furiously reeling the line in, an ideal follow-up shot would be the fish being pulled out of the water, and so on.

But even still, the question lingers about when exactly to cut from one shot to the next. Every single shot has to start and end somewhere. Every edit is an opportunity to create a smooth, slick transition, but a clumsy edit can disrupt the flow and kick your viewers out of the story.

The best way to make your edits feel seamless is to find a moment when the same action is going on in two shots and to cut right in the middle of that action. In Lesson 7, you learned about getting shots in pairs. This is exactly when and where you can put those shot pairs to work.

If you have a close-up of the fish being lifted into the boat and a wider shot of someone lifting a fish (even if it's a different fish from later in the day), cut from one to the other halfway through the lifting action and you'll have a perfect invisible edit. The viewer will be so busy watching the fish moving in the frame that they'll hardly notice you cut to a new shot.

Improving an Edit

Those editing tips are general rules that can be put into practice regardless of the kind of footage you're working with. The rest of this lesson focuses more on specific tasks to help you make the most of various editing situations. To get started, first get familiar with the project you'll be working on.

1   Click the Project Library button in the upper-left corner of the iMovie window to open the Project Library.

2   Click the **ATS-Bhutan - (Start)** project.

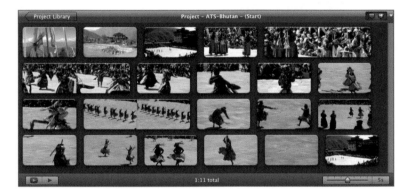

3   Press \ (backslash) to play from the beginning of the project.

The flags and the wide shots of the building serve as a nice establishing sequence to bring us into the location where the festival is happening, but the transition from those wide shots to the first performers feels a little abrupt.

Adding a shot of the crowd getting settled would be an ideal choice. But if you skim the footage in the Event Browser, there isn't such a shot available. Fortunately, someone thought ahead and shot some video of the same event with her still camera.

Adding Video from iPhoto

Most modern still cameras shoot video in addition to still photos. There's not a whole lot of use for viewing such videos in iPhoto's library, but if you've got movies mixed in with your iPhoto Events, you can access them directly from iMovie's Event Library.

1 In the Event Library, click the iPhoto Videos logo to load any such movies into the Event Browser.

Videos will be sorted by Event name. You should have an Event called Bhutan, containing a single video clip.

NOTE ▶ If you did not complete Lesson 1 in the iPhoto section, you can import the same file by choosing File > Import > Import Movies and navigating to Desktop/iLife09_Book_Files/Lesson_08/FestCrowd.mov For more on importing movies, see Lesson 7.

2 Click the clip once to select the default four-second section, and drag it in between the wide shot of the stadium and the full shot of the musicians.

The clip is added to the sequence, providing a natural bridge between the two shots.

Inserting a New Clip

Go ahead and watch the whole project. There's a wide shot of a group of dancers in blue frocks and yellow skirts. The shot is great. It allows you to get a sense of the scope of the event and it's one of the only shots that show a group moving in (near-) perfect formation. However, it does go on a little long.

You learned several ways to shorten a clip in Lesson 5, and you'll learn some other similar techniques in the next few exercises. But in this instance, rather than shorten it, you'll insert a new shot in the middle of it, thereby breaking it into two separate shorter pieces.

1   In the Event Library, click ATS – Bhutan.

2   Skim the clips until you find the shot of the same yellow-skirt dancers, but in a tighter framing.

3   Click near the beginning of the shot to select the default four-second region. Then, drag the selection on top of the wide shot in the Project Browser. Try to drag it about one-third of the way into the clip.

When you drop the clip, a menu of options appears. These are all different kinds of edits and effects you can apply.

4   Choose Insert.

The wide shot of the dancers is broken into two pieces and the new tighter shot is added in between.

TIP ▶ Inserting a new clip will always make your project longer and it will never delete any part of the clips that it's inserted between.

The insert occurs exactly where you dropped the clip. So if you drop it near the beginning of the clip, the second part of the clip will be longer than the first section, and if you drop it near the end of the clip, the second part will be shorter than the first.

Adding a Cutaway

Another way to add a clip in the middle of a shot that's already in your project is to use a cutaway edit. A cutaway is different from an insert because it covers up the footage in the project. Instead of your whole project getting longer, it stays the same length. Also, a cutaway uses a second video track, which makes it easy to move the shot around to fine-tune the timing after you've made the edit.

In this project, the main focus is the festival performers, but in addition to how remarkable the dancers and musicians are, the crowd in the stadium is also somewhat unusual. By showing who's watching the show, you add to the depth and complexity of the event and make a better movie.

It's also a great way to cover a mistake.

1   Play the project from the beginning.

After the close-up shot of the horn players, there's a pretty long shot of dancers in blue and red costumes, and midway through, the shot briefly goes out of focus.

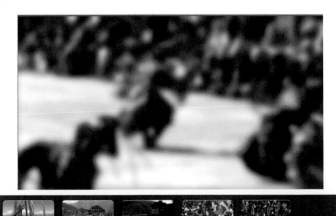

This is a perfect place to try out the cutaway edit.

2   In the Event Browser, find the shot of the group of monks in the stands.

3   Click the monks clip to select the shot and drag it right on top of the blurry clip.

When you release the mouse button, the Edit Options menu appears.

4   Choose Cutaway.

The shot is added to the project on a new track, covering part of the blurry dancers clip.

When you play across this section of the project, the movie *cuts away* to the monks while the other clip is out of focus.

You can adjust the length and position of the cutaway by dragging the cutaway clip in the Project Browser.

5   Drag the monks clip to the left or right as necessary to ensure that it covers the blurry section.

TIP ▶ In addition to fixing mistakes, the cutaway edit is also perfect for interviews; if you have footage showing what the person is talking about, *cut away* to that shot and you'll still hear the person talking at the same time.

Creating a Picture-in-Picture Effect

Very similar to the cutaway edit is the picture-in-picture edit. It works exactly the same as the cutaway, but instead of selecting Cutaway in the Edit Options menu you choose Picture in Picture.

In this case, instead of the cutaway covering the whole background clip, the new shot is placed in a little window on top of the background.

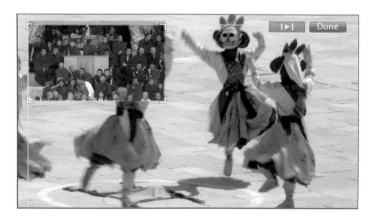

You can resize and reposition the picture-in-picture directly in the Viewer.

Replacing a Shot

Now that you're getting the hang of all the different ways to add a clip to your project, you can see just how versatile an editor iMovie really is. The one type of edit you haven't yet explored is replacing one shot with another.

iMovie has four different ways to replace a shot: Replace, Replace from Start, Replace from End, and Replace at Playhead.

The basic replace means the clip in the project is simply exchanged with the clip you drag from the Event Browser. If the new clip is shorter or longer, your project gets shorter or longer to accommodate it.

The other replace methods always keep the duration of the clip being replaced. If you drag a ten-second clip onto a five-second shot in the project, you're only going to get five seconds of your new shot in the project.

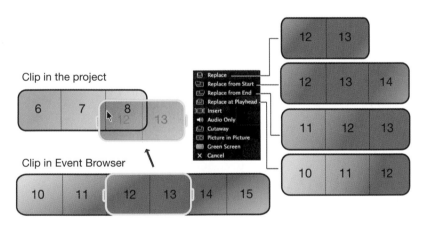

Which five seconds you end up with depends on which edit type you choose:

▶ Replace from Start will use the first five seconds of your selection.

▶ Replace from End will use the last five seconds of your selection.

▶ Replace at Playhead will place the beginning of your selection precisely where you dropped the clip. (So, in the figure above, frame 12 of the new clip is placed where frame 8 of the old clip was, because that's where the pointer is.)

And remember, in these examples, the reason the clips are all five seconds long is that the clip being replaced is five seconds long. If you were replacing a three- or eighteen-second clip, the new clip would be exactly three or eighteen seconds long.

> **NOTE** ▸ If your new clip isn't long enough to fill the hole, iMovie will warn you, and you can either cancel or just use as much footage as you have available.

In the project you're working on, you'll use a simple replace to exchange a repetitive shot with something more exciting.

1 In the Project Browser, look at the shot directly after the cutaway shot. It's almost exactly the same as the previous shot (the one you cut away from).

There's no need to see two such similar shots back to back. In this case, you'll replace the second shot with a different shot.

2 In the Event Browser, find the shot of the single man in the big red skirt twirling.

3   Skim the red-skirt shot and drag from just before he makes his big turn until just after he spins around completely (about 2 seconds).

4   Drag the selection onto the repetitive shot in the Project Browser.

When you release the mouse button, the Edit Options menu appears.

5   Choose Replace to exchange one shot with the other.

Excellent work! Little by little, you're refining this rough cut into a polished, finished work of art.

Using the Clip Trimmer

Often you'll want to make some adjustments to the timing of a clip after it's been added to your project. For example, in this project the close-up shot of the two horn players begins with a bit of camera jostle that's distracting and also ruins the smooth cut between the wide shot of the horn players and the close-up.

You learned some ways to modify a clip in the project in Lesson 5, but there are other, more powerful ways to adjust individual clips, such as the Clip Trimmer.

1   Position your pointer over the close-up shot of the horn players, and when the Action menu pop-up appears, click it and choose Clip Trimmer.

A new pane appears on top of the Event Browser. All of the footage from the selected clip is visible, with the area used in the project highlighted.

2 Adjust the Zoom slider in the lower-right corner until it says 2s (two seconds).

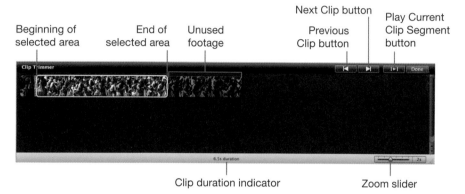

You can drag either edge to shorten the beginning or end of the clip, or you can drag the yellow box to move the selection without changing the duration of the clip.

In this case you need to remove a few frames from the beginning of the shot.

3 Click the left handle and, while watching the viewer, drag right until the camera jostle settles (until the duration reads approximately 5.3 seconds).

4 Click the Play Current Clip Segment button to watch just the selected area.

TIP To trim another clip in the project, click the Previous Clip or Next Clip button, or click any clip directly in the Project Browser, and the Clip Trimmer will update to show the new clip. In this case you don't need to trim any other clips.

5 Click Done in the upper-right corner of the Clip Trimmer to close the pane.

Fine-Tuning an Edit

The Clip Trimmer is a powerful tool to make changes to an individual clip, but sometimes you want to manipulate the edit point between two clips at the same time. The Precision Editor is similar to the Clip Trimmer, but it shows the two adjacent clips on either side of an edit and allows you to adjust either one or both.

To demonstrate this, you'll adjust the edit between the wide shot and the close-up of the dancers in the yellow skirts and blue tops.

1   Position your pointer over the close-up shot of the yellow-skirt dancers (the same shot you Inserted earlier in the lesson.). When the Action pop-up menu appears, click it and choose Precision Editor.

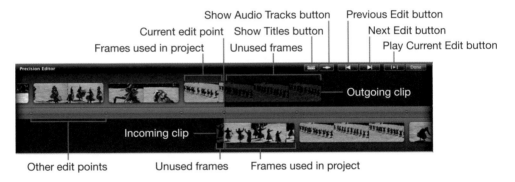

The Precision Editor pane opens. This window shows the outgoing clip on the top, and the incoming clip on the bottom. As in the Clip Trimmer, you can see both the part of the clip currently in use in the project, as well as the extra footage that you're not using.

If you position your pointer over the top clip, the dimmed area after the edit point lights up, and you can skim or play the whole clip by pressing the spacebar.

If you position your pointer over the bottom clip, the dimmed area before the edit lights up and you can skim or play that whole clip.

If you position your pointer over the gray edit bar area between the two clips, you can skim or play the clips as they appear in the project, reflecting the current edit.

You can shorten or lengthen either clip, thus changing the edit point. In this case, you'll try to match the jumping action that occurs in both clips to create a smooth edit.

In general, the easiest way to get a *continuity cut*—where the action feels fluid and smooth across the edit—is to begin by finding a clear similar action that is visible in both shots and then lining the edit up there.

2   To make the exercise easier, zoom in on the edit by dragging the Zoom slider to the left until it reads 1s (one second).

3   Skim the top (outgoing) clip until you find the frame where the dancers' feet land, and click there.

The extra frames you identified are added to (or subtracted from) the outgoing shot so that the frame you selected becomes the very last frame before the cut.

NOTE ▶ Earlier in this lesson, you inserted the close-up shot into the wide shot, and because you may have inserted it at a slightly different location, your edit may look slightly different from the figures here. Have no fear: The edit should still work if you focus on finding the matching action in both shots.

4   Now, skim the bottom (incoming) clip, find the frame where the dancers'
feet land, and click to commit the edit.

NOTE ► The dancers don't all land at exactly the same time. Just try to
focus on the one or two in the middle.

Now you've fixed both clips so that the edit hinges on matching action.

5   Click the Play Current Edit button to see the results of your work.

Cutting on matching action is the heart of effective editing. This is the stuff
the pros spend all day getting just right. The reason it works is that the viewer's
mind is so busy following the movement within the frame that they don't
notice the fact that the angle has changed.

But to create a truly *invisible edit*, there's another step you must take. If the
goal is to hide the edit point, cutting just as the dancers' feet land on the
ground is actually drawing attention to the cut: He lands, and that seems to
make the cut happen.

A more effective edit would cut a few frames earlier, so the cut happens *midway
through the action*. This way, the act of the dancer's landing happens fluidly
across the edit, and by the time he's landed, we've already sneaked the edit point
past the viewer.

You've already got the timing just right, but now you just need to adjust both clips together so that the cut happens a few frames earlier.

6   Drag the cut point (the blue ball) on the gray edit bar to the left while watching the Viewer.

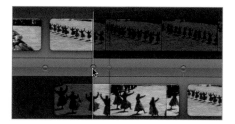

7   Select a frame somewhere between the apex of the jump (when they're highest in the air) and the moment of landing, and release the mouse button.

8   Click the Play Current Edit button again to see the new cut.

Even if your picture cut is perfect, there's something else that's making the edit feel abrupt: the sound. Hearing the audio shift so clearly calls out the edit point, defeating your best efforts to create a seamless cut.

Fortunately, iMovie's Precision Editor can edit the clip's audio as well.

9   Click the Show Audio Tracks button.

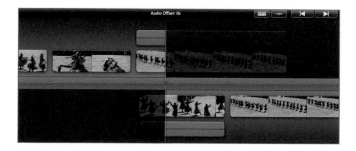

Just as with the video, the Precision Editor shows both the part of the clip currently in use, as well as the audio from the original footage that isn't active (and that part is dimmed until you move your pointer over it). However, unlike the video, the two audio tracks can overlap so you hear both.

In this case, the problem is that the bells in the second clip turn off abruptly at the same instant that the picture cuts, making the cut feel abrupt. If the audio from the second clip started earlier, before the picture edit, the whole cut would suddenly feel much more organic.

10 Position your pointer over the blue audio bar for the top (outgoing) clip.

A red playhead appears under your pointer.

11 Line up the red playhead with the edit point line, and the pointer changes into a drag arrow.

12 Drag the red playhead line to the right until it is past the end of the close-up shot.

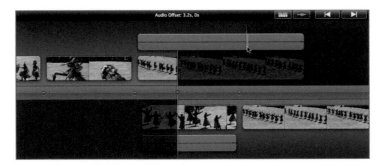

The audio for the first clip will now play all the way through the next shot.

13 Click the Play Current Edit button one more time.

14 If you're satisfied, click the Done button to close the Precision Editor.

The edit should now look and sound perfect. In fact, if you've done your job right, the edit will look transparent—no one will even notice it.

But don't despair; you know how much work went into constructing that perfect edit and you've done it in the service of the movie you're making. And even if they don't realize it, your viewers will appreciate the results.

Lesson Review

1. Where can you access videos shot with a still camera or otherwise imported into iPhoto?

2. Does inserting a clip cover up existing footage?

3. Does a cutaway cover up existing footage?

4. How many ways are there to replace a shot?

5. If you replace a five-second shot with a ten-second shot, how long will the resulting shot be?

6. How do you open the Clip Trimmer?

7. How do you open the Precision Editor?

8. Can you modify both clips in the Precision Editor at the same time?

9. Can the Precision Editor modify audio or just video?

Answers

1. In the iPhoto Videos section of the Event Library.

2. No. It pushes the old footage out of the way to make room for the new shot.

3. Yes. Cutaways cover the footage under them.

4. There are four: Replace, Replace from Start, Replace from End and Replace at Playhead.

5. It depends on which kind of replace you choose. A simple replace will result in the whole ten-second new clip. All the other replace methods will result in a five-second clip.

6. Select Clip Trimmer from the Action pop-up menu for any clip.

7. Select Precision Editor from the Action pop-up menu on any clip, or double-click the space between two clips.

8. Yes. Drag the blue ball in the gray edit bar.

9. The Precision Editor can trim both audio and video.

9

Lesson Files   After installation:

iLife09_Book_Files > Lesson_07 > Unlikely Hero.mov

iLife09_Book_Files > Lesson_07 > Flying Background.mov

ILife09_Book_Files > Lesson_09 > VietNamMotorcycle.mov

Time   This lesson takes approximately 45 minutes to complete.

Goals   Incorporate still images and animate them using the Ken Burns tool

Add and customize animated titles

Apply video effects to create unique visual looks

Modify clip speed to create slow motion and backward playback

Create a freeze frame effect

Use the Video Adjustments inspector to fix color and contrast errors

Learn to use and control the video stabilization feature

Create special compositing effects using green-screen footage

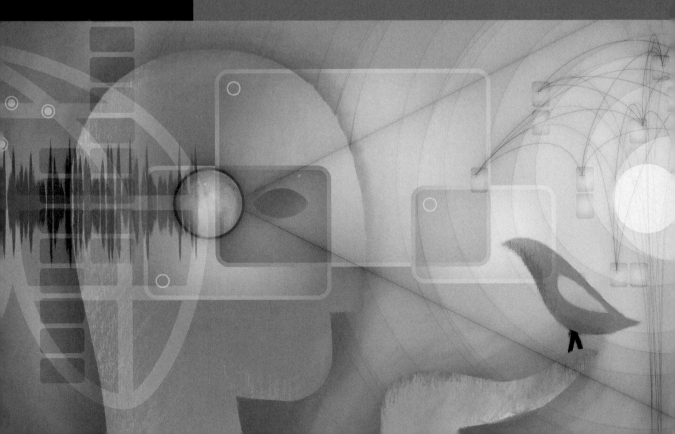

Hollywood, Here I Come: Creating Visual Effects

The term *visual effects* generally refers to anything other than simple editing. This includes creating cool titles, animating still images, adding transition effects between shots, working with slow-motion and speed effects, performing color correction, applying video filters, and even executing complex compositing using green-screen footage.

Using iMovie, you can perform all of these effects with great ease. In fact, your greatest danger is overdoing it, using so many visual effects that they overpower the content they are applied to. The truth is, such effects are best used in moderation. Always let the specific footage you're working with dictate what kind of effects you employ.

Also, mixing and matching different kinds of effects diminishes the impact of any individual shot. Imagine reading a book where every line was written in a different font. You'd hardly be able to concentrate on the words themselves because you'd be distracted by the graphical treatment applied to them. Instead of using different effects on every shot, you'll create a more enjoyable movie if you select one or two similar effects and use them sparingly.

Still, adding a nice collection of well-chosen visual effects is one of the best ways to give a professional polish to your work and really impress your audience.

Creating a Polished Opening

A strong opening is critical for every video project, and since you're not deep into the body of your story yet, it's one of the least distracting places to try out different visual effects.

Remember, however, that your opening shots set the tone and the mood for the rest of the piece. If you keep this in mind, you can effectively prepare your viewers for what's to come and engage them in your movie from the opening moments.

Adding a Still Image from iPhoto

One way to give the movie a nice introduction is to grab a still photo and put a title over it. In many situations, you'll have both video and still photos of the same event. Fortunately, you can view your iPhoto library from right inside iMovie.

1   From the Project Library, open **ATS-Bhutan - (Lesson 9)**.

    This is a project containing all the edits made in Lesson 8. If you completed Lesson 8, you can also continue working in the **ATS-Bhutan - (Start)** project.

2   Click the Photos button in the Event Browser.

Photos button

The Photos Browser opens, showing all the Events from your iPhoto library. You can navigate to other iPhoto albums using the icons at the top of the iPhoto library.

3   Find the Bhutan Event, and double-click it.

TIP ▶ You can limit the Photos Browser to show only pictures from the same date as the Event currently open in the iMovie Event Browser or from a date range. The clips in this project had to be modified, so they're no longer linked to the photos from the same Event. In your own projects, however, this is a quick way to find photos from the same Event as your video.

4   Find the photo of the mountain vista pictured below.

5   Drag the photo into the project, adding it before the first shot. Play the project.

The still photo is added and an automatic zoom-out effect is applied. You can customize that effect in the Crop window.

6   Click the still photo in the Project Browser, and press C to open the Crop window.

Swap Start and End button

The green box indicates the starting frame, and the red box indicates the ending frame. iMovie automatically animates from the start to the end, creating the zoom effect.

Because this is the opening of the show, we want to invite the viewer into the location. A zoom in, instead of a zoom out, would be more effective.

7   Click the Swap Start and End button, then press the Spacebar to play.

That switches the zoom out to a zoom in. You can also click the green or red box and manually adjust it to create a custom movement.

8   Click Done to close the Crop window.

Adding a Title

Now that you've added this great background picture, you can add a title on top of it using one of iMovie's built-in animated title effects.

1   Click the Titles button or press Command-3 to open the Titles Browser. Move your pointer over the different titles to see the animated effects.

2   Drag the Soft Edge title onto the center of the still image at the beginning of the project.

The title is automatically placed above the clip, and the text becomes visible in the Viewer.

3   Click the text in the Viewer to select it, type *Bhutan: Land of the Thunder Dragon*, and then press Return.

Some of the words you typed may not be visible. iMovie allows you to customize the font, color, and size so all of your text fits on the screen.

4   Click the Fonts button in the upper-left corner of the Viewer.

The iMovie Fonts window appears. This window is interactive.

5   Move your pointer over the different fonts, colors, and font sizes to preview how your title looks in each of those settings.

As you drag from left to right over the box containing the font, color, or size in the Fonts window, you skim the title to see the animation in effect.

6   Choose Impact, Yellow, and font size 3, and then click Done.

TIP ▶ You can customize which fonts and colors appear in the Fonts window in iMovie preferences.

Applying Video Effects

Another thing you can do to give this opening graphic a bit more panache is to add a video effect to the image.

1 Double-click the still image of the mountain in the Project Browser to open the Clip inspector.

2 Click the Video Effect button (currently reads "None").

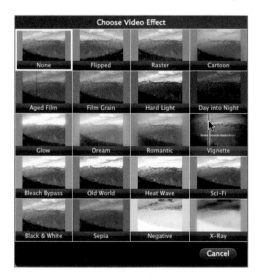

The window flips over and reveals the Video Effects Browser. Just like the Fonts window (and the Transition Browser you used in Lesson 5), this window is interactive.

3 Move your pointer over the different effects to see how the filters look applied to your clip in the Viewer.

4 Press the spacebar to play. While it's playing, move your pointer over the different effects.

The video will keep looping until you click one of the effects to apply it.

5 Click Vignette.

This adds a subtle darkening to the four corners of the image and helps give more depth to the shot.

Adding a Single-Point Map

In Lesson 5, you used the Map feature to show a travel line from the North Pole to Atlanta. In this project, you'll add a map but with only one point.

1 Click the Show Maps and Backgrounds Browser button or press Command-5.

2 Drag the Educational Map into the project, putting it after the still image and before the first clip.

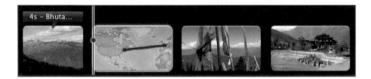

3 In the Map inspector, click the Start Location button (currently reads "San Francisco").

4 In the Choose City or Airport field, type *Bhutan.*

5 Choose the first item in the list (Bhutan) and click OK.

6 Instead of choosing an End Location, just click Done.

7 Play or skim over the map to see the results of your work.

Playing a Clip Backward

So far you've built a very engaging introduction to the movie and set the stage for what's to come. But there's something that isn't working as well as it could.

The wide shot of the building, where the camera zooms out to show the flags, is visually taking the viewer away from the location where the event is taking place. It would be much more effective if it zoomed into the building, but unfortunately that's not what the cameraman shot at the time.

Luckily for us, iMovie allows you to play clips in reverse, which gives you exactly what you need.

1   Position your pointer over the shot of the exterior of the building. When the Action menu appears, click it and choose Clip Adjustments to open the inspector.

2   Select the Reverse checkbox and click Done.

3   Play the beginning of your project again.

Now the shot is inviting us into the location. No one will ever know it wasn't shot this way in the first place.

TIP▶ Many shots will look funny when played in reverse, so apply this effect judiciously. But in some cases, it's the perfect tool for the job.

Changing Clip Speed

You can also change a clip so it plays in fast motion or slow motion. This can be a dramatic special effect when used with the right footage.

In this project, slowing down the speed on some of the shots of the dancers can add a subtle magical quality to the shots, reinforcing the mythic aspect of this ancient tribal ritual.

1   Position your pointer over the first shot of a single dancer (the twirling man in the red skirts). When the Action menu appears, choose Clip Adjustments.

In the inspector, there's a Speed slider with a tortoise on one side and a hare on the other.

Dragging toward the tortoise will slow your shot down, and dragging toward the hare will speed your shot up. You can also type a number directly in the Speed Percentage field or in the Speed Duration field.

2   Drag the Speed slider toward the tortoise until the speed percentage reads 50% and click Done.

TIP Changing the speed of your clips automatically changes their duration. If you had a five-second clip that you play at 50% speed, it's going to last ten seconds. You can always change the clip duration after applying the speed effect by using any of the editing tools described in Lesson 8.

3   Experiment with changing the speed of other clips in the project.

> **NOTE** ▶ Some clips can't have speed effects applied until they're converted
> to a different format. For example, the video clip that came from the iPhoto
> library was shot using a still camera in an uncommon video format. Clips
> recorded in MPEG or H.264 will also need similar conversion.

If you open the Clip Adjustments inspector for such a clip, instead of the
tortoise-and-hare slider, you'll see a Convert Entire Clip button. Once the
clip has been converted, the speed controls will be available.

Creating a Freeze Frame

Another speed-related effect you can perform in iMovie is to make a freeze
frame of your video. This is a great way to create a dramatic ending for your
movie.

1   Skim the second-to-last shot in the project, and find the frame where the
dancer is at the apex of his jump.

Freezing this frame will add excitement to the shot, emphasizing how high
the dancer jumps and providing great punctuation to all the quick cuts
that came before it.

2   With your pointer over the exact frame you want to freeze, Control-click (or right-click). From the shortcut menu, choose Add Freeze Frame.

The clip containing that frame is split in two and the freeze frame appears as a new clip between them. By default, it's four seconds long. You can change the default in the Timing pane of the Properties window.

3   Play over those last few clips to see the freeze frame effect.

4   Click the leftover part of the shot after the freeze frame and press Delete.

For extra-dramatic results, you can apply a Ken Burns effect to add a little zoom-in on the frozen frame.

5   Select the freeze frame shot and press C to open the Crop, Rotate and Ken Burns window.

6   In the Viewer, click the Ken Burns button in the upper left to select that mode.

The Start (green) box is selected by default, but you don't want to modify that.

7   Click the image to make the End (red) box active, then drag one of the corners to shrink the box and position it around the dancer. Click Done.

TIP ▶ If you accidentally drag the green box instead of the red one, you can easily swap the beginning and ending frames using the Swap Start and End button in the upper-left corner of the frame.

Adding Transitions

Your movie is really coming along with a great beginning, middle, and ending. You've employed a variety of visual effects, but none of them overshadow the content of the shots and they all work seamlessly together.

There's another arrow in your quiver that can go a long way toward giving your movie that professional finished look: transition effects. iMovie has many different types of transition effects, from simple cross-dissolves to 3D cube-spins and various wipes.

You can add individual transitions by dragging them from the Transitions Browser to the space between any two clips (as you did in Lesson 5), but you can also add a transition between every shot in one fell swoop.

1   Choose File > Project Properties or press Command-J to open the Project Properties window.

2   Beneath the Themes, select the "Automatically add" checkbox. Leave the transition pop-up set to Cross Dissolve.

The window expands to show the automatic transition options.

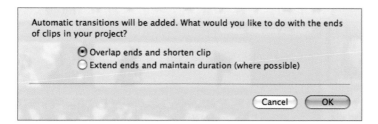

When you add a transition, the effect requires additional frames outside the original duration you selected when you added your clips to the project.

You must now decide whether to make the clips shorter to account for the transitions, or to add more frames from the original footage. For this lesson, you can leave the setting in the default ("Overlap ends and shorten clip").

3   Click the Timing button to open the Timing pane.

4   Set the Transition Duration slider to 1.0 seconds and click OK.

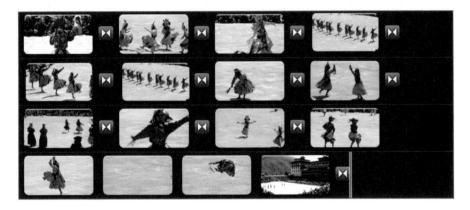

Cross-dissolve transitions are added between each clip, including a fade-in on the first clip and a fade-out on the last clip. When the clip is not long enough, no transition is added, as you see in the last few short shots.

5   Play the whole project to see the results.

The automatic transitions setting is very handy to quickly add all these effects in one step, but it doesn't mean you can't customize the effects once they're applied.

For example, the automatic transitions setting didn't add an effect between the freeze frame and the ending shot of the crowd, but that doesn't mean you can't add one.

6   Click the Transitions button or press Command-4. Drag the Fade to White transition between those last two clips.

iMovie warns you that you have to turn off automatic transitions in order to make any changes, but that's okay. The transitions it added won't go away.

7 Click Turn Off Automatic Transitions.

Your custom transition is added between those two last shots.

8 Double-click the Fade to White transition to open the inspector.

9 Set the Duration to 2.0 seconds and click Done.

This adds emphasis to the final beat and creates a nice transition to the final crowd shot.

You can also replace any existing transition effect with another.

10 From the Transitions Browser, drag the Cross Blur effect onto the very last transition in the project (the fade-out from that final crowd shot).

Also, there are several edits that don't work as well as fades and would be better as cuts. For example, see the edit you adjusted with the Precision Editor in Lesson 8 between the wide shot of the dancers and the close-up or the very quick cuts at the end of the project.

11 Command-click any transitions you want to remove, and then press
Delete.

The unwanted transitions are removed.

12 Play the whole project beginning to end to see the results of your work.

Color Correction

You've really transformed this collection of shots into a finished movie to be
proud of. But there is one more thing that can be done to give it that final
polish.

Some of the shots are not quite as beautiful as they could be. iMovie has powerful image adjustment tools similar to those in iPhoto, which let you correct
white-balance errors, improve image contrast, and even create custom "looks"
to really make a movie your own.

In this project, there are two shots in particular that can use a little color correction. The cutaway shot of the monks is very washed out, and the opening
shot of the flags seems a bit too orange. Both can be fixed quickly and easily
using the Video Adjustments inspector.

1 Position your pointer over the cutaway shot. When the Action menu
appears, click it and choose Video Adjustments.

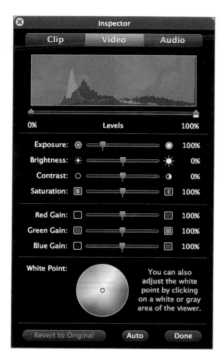

There are many sliders you can manually adjust to improve the image quality (as you learned in Lesson 5), but iMovie also has a magic one-click button to make your shots look their best.

2   Click the Auto button at the bottom of the inspector and then click Done.

Your shot looks sharper and richer instantly.

The Auto button improves the contrast of the shot, making the darkest areas darker and the lightest areas lighter. In many projects, every single shot will look better if you simply click the Auto button.

3   Position your pointer over the first flags shot. When the Action menu appears, click it and choose Video Adjustments.

This shot doesn't have a contrast problem (though clicking the Auto button might make some minor improvement). It has a white-balance problem.

You can manually drag the white dot in the center of the color wheel or, even easier, just click a white or gray spot in your image.

4   Move your pointer over the Viewer.

The pointer turns into an eyedropper.

5   Click a gray area of the clouds in the background.

iMovie automatically recalibrates the image.

6   Click Done to close the inspector.

TIP ▶ Although in some images you can click either a white or a gray spot, this might not result in an adequate correction if the white area is overexposed (as the clouds are in this shot). In general, if there is true gray in your shot, that's the best target to use.

Stabilizing Your Clips

Video stabilization is going to change the way movies are made. Although it's long been available as a high-end feature in digital video editing tools, those folks at the high end also have had access to Steadicams and fancy camera dollies, which are more reliable and offer far more flexibility than cranking up the video stabilizer.

Don't be fooled into thinking that software can magically fix any poorly shot footage. It can't. You still have to do your very best to keep the camera steady and you still have to limit camera movement to the cases described in Lesson 7.

But the difference between the unwatchable handheld movement, so common in amateur and home videos, and the slightly improved stabilized version is going to save countless precious memories and last-minute celebrations from the cutting-room floor.

Make no mistake: Video stabilization isn't perfect. It can take a long time to process your video, all of the blurriness you get from moving the camera quickly isn't going to go away, and, in order to stabilize a shot, you must zoom in on it a little bit, which lowers the video quality and alters the framing from your original intent. Plus, there are going to be sections of your video just too shaky to stabilize at all, and iMovie will let you know about that.

But these downsides are a reasonable compromise when the alternative is that you miss the opportunity to share your amazing footage of Sasquatch rummaging through your backyard barbecue or, more realistically, when your baby takes his very first step.

1 Choose File > Import > Movies. Navigate to to iLife09_Book_Files > Lesson_09 on your Desktop and and select **VietNamMotorcycle.mov**.

2   Create a new Event called ATS – Vietnam, leave the rest of the settings at their defaults, and click Import.

The clip is imported and the new Event is loaded into the Event Browser.

3   Press the Spacebar to see the clip.

Shot from a motorcycle, the clip is very shaky.

4   Click the clip once to select it (anywhere is fine) and choose File > Analyze for Stabilization.

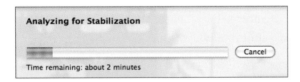

iMovie analyzes the clip. This analysis can take as long as 4–8 minutes per minute of source video.

TIP▶ When you import footage from a camera, there's a checkbox you can select to automatically have all the clips analyzed as they're imported.

When the analysis is done, you'll see some red squiggly lines on certain parts of the clip in the Event Browser.

The squiggly areas are sections of your video that are so shaky that iMovie can't stabilize them. This can also occur because someone walks in front of the lens.

You can choose to automatically hide those squiggly sections.

Hide Segments with Excessive Shake button

5 Click the Hide Segments with Excessive Shake button.

The Event Browser updates to show only the sections of your video with manageable shakiness.

Unfortunately, you can't see the effect of the stabilizer until you add your clips to a project.

It doesn't make much sense to add this shot to the existing Bhutan project, so you'll create a new project just for this example.

6 Choose File > New Project or press Command-N. Name the project *Stabilized*, leave the rest of the settings at their defaults, and click Create.

The new project is created and automatically opened.

7 In the Event Browser, click the second chunk of video, press Command-A to select the whole clip, and drag it into the Project Browser.

8 Move your pointer over the Project Browser area and press \ (backslash) to play the project.

The clip looks dramatically different. To compare it to the original, just move your pointer over the version in the Event Browser and play that one.

While the effect is certainly impressive, it may actually be a little too smooth. A little bumpiness feels natural, and this has none.

9   Double-click the clip in the Project Browser.

The inspector opens. The Stabilization checkbox is selected and the Maximum Zoom slider is all the way to the right, at around 134%.

NOTE ▶ The maximum zoom is determined automatically by the amount of shakiness in each shot, but iMovie will never zoom anything past 150%.

10 Press the Spacebar to play the clip, and while it plays, adjust the Maximum Zoom slider.

The lower you set the slider, the more shakiness you allow in the clip.

11 Set the slider to about 120% and click Done.

NOTE ▶ Video cameras use one of a few different technologies to capture video. Cameras using CMOS can sometimes generate a strange smearing effect when stabilized. Check the documentation for your video camera to identify whether it uses CMOS or CCD chips.

Using Green-Screen Shots

One of the most impressive new features in iMovie '09 is the ability to work with green-screen shots. This allows you to create amazing *compositing* effects where a person (or object) shot in one location can be magically transplanted and integrated into another location.

The good news is that in iMovie '09, achieving such an effect is truly effortless, as you'll learn in the next few steps. The not-as-good news is that you do have to shoot your green-screen footage carefully to get a realistic effect.

▶ **Tips for Shooting Green-Screen Footage**

The quality of your final effect will be limited by the quality of the footage you begin with. This is always true, but it's absolutely critical with green-screen footage.

To create high-quality green-screen effects in iMovie, follow these specific guidelines.

1. *Use a clean, smooth, evenly colored background that must be true green.*

   Using a proper background is important. You can buy inexpensive green backdrops in paper, fabric, and other materials, or you can just buy paint. Be sure whatever you get is specifically called *chroma green*.

   Continues on next page

▶ **Tips for Shooting Green-Screen Footage** *(continued)*

It's also critical that the background is lit evenly. Outdoors on a cloudy day is the best option of all; otherwise, you will likely need two identical lights shining on the screen from opposite angles. Avoid any shadows (such as from your subject) or uneven lighting (such as from the subject's key light).

2. *Keep your subject as far away from the screen as possible and the camera as far from the subject as possible.*

   One very common mistake is to have the subject stand too close to the background. This can cause some of the green to reflect onto her, and that can be very difficult to fix.

   Also, the further away the camera is from the subject, the easier it is to frame her entirely within the green background (by zooming in). You must have the green color completely surround the subject. You'll probably need a bigger green backdrop than you expect!

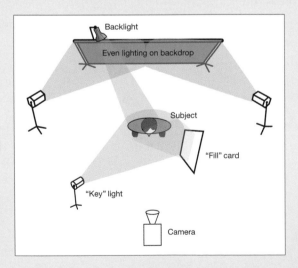

   For best results, add a light behind the subject (called a *backlight* or a *rim light*) to add a rim of light on the edge of the subject's head and shoulders. This creates separation between the subject and the background

Continues on next page

▶ **Tips for Shooting Green-Screen Footage** *(continued)*

and will help create a better effect. Just be sure the backlight isn't spilling onto the screen or shining direct into the camera lens.

3. *Use the same lens and lighting as the background shot.*

The most commonly overlooked aspect of making a good green-screen composite is careful planning about what the background is going to be. To make a convincing shot, the camera should be shooting the subject and the background from the same angle and using the same zoom setting. If the background was shot from a high angle but the subject is shot dead-on, something will look askew when you combine the two shots.

Also, if the sun is clearly shining from the left side in your background, and the subject is lit evenly (or, worse, from the right) in your green-screen shot, the shot will never match naturally.

4. *Make sure the subject doesn't wear anything green.*

This may seem obvious, but it's another common mistake. Everything that's green is going to turn invisible. So if your subject has green stripes on his tie or even very green eyes, those spots will become transparent when you add the effect in iMovie.

5. *Have the subject leave the frame before you shut off the camera.*

One of the tricks iMovie uses to get such clean green-screen effects is that it (optionally) examines the last frame of the movie and subtracts whatever is there from the rest of the shot. If you remove your subject from the frame before turning off the camera, the last frame shows just the empty green screen.

Performing a Green-Screen Edit

In order to make a green-screen shot work, you need two different clips, the foreground and the background. When creating such an effect in iMovie, you must add the background first.

1 Choose File > New Project, or press Command-N to create a new project. Name the project *Green Screen Example*, leave the aspect ratio at 16:9, do not select a theme, and click Create.

The new project is opened in the Project Browser.

2 In the Event Library, click the Greenscreen Shots Event you created in Lesson 7.

The two shots are loaded into the Event Browser.

NOTE ▶ If you didn't complete Lesson 7, you'll need to import the two shots (**Unlikely Hero.mov** and **Flying Background.mov**) needed for this lesson now. They're located in iLife09_Book_Files > Lesson_07.

3 Click the background shot (the one that's not the green screen) and drag it into the project.

4 In the Event Browser, click near the beginning of the green-screen shot to select the default four-second selection.

5 Drag the selection on top of the background shot in the Project Browser.

The Edit Options menu appears.

6   Choose Green Screen.

The shot is added on a new track above the background shot. The Viewer shows the composited effect.

7   Press \ (backslash) to play the project from the beginning.

The shot mostly works, but there is some junk on the left side and the bottom of the green-screen shot that is visible and ruining the effect.

8   In the Viewer, click the Cropped button.

Four control points appear in each of the corners of the Viewer. Video outside the control points will not be visible in the project.

9   Drag the points to hide the elements on the left and bottom of the screen. Click Done.

10 Play the project again to see how that adjustment improves the shot.

The effect mostly works, but there's still a visible white line beneath the hero's chest. This is a reflection of the white suit on the green background that was not automatically removed.

Unwanted reflection

11 Double-click the green-screen shot in the Project Browser to open the inspector. In the Background section of the inspector, select the "Subtract last frame" checkbox. Click Done in the Inspector and Viewer.

This makes the white line go away and you're left with an amazing shot of the unlikely hero flying through downtown Los Angeles. Add a little wind sound effect and *voilà*, instant superhero.

Lesson Review

1. Where are still photos from iPhoto available in iMovie?

2. How do you apply video effects like Aged Film or Vignette?

3. If you play a five-second clip at 50% speed (slow motion), how long will the clip be?

4. True or false: Once you apply automatic transitions, you can't add or modify any transitions in the project.

5. Does the Auto button in the Video Adjustments inspector fix white-balance errors?

6. True or false: Video stabilization can stabilize any footage, no matter how shaky.

7. What do the red squiggly lines indicate?

8. True or False: The green-screen function will work on shots with a blue background.

9. True or false: The green background must cover the entire background.

10. Does wearing tights and a cape automatically make you a superhero?

Answers

1. In the Photos Browser.

2. In the Clip Adjustments inspector, click the Video Effects button.

3. Ten seconds.

4. False. But making any changes requires turning off automatic transitions.

5. No. It improves contrast.

6. False.

7. Areas of excessive shakiness that iMovie can't stabilize.

8. False. The background must be green.

9. False. You can crop out areas that are not green.

10. No, but with iMovie and a little ingenuity, you can sure look like one.

10

Lesson Files

After installation:

~/Movies/iMovie Projects/ATS-Bhutan - (Lesson 10)

~/Movies/iMovie Projects/ATS-Christmas Morning - (Lesson 10)

Time

This lesson takes approximately 30 minutes to complete.

Goals

Normalize clip volumes to ensure consistency

Perform an Audio Only edit

Add music and sound effects to your project

Adjust audio levels and audio fades

Record and adjust a voiceover track

Understand ducking to control other audio clips

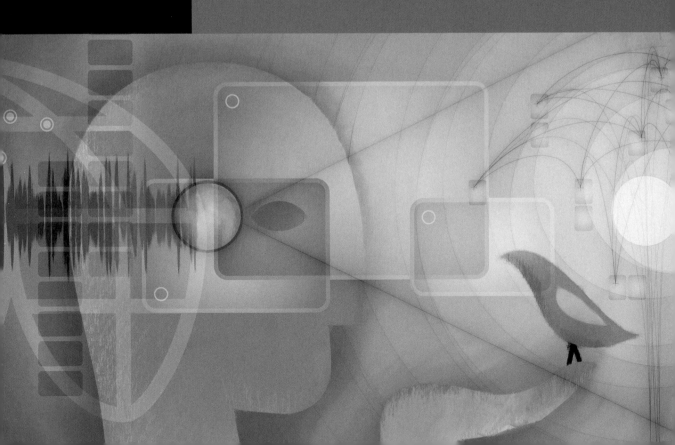

If Seeing Is Believing: Working with Audio

Most video hobbyists don't appreciate the importance of sound, so they put most of their emphasis on how things look—after all, sound is literally invisible. But that doesn't mean it's not a critical component of a finished movie.

In some ways, having a quality audio track may be even more important than having great visuals. Although the picture contains the information (who, what, where, and so on), it's the sound that conveys the emotional tone (how someone is feeling, the musical vibe, and so on). Or put another way, if seeing is believing, then hearing is feeling.

Good audio starts during shooting. If you don't record your audio properly, it's nearly impossible to magically restore it while editing. However, iMovie does provide a wide range of powerful and flexible audio tools to help you make the most of whatever you have recorded. And like the rest of the program, those tools are both easy and fun to use.

Your camera is always recording sound, so virtually all of your footage will have an audio track running alongside the video. When you edit pieces of that footage into a project, you can choose which parts of the sound to keep and at what volume. Additionally, you can add new sounds such as sound effects and music and even a voiceover to enhance your movie and add depth and a professional polish.

Adjusting Audio Levels

Many times you'll want to simply turn off the sound from your original footage and use a music track or voiceover recording instead of the audio your camera recorded. In other cases, you may want to raise or lower the volume of different sections to control the story. Nearly always, audio clips should incorporate a little *fade in* and *fade out* so they don't start or end abruptly, which can be very unpleasant for the viewer. Fortunately, iMovie applies such an effect automatically to every shot.

It's also preferable to have all of the sound in your project set to approximately the same volume. Nothing is more annoying than watching a program where one section is too quiet and another is too loud. Creating an even, consistent audio level is probably the most important thing you can do to make your movie sound its best.

Unfortunately, it's often very hard to ensure the audio levels are consistent, because in one case the camera might be very close to the subject, and in another case, it might be far away. What's more, the people within the shots may talk at very different volumes, further complicating your efforts.

1   Click the Project Library button to open the Project Library.

2   Double-click the **Christmas Morning – (Lesson 10)** project.

This is a completed version of the project you created in Lesson 5. Although the edits you made in that lesson resulted in a satisfying final movie, you can improve it further using the audio tools described in this lesson.

3   Press \ (backslash) to play the project from the beginning and pay extra attention to the sound.

The first two clips have a consistent sound level, but the next couple clips are quite a bit quieter.

4   Position your pointer over the third video clip (of the girl lifting the pink and blue pajamas).

5   When the Action menu appears, choose Audio Adjustments.

The Audio inspector opens. Here you can adjust the audio level of the clip, as well as control a variety of other aspects of the audio. In this case, you know you want to make the sound louder, but how much louder?

The goal is not just to make everything audible, but also to make the sound consistent so it naturally flows from one clip to the next. You could adjust the Volume slider, but that's no guarantee that the results will match those of the previous clips.

Instead, you can use the Normalize feature. When you *normalize* a clip, iMovie analyzes the volume to determine just how loud it actually is (regardless of the setting on the Volume slider). Then the volume is changed to a standard, even level that will be the same, clip to clip.

TIP In general, normalization works best when you apply it to all of your clips, so they're all changed to a consistent level.

6 Click the Normalize Clip Volume button.

iMovie analyzes the clip and adjusts the volume accordingly.

7 Press the spacebar to play the clip and hear the difference.

TIP If you click Done, the Audio inspector will close, but because you know you're going to want to normalize some of the other clips too, you can save some time by leaving the inspector open.

8 With the inspector still open, move your pointer over the next clip in the project.

The pointer has a little speaker attached to it. If you click another clip, the inspector will update to show the settings for that clip.

9   Click the next clip in the project. Then, in the inspector, click the Normalize Clip Volume button.

This clip is also adjusted, and the two clips now have consistent levels.

10   Click Done to close the Audio inspector.

Adding Sound

Remember that your project isn't restricted to video clips. You've already used still images and other effects, and you can add audio elements too. Professional films utilize thousands of audio-only elements, ranging from sound effects to background ambiances to music to other voices. You don't have to match that level of detail, but you should always consider whether adding some additional sounds to your movie can make it more complete.

In iMovie, you can add an audio-only clip—for example, one of the hundreds of sound effects that come with iLife '09, or a music track created in GarageBand. You can also add just the audio from a video clip. To make the Christmas project reach its full potential, you'll do both.

1   In the Event Library, click More Christmas.

There's only one clip in this Event.

2   Press the spacebar to play the clip.

The picture isn't necessarily anything special, but the audio of the girl saying "It's Christmas" can serve as a great introduction to the movie.

3   Drag from the beginning of the clip until after she says "It's Christmas" (about 5 seconds).

4   Drag the selection onto the middle of the first clip in the project.

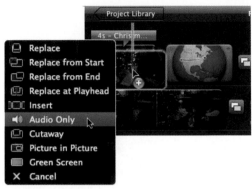

5   When the edit menu appears, choose Audio Only.

The audio for the clip is added to the project and appears as a bar underneath the clip.

6   Press \ (backslash) to play the project from the beginning and hear how the sound fits.

7   Adjust the timing of the audio clip by dragging the audio bar to the left or right.

Adding Background Music

Next you'll add some music, which was created especially for this project in GarageBand. In Lesson 5 you added a little sleigh bells sound, but that sound has been removed in this version of the project.

1   Click the Show Music and Sound Effects Browser button.

2   In the Audio Browser, click the disclosure triangle next to GarageBand
to expand it.

3   Click the GarageBand folder.

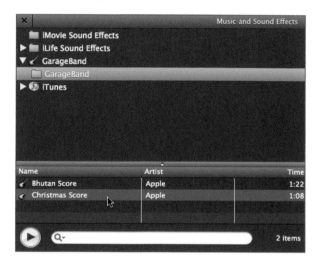

A list of songs created in GarageBand appears.

4   Click **Christmas Score** and press the Play button to preview the music.

5   Drag **Christmas Score** to the Project Browser, and when you see the background light up green, drop it.

NOTE ▶ Be careful not to drop the music onto a specific clip or the music
will only play over that one item. The green background is your clue that
you're dropping it in the right place.

The music track is added to the background of the project.

6   Play the project to hear how the music integrates with the existing audio.

You can begin the music at a specific point of your choosing. In this case, you'll move it to begin just as the girl says "It's Christmas."

7   Drag the name of the background music track to the right until it starts just as the clip of the girl's voice begins.

Congratulations! You've just made a great Christmas movie.

But before you celebrate too much, you're going to add the same level of polish to the Bhutan movie and learn just a few more of the audio tools available to you in iMovie.

8 Click the Project Library button to open the Project Library.

9 In the Project Library, double-click the **ATS-Bhutan – (Lesson 10)** project.

This is a completed edit of the Bhutan project, but it still needs some audio work.

10 In the Music and Sound Effects browser, click **Bhutan Score** and press the Play button to preview it.

11 Drag **Bhutan Score** into the project and drop it on the background. (Be careful not to drop it on a specific clip).

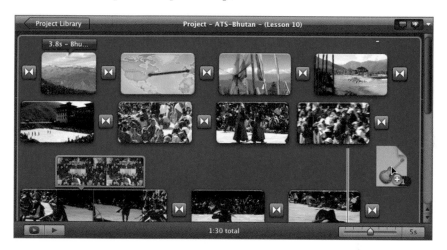

Adding Sound Effects to a Clip

Adding music takes this piece to new heights, but the ending still feels a little empty. Given that you've got that wide shot of the crowd at the end, what about supplementing it with some applause? The shot is wide enough that you can't really see what people are doing, so no one will really even know if they applauded or not in real life.

1 In the Music and Sound Effects Browser, click the iLife Sound Effects item.

2   In the search field at the bottom, type *crowd applause.*

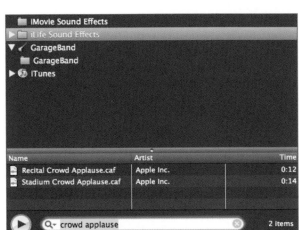

Two items appear in the list.

3   Preview the two sound effects tracks.

The recital track sounds like it was recorded indoors and the stadium track sounds like it was recorded outdoors. Because the Bhutan festival is outdoors, the stadium track will make a better fit.

4   Drag the stadium crowd applause sound into the Project Browser, and drop it directly on the last clip. (You may need to first scroll the Project Browser so you can see the last clip.)

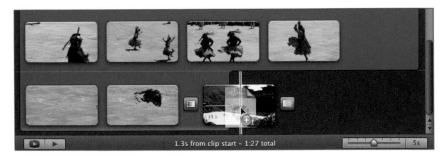

This time, instead of the sound being added to the background, it's added as a new green bar directly under the clip.

To make the sound feel more integrated into the movie, you can make it begin a moment before the video cuts to the crowd visual.

5   Drag the crowd sound effect to the left until it starts halfway through the freeze frame of the dancer.

6   Drag the right edge of the sound effect to the right, to lengthen the sound so it extends all the way through the last clip and to the end of the transition effect.

7   Play the project to hear how this sound work you've done enhances the movie.

Oops! The crowd sounds great, but you can still hear the audio from the original clip.

8   Select that last clip and press A to open the Audio inspector.

9   Drag the Volume slider to 0 to silence the clip, and then click Done.

Adding a Voiceover

Some movies may benefit from incorporating narration or commentary that you record during the editing process. iMovie has a built-in recording tool to help you make such recordings and integrate them seamlessly into your movie.

> **NOTE** ▸ In order to do the following exercise, you need to have a built-in microphone on your Mac, or have an external mic attached via the Audio In jack.

1   Click the Voiceover button or press O.

The Voiceover inspector opens. In order to begin recording a voiceover you want to first make sure the microphone is working and recording a good level.

2   Set the Record From menu to Built-in Microphone if you're using the built-in mic, or to Built-in Input if you're using an external mic.

3   Count to ten and watch the audio meters to ensure that you're getting a clear level.

TIP If the audio meters are showing red, your input is too loud. If you're just seeing a few bars of green, your input is too soft.

4 Adjust the Input Volume slider if necessary to get a good level.

5 Practice reading the text in step 7 a few times before you begin recording.

6 Click the clip in the project showing the close-up of the horn players.

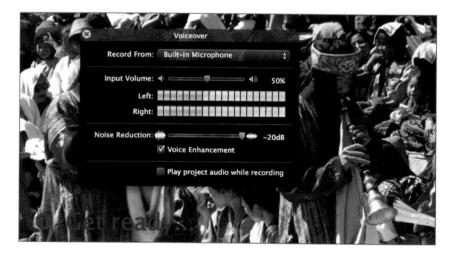

iMovie counts down from three, and when it finishes, you're live!

7   Read the following text aloud:

"The Cham dance is a traditional mask-dance performed by practitioners of certain sects of Buddhism. The dance is considered to be a form of meditation, and an offering to the gods."

8   When you're done recording, click anywhere or press any key.

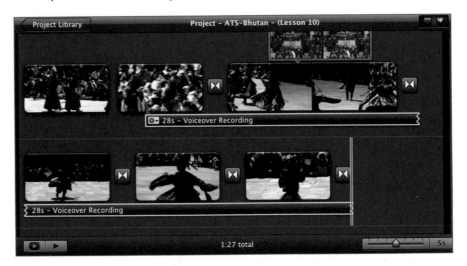

The voiceover is added as a purple bar beneath the clips.

You can drag the left or right edge to trim off the beginning or ending of the recording, or if you don't like the recording at all, select it and press Delete.

9   Close the Voiceover inspector to end Voiceover recording.

Mixing Levels

Now that you've incorporated so many different audio elements into your project, you must play the whole project and make sure the audio is mixing together in a clear and sensible way.

1   Press \ (backslash) to play the project from the beginning.

You may notice that when the voiceover begins, the music and other audio tracks seem to get quieter. This is because iMovie automatically turns on *ducking* for voiceover recordings. Ducking is a way to change the volume of everything but the track you're listening to.

2   Double-click the Voiceover bar, and in the inspector, click the Audio button at the top.

Notice that the Ducking checkbox is selected and the slider is set to 15%.

This tells iMovie to turn down the volume of the background music, the sound from the video clips, and any sound effects (if there are any) so you can hear the voiceover more clearly.

You can select the Ducking checkbox for any clip in your project to perform a similar audio adjustment.

3   Play the remainder of your project.

Everything should sound pretty good, but the applause at the end might seem too loud.

4   Click the Action menu icon on the green sound effects bar for the applause, and choose Audio Adjustments to open the Audio inspector.

5   Press the spacebar to preview the sound effect.

6   Lower the volume to about 50%, and press the spacebar again to check the new level.

That gets the overall volume of the clip more in line with the rest of the program, but it still needs a little fade out to end along with the picture.

7   Adjust the Manual Fade Out slider to about 1.5s (1.5 seconds).

8   Click Done to close the Audio inspector.

9   Play the whole movie one more time from the beginning.

Congratulations! You've now made a great, polished movie with a professional-sounding soundtrack.

Remember, in order to make the sound elements you add to your project feel integrated, you can't just drop them in and forget about them. You may need to make additional adjustments such as the ones you've done in this lesson.

Lesson Review

1.   What does it mean to normalize a clip?

2.   Does ducking change the volume of the selected audio track?

3.   Are audio fades added automatically to video clips?

4.   How can you add realistic sound effects to your movie?

5.   How can you change where background music begins in your project?

Answers

1.   To normalize clip volume means to bring the audio of a clip to a preset uniform level.

2.   No. Ducking reduces the volume of any audio that overlaps the track for which ducking has been selected.

3.   Yes. iMovie adds an automatic half-second fade to the start and end of every video clip. To remove the fade, open the Audio Adjustments window and slide the Manual Fade slider to zero seconds.

4.   Don't just place a sound effect and move on. When you add a sound effect to your movie, be sure to adjust the volume level and fade to fit appropriately within the aural context of your movie.

5.   Drag the background music by its name to where you want it to start.

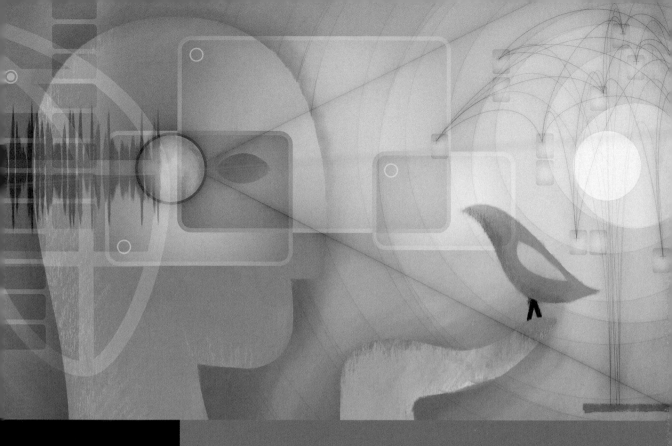

GarageBand: A Musical Sampler

Mary Plummer is a professional musician, composer, and video editor who has edited and scored music videos, documentaries, and independent feature films. An Apple Certified Trainer, she is the co-owner of InVision Digital and Media Arts Inc., an Apple Authorized Training Center located at Universal Studios in Orlando, Florida. Mary's other books include *Apple Pro Training Series: Soundtrack Pro* and the forthcoming *Apple Training Series: GarageBand '09*.

11

Lesson Files No new files for this lesson

Time This lesson takes approximately 30 minutes to complete.

Goals Connect instruments to the computer

Explore the Learn to Play interface

Customize the Learn To Play appearance

Download additional Learn To Play lessons

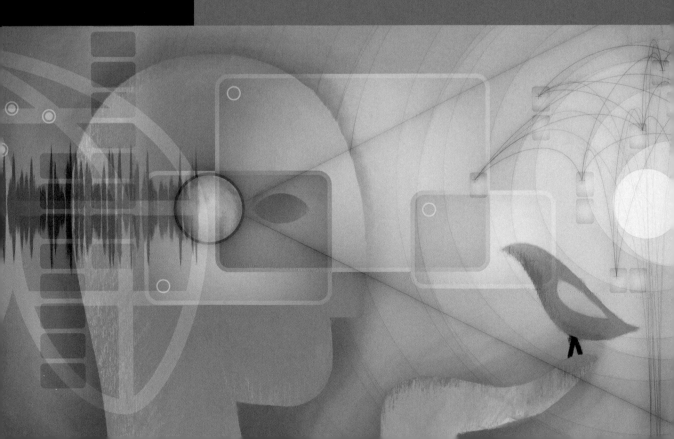

Learning to Play Music with GarageBand

Whether you're an accomplished musician or hobbyist, or simply someone who enjoys other people's music, GarageBand can help you take your musical aspirations to the next level—no experience required!

GarageBand '09 has evolved into a fully functional musician's workshop with all of the tools you need to learn, record, compose, produce, mix, and share your music.

This lesson focuses on the Learn to Play Lessons that can teach you to play either guitar or piano.

If you don't have an instrument at this time, feel free to read along with the lesson to get an idea of how GarageBand Learn to Play lessons work.

Opening GarageBand

In this section, you're going to open GarageBand and take a look at the various options available for learning music, playing along, composing, and recording music.

1   Click the GarageBand icon in the Dock to open it.

The GarageBand welcome screen opens.

This window includes links to play the GarageBand video tutorials, as well as information on getting hands-on help.

For now let's close the window and move on to the actual interface.

TIP▸ If you don't care to see the welcome screen every time that you launch GarageBand, deselect the checkbox in the lower-left corner of the window before closing it.

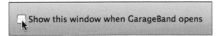

Show this window when GarageBand opens

2 Press Command-W to close the welcome screen.

The New Project dialog appears, with buttons for all of the different project types, including New Project, Magic GarageBand, and iPhone Ringtone.

3 Click the New Project button to see a list of project templates appear in the main area of the window. Templates are included for piano, electric guitar, voice, loops, keyboards, acoustic instruments, songwriting, podcast, and movie scoring.

You'll work more with the project templates in Lesson 13, Creating an iPhone Ringtone. For now, you can leave the New Project dialog open while you connect your instrument in the next section.

Connecting Musical Instruments to Your Computer

There are two types of musical instruments: electric and acoustic. An electric instrument has a built-in interface for output of its sound, but an acoustic instrument needs a microphone to record its sound.

Electric instruments include electric guitars, electric keyboards, and electric bass. You can connect an electric instrument directly to your computer's audio-in port, if your computer has one. The computer audio-in port is a ⅛″ mini input, so you'll need an adapter or cable to convert the ¼″ output from your instrument to the ⅛″ audio-in port (mini input) on the computer.

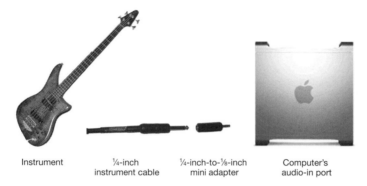

| Instrument | ¼-inch instrument cable | ¼-inch-to-⅛-inch mini adapter | Computer's audio-in port |

To record an acoustic instrument or vocals, you can connect a microphone to your computer through the audio-in port. Mac Pro computers also include optical digital audio in/out ports for higher-end audio recording equipment.

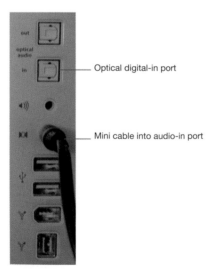

Optical digital-in port

Mini cable into audio-in port

You can also connect an audio interface to your computer and then connect your microphone or instruments to the audio interface. There is a wide range of audio interfaces and compatible formats, including USB, FireWire, PCI, and

PC cards. With the addition of an audio interface, GarageBand allows you to record up to eight Real Instrument tracks and one Software Instrument track simultaneously. An audio mixer or console will also record more than one instrument or microphone at once, but it will mix all the inputs into only one stereo track.

Make sure that whatever audio interface you use is compatible with Mac OS X 10.5.6 or later (for GarageBand '09) and that your computer supports the format used by the interface. Your interface documents should state whether it's compatible with your Mac.

To set up recording using your Mac's built-in port, do the following:

1   Choose System Preferences > Sound > Input and select Line In > Audio line-in port as your sound input device.

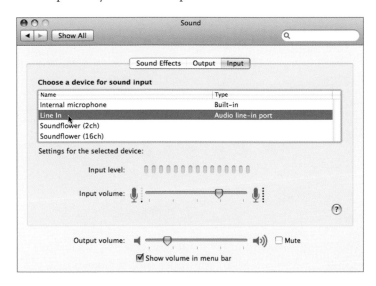

2   Play your instrument and adjust the Input Level slider until you achieve a good level without peaking/clipping.

Once you've finished connecting your instrument you can continue to the next sections to explore the Learn to Play exercises for guitar and piano, or move on to Lesson 12, Jamming With a Virtual Band, to play along with other virtual musicians.

MORE INFO ▶ For more information on arranging and creating music in GarageBand, check out *Apple Training Series: GarageBand '09* by Mary Plummer, or consult the Getting Started with GarageBand document available through the Help menu.

Connecting a MIDI Instrument to the Computer

MIDI stands for Musical Instrument Digital Interface. It's an industry standard that allows all devices such as synthesizers and computers to communicate with each other.

A USB MIDI keyboard or other MIDI controller connects directly to the computer and to the keyboard with a USB cable.

To connect a USB MIDI keyboard to the computer, simply plug it into a spare USB port. To connect a standard MIDI controller such as a keyboard, you'll need a USB-to-MIDI interface. Connect the keyboard to the MIDI interface device using standard MIDI cables. Then connect the interface to your computer using the USB cable. Carefully read the instructions that come with the keyboard and MIDI interface, and be sure to install all of the necessary drivers.

MORE INFO ▶ For more information about GarageBand accessories, including MIDI keyboards, USB keyboards, or MIDI interfaces, visit Apple's website.

Learning to Play Guitar or Piano

Are you one of the millions of people who say they wish they had learned how to play piano or guitar when they had the chance? Well, if you have a Mac, a guitar, a piano or MIDI keyboard, and GarageBand '09, this is your chance! Many of you already have an instrument in the house (or garage, or attic collecting dust), and if not you probably know someone who will loan you one.

GarageBand's new Learn to Play lessons are perfect for anyone who is ready to start taking lessons, or who took lessons a long time ago and needs a refresher, or even for a student who is currently taking lessons and would like some personal tutoring at home.

Rather than guide you through an entire basic lesson, the next few exercises are designed to introduce you to the Learn to Play lessons interface, as well as the recording and customizable features so that when you're ready to sit down for a full Learn to Play lesson you'll be ready to rock and roll (literally).

Taking a Guitar or Piano Lesson

This section will cover the features of both the Intro to Guitar and Intro to Piano Learn to Play lessons. If you have an instrument connected to the computer, follow along with the steps appropriate for that instrument. Most of the steps will be the same for both guitar and piano lessons.

GarageBand '09 includes nine free basic guitar and piano lessons. The first lesson for both instruments is automatically installed on your computer when you install iLife '09.

You don't need to have a guitar or piano handy to follow along with this exercise. When you're ready to take an actual Learn to Play lesson, you'll need to connect your instrument to the computer to fully explore interactive features such as tuning and recording your practice.

You can open the first Learn to Play lessons from the GarageBand Project window.

> **NOTE ▶** If you don't want to learn about the Learn to Play lessons at this time, feel free to jump to Lesson 12, Jamming With a Virtual Band.

1   Open GarageBand and select Learn to Play from the projects list on the GarageBand Project window.

2   Select either Guitar Lesson 1 or Piano Lesson 1, then click Choose or press Return.

The screen fades out and the lesson opens.

NOTE ▸ You can also open a Learn to Play lesson by double-clicking a lesson icon on the GarageBand Project window.

Exploring the Interface

Now that the Intro to Guitar lesson is open, you can see the default interface. The default lesson interface includes a Video area in the upper part of the screen and an animated guitar fretboard in the lower part of the screen. Transport controls are located in the dark gray Control Bar at the bottom of the screen. You can use these controls to record, play/pause, or repeat parts of the lesson.

Video Area   Control Bar   Animated Instrument

Each lesson includes at least two chapters; in these examples the chapters explain how you can Learn (take a lesson) or Play (watch and listen to the instructor playing the lesson song). It's a good idea to start with the Play chapter first to familiarize yourself with the music that you'll be learning during the lesson. In this case, the music is simply the strumming of an E chord.

Let's play the music, and explore some of the different controls to adjust the playback while the music and video play.

1   Double-click the Play Chapter button in the upper-left corner of the Video area.

The music starts and the Video area shows two views of the instructor playing the guitar or piano.

NOTE ► To exit the lesson at any time, click the X (close button) in the upper-left corner of the screen.

2   Move the pointer to the empty gray space below the Video area to see the entire video, without any overlays.

The left side of the Video area will always show the instructor and the full guitar or piano. For the guitar lessons the right side can show either the guitar with the instructor's hands only, or the top of the fretboard.

3   If you're following the guitar lesson, move the pointer to the lower-right corner of the Video area and click back and forth between the two view buttons to change views of the guitar.

4   Click the Play button in the Control bar, or press the spacebar to pause playback.

5   While playback is stopped, drag the playhead left or right to move to a point earlier or later in the song.

6   Press the Right or Left Arrow keys to move the playhead incrementally left or right.

7   Press Return to move the playhead to the beginning of the song.

8   Press the spacebar, or click the Play button to start playback again.

NOTE ▶ The Volume slider in the lesson interface works independently of the volume controls for your Mac, and controls only the volume level of the lesson playback. You can adjust the levels within the lesson interface as needed. If you don't hear anything at all, check to make sure that your computer volume levels are not muted or too low.

9   Click the Metronome button to turn on the click track while the music plays. Feel free to click the Metronome button again to turn off the metronome whenever you like.

10   Drag the Playback Speed slider to the left to slow down the tempo (speed) of the music playback.

When you adjust the playback speed for the first time a warning dialog appears to tell you that slowing down the speed will mute the instructor's voice. If you don't want to see this warning every time you adjust the speed, select the "Don't show again" checkbox.

11   Click OK to close the dialog and slow down the playback tempo.

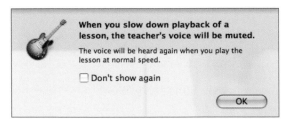

12   Experiment with the different controls, then click the Play button, or press the spacebar to stop playback. Be sure to return the Speed slider to the normal (full right) position.

Now that you're familiar with some of the different playback options and controls, let's move on to the lesson.

13 Double-click the word *Learn* in the upper-left corner of the Video area to switch to the lesson interface.

The lesson starts with an introduction of the instructor, Tim.

14 Stop playback.

You can follow the entire lesson shortly if you'd like. But first, let's take a few minutes to learn how to navigate between sections, and explore some of the customizing features available to enhance your lesson experience.

Navigating Between Lesson Sections

Each Learn to Play lesson comes with at least two chapters. The sections are listed in order along the playhead scrub area above the transport controls.

As you can see, the Intro to Guitar lesson includes seven sections: Learn, Acoustic Guitar, Electric Guitar, Holding the Guitar, Tuning, Picking and Strumming, and Strumming an E Chord.

The Intro to Piano lesson includes eight sections: Learn, Black and White Keys, Playing Position, Sustain Pedal, Chords, Chord Progressions, Rhythm, and Next Steps.

The playback controls and keyboard shortcuts work the same for the Learn (lesson) interface as they did in the Play interface. The difference is the ability to jump around from section to section, or cycle (loop) a specific section.

1   Start playback of the lesson.

2   Click any of the section titles listed in the playhead scrubber area to jump to the beginning of that chapter.

3   Click the Cycle button in the Control bar to cycle (repeat/loop) the selected section.

The selected section title turns yellow to indicate that a cycle region has been created for that section. It will cycle (repeat) continuously until playback is stopped, another section is selected, or the Cycle button is turned off.

NOTE ► If all of the section titles turn yellow at once, the entire lesson is included in the cycle region. Click any specific section title to limit the Cycle Region to the selected section.

4   Turn off the Cycle button and pause playback.

Now that you've learned how to select, navigate, and cycle through sections within the lesson, let's move on to some of the cool customizing features.

Customizing the Lesson Workspace

One of most helpful features for taking a lesson is the ability to customize the lesson's appearance at any time to suit your specific needs. For example, you can show or hide the animated instrument, or change the Notation view. For guitar lessons you can show a Notation view between the Video area and the animated fretboard, or hide the animated fretboard and view only the notation with the video.

All of the customizing choices are available in the Setup menu that can be accessed near the upper-right corner of the screen.

1 Click the Setup menu button.

The Setup menu appears with choices for Notation and Appearance.

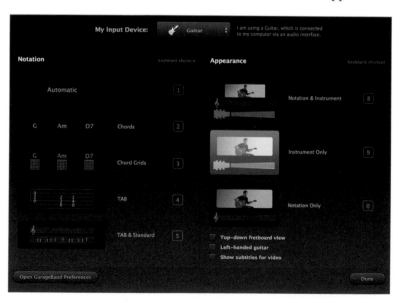

Notice the numeric keyboard shortcut next to each choice. These can be used to change the lesson appearance instantly without interrupting playback.

2   For the Guitar lesson, select TAB & Standard under the Notation column.

This view includes a combination of two common types of guitar notation.

For the Piano lesson, select Both Hands under the Notation column.

NOTE ▶ In the Automatic view, the notation appearance will change automatically, depending on what is being presented in the lesson. For the guitar lesson, because this particular lesson includes only basic picking and strumming, the automatic view actually hides the notation for most of the lesson.

3   Select Notation & Instrument under the Appearance column.

4   Click Done to return to the lesson.

5   For the Guitar Lesson, play the Picking and Strumming chapter.

6   For the Piano Lesson, play the Chord Progressions chapter.

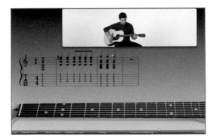 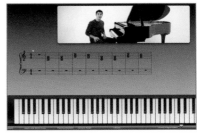

The Notation view appears in the middle of the screen whenever the instructor plays the guitar or piano.

Notice that the animated instrument also shows which notes are played in unison with the notation.

7   Press the numeric keys 2-5 to alternate between chord symbols, chord fingering grids, tablature (TAB), or standard notation. Press 6-9 to change the appearance to show or hide the Notation view and animated instrument.

When you're finished experimenting with the different views, stop the lesson playback.

NOTE ▶ The setup menu also includes checkboxes to select a left-handed guitar, top-down fretboard, and subtitles for the video. You can also use the My Input Device Menu at the top of the Setup pane to change your guitar input settings for the lesson.

Tuning and Recording During a Lesson

In addition to taking a lesson, you can also tune your guitar and record your practice during the lesson. Because both of these features require a guitar or keyboard that is connected to the computer, they won't be included as exercises in this lesson.

The Tuner is located next to the Setup button near the upper-right corner of the screen.

To tune your guitar, simply click the Tuner button and play the string that you want to tune. The visual tuner works the same as most professional guitar tuners.

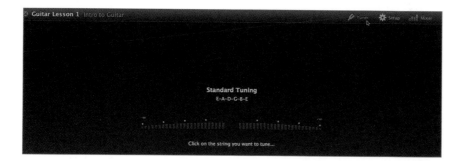

To record your practice, move the playhead to the place where you want to start recording, click the Record button in the Control bar, and play your guitar. Click the Play button when you're finished. For a guitar recording, a purple Real Instrument region appears below the playhead; for a piano recording, you'll see a green Software Instrument region. You'll learn more about the different types of regions in the next lesson.

Recording

Finished region

TIP ▶ To record multiple takes, turn on the Cycle button, and select the chapter you want to record. Record as many takes as you want; when you stop recording a number appears indicating the number of takes. You can click the take number in the upper-left corner of the purple recording region to choose a different take.

Changing a Lesson Mix

Because practice, practice, and more practice are an important part of any successful music lesson, you may want to adjust the lesson mix as you progress to better suit your practice needs. For example, you would probably grow tired of the instructor's voice saying the same thing over and over when all you want to focus on is the sound of his guitar or piano, or perhaps the sound of your own instrument. Let's take a look at the lesson mixer and see how to change the lesson mix.

1   Click the Mixer button, located in the upper-right corner of the screen.

The Mixer appears as an overlay over the lesson window.

Each track includes a Mute Button to silence a track, a Solo button to play only that track, and a Volume slider to adjust the track's volume.

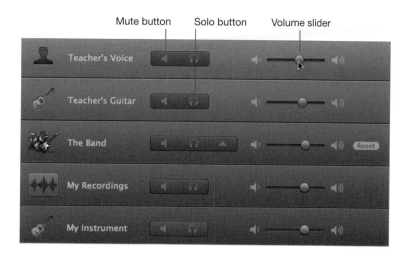

Mute button   Solo button   Volume slider

NOTE ▶ The My Recordings track appears only if you've recorded your instrument with the lesson.

2   For the guitar lesson, play the Picking and Strumming chapter.

3   For the piano lesson, play the Chord Progressions chapter.

While the lesson plays, click the Mute button on the Teacher's Voice track to mute the track.

The Mixer buttons, like other controls within GarageBand, turn blue to indicate that they're on.

4   Click the Mute button again to unmute the track.

5   Experiment with the different mixer controls. When you're finished, click the Mixer button to hide the mixer.

6   Click the X (close) button in the upper-left corner of the lesson window to close the lesson.

That's it. Now you know your way around a Learn to Play lesson.

Downloading Additional Learn to Play Lessons

So you've finished the first Learn to Play lesson. Are you ready for more? GarageBand now includes eight more Learn to Play basic guitar or piano lessons that you can download right to your computer—and they're free!

The additional Learn to Play guitar lessons are as follows:

- ▶ Guitar Lesson 2   Chords – G, C
- ▶ Guitar Lesson 3   Chords – A, D
- ▶ Guitar Lesson 4   Minor chords
- ▶ Guitar Lesson 5   Single Note Melodies
- ▶ Guitar Lesson 6   Power Chords
- ▶ Guitar Lesson 7   Major Barre Chords
- ▶ Guitar Lesson 8   Minor Barre Chords
- ▶ Guitar Lesson 9   Blues Lead

The additional Learn to Play piano lessons are as follows:

- ▶ Piano Lesson 2   Right Hand
- ▶ Piano Lesson 3   Left Hand
- ▶ Piano Lesson 4   Rhythm
- ▶ Piano Lesson 5   Sharps and Flats
- ▶ Piano Lesson 6   Rhythmic Accents
- ▶ Piano Lesson 7   Major and Minor Chords
- ▶ Piano Lesson 8   Scales
- ▶ Piano Lesson 9   Playing the Blues

To download your next lesson, you'll need to choose it from the Lesson Store.

> **NOTE** ▶ If you don't want to download another lesson, you can still follow along with this exercise; just don't click the Download button when prompted to do so.

1   Select the Lesson Store in the GarageBand Project window.

The Learn to Play piano and guitar lessons are listed.

2   Click the Basic Lessons button at the top of the dialog, if it isn't already selected.

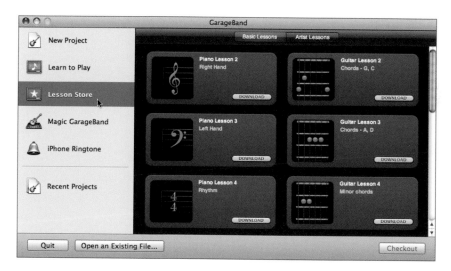

3   Click the Download button on the specific lesson that you'd like to download.

A dialog appears confirming the download.

4   Click Download in the dialog to begin the download.

The lesson is downloaded to your computer and an icon for the lesson appears in the Learn to Play lessons list in your Project window.

Taking an Artist Lesson

If your piano and guitar skills have grown beyond the basic lessons, you're ready to learn from the pros. Artist Lessons use the same interface as the basic Learn to Play lessons with the advantage that your instructor is the actual recording artist who made the music a hit. Want to learn "Roxanne" from Sting, "Thinking About You" from Norah Jones, or "Proud Mary" from John Fogerty? You can do it in GarageBand. The Artist lessons also include personal stories told by the artists about their songs.

These more advanced lessons are also available for purchase from the Lesson Store.

To purchase an Artist Lesson, click the Lesson Store button in the New Project dialog, then click the Artist Lessons button to see the list. From there you can view the different choices and click Add to Cart; then follow the instructions to purchase and download the lesson.

Lesson Review

1. Which instruments have Learn to Play lessons included with GarageBand?

2. How do you download additional lessons?

3. Do you have to have an instrument connected to the computer to take a Learn to Play lesson?

Answers

1. GarageBand includes Learn to Play lessons for both Piano and Guitar.

2. You click the Lessons Store button on the GarageBand Project dialog, then choose the lesson that you want to download.

3. You can take a Learn to Play lesson with or without an instrument; however, having a Guitar or Keyboard connected to the computer allows you to tune (for guitars) and play along with the instructor during the lesson.

12

Lesson Files

After installation:

iLife09_Book_Files > Lesson_12 > Magic Rock Song.band

Time

This lesson takes approximately 30 minutes to complete.

Goals

Choose a Magic GarageBand Jam genre

Audition and select instrument parts

Work with the mixer during an audition

Select and customize your instrument part

Record a keyboard part using musical typing

Open and save a finished song

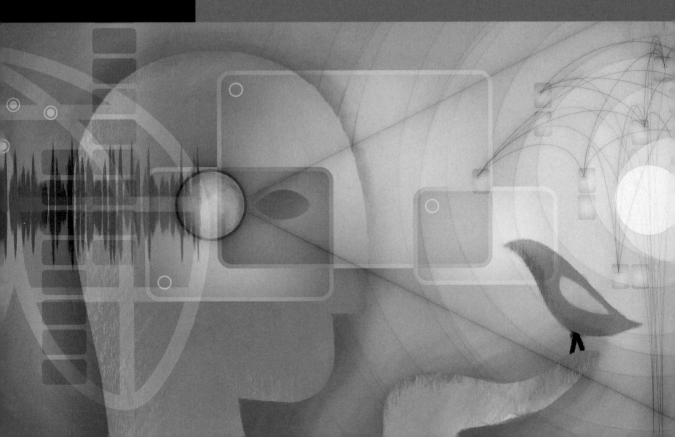

Lesson 12

Jamming with a Virtual Band

One of the greatest pleasures of being a musician is performing with a band on stage in front of a huge crowd of screaming fans. That might not be a reality for everyone, but playing along with GarageBand's virtual musicians is a great way to practice, create music quickly, play and record original riffs, or just jam along and enjoy the process (screaming fans optional). Magic GarageBand Jam puts you at center stage as the leader of a virtual band and offers nine different genres of music to choose from.

Whether you're a professional musician, or have just finished your Learn to Play lessons, Magic GarageBand Jam offers a flexible performance experience to take your musical skills to the next level.

The next series of exercises will lead you through a hands-on tour of Magic GarageBand Jam. Along the way you'll choose a genre, audition musicians, select your own instrument, record a simple part, and finally open and save the finished song in GarageBand.

Let's get started.

Selecting a Musical Genre

Magic GarageBand Jam offers nine different musical genres to choose from, including Blues, Rock, Jazz, Country, Reggae, Funk, Latin, Roots Rock, and Slow Blues.

You can preview the various genres right in the GarageBand Project window.

1   Launch GarageBand. If GarageBand is already open, choose File > New.

2   In the GarageBand Project window, click the Magic GarageBand button.

An icon for each of the nine genres appears in the project list. To preview a genre, simply move your pointer over a genre icon until you see the preview overlay appear. Then click the small Play Preview button.

3   Move your pointer over the Blues icon and click the Play Preview button to hear the blues song. Click the button again to stop the preview.

> **TIP** You can use your computer volume level controls to adjust the preview volume levels.

4   Preview some of the different genres to hear the variety of music that you can jam along with in Magic GarageBand Jam.

For this lesson, let's use the Rock genre.

5   Double-click the Rock genre icon to open that project.

After a moment The Magic GarageBand stage appears along with the default instruments used in the song.

Navigating and Controlling Playback

Now that you've opened a Magic GarageBand project, it's a good idea to learn how to navigate your way around a song and control playback.

If you already completed the Learn to Play exercises in Lesson 11, you'll see some familiar features in the Control bar at the bottom of the window. If you skipped ahead to this lesson, no problem; you'll be acquainted with the controls soon.

1   Click the Play button in the Control bar to play the song.

The music plays in its default arrangement. You can use the volume slider if you need to increase the song's volume temporarily.

2   Press the spacebar to pause playback.

3   Press Return to move the playhead back to the beginning of the song.

Each Magic GarageBand song includes an Intro, two Verses, a Chorus, and an Ending. You can quickly navigate to the beginning of one of these sections by clicking the corresponding part above the Control bar.

4   Click Verse 1 to select that section of the song.

The selected section turns yellow, and the playhead jumps to the beginning of that section.

5   Press the spacebar or click the Play button to start playback again.

Notice that this time the playback includes only the selected snippet of the song. This feature comes in really handy if you want to practice or play along with just one part of the song at a time.

6   Click the Snippet/Entire Song switch to set it back to Entire Song and pause playback.

The yellow highlighted section of the song disappears, and the entire song plays again.

You can also play the project full screen by clicking the small View button in the lower-right corner of the stage.

You can click the View button again at any time to return to the window view.

NOTE ► If you're using the full-screen view, you can click the X (close button) in the upper-left corner of the screen to close Magic GarageBand at any time.

Auditioning Virtual Musicians (Instrument Parts)

Now that you've opened the song and know how to control playback, you can audition the different instrument parts.

Each Magic GarageBand song includes Guitar, Bass, Drums, Keyboard and Melody instruments, and a place for you (My Instrument) at the center of the stage. As the leader of the virtual band, you control which musicians get to play, as well as the instrument and feeling of the part.

The good news is that your job is much easier than auditioning musicians in the real world. In Magic GarageBand the virtual musicians are very professional, which means you don't have to deal with egos, tardiness, attitude, or poor playing. Instead, you can focus on choosing the right parts for your unique version of the song—there are more than 3,000 possible combinations of sounds for each genre.

1   Roll the pointer over each instrument on the stage to see the name of each instrument part.

The spotlight illuminates whichever instrument you roll over, and the name of the instrument or part appears.

2 Click the Guitar on the left side of the stage to select that instrument part.

The Instrument list below the stage changes to show the other instrument choices for the song's guitar part. In this case, there are seven different guitar styles from which to choose: Jangle, Strumming, Honky Tonk, Punk, Windmills, Big Stack, and Glam.

The No Instrument choice on the far right of the instrument list is also available if you don't want to include a particular instrument in the song at all.

If you aren't familiar with these different styles of guitar, no problem. You can simply change them while the song is playing to hear how they change the feel and sound of the song.

TIP It's a good idea to audition instruments against one section (snippet) of the song, such as the verse or chorus, so that you hear all of the different choices in the same context.

3 Play the song, and click Verse 1 to loop playback of that section (snippet) of the song.

4   Click each of the different guitar sounds in the list to audition them with the first verse of the song.

When you change instrument sounds, the new instrument (virtual musician) needs to wait until the next measure to jump in—so be sure to give each guitar a chance to play before moving on to the next one.

You should notice a clear difference in the sound of the guitars.

NOTE ▶ GarageBand comes with an awesome set of guitar amps and stompbox effects to create these sounds—and more—with your own guitar recordings.

5   Choose your favorite guitar sound.

If you're having trouble deciding, try the Big Stack for a nice, over-the-top, heavy electric guitar with plenty of effects. I like this one because it reminds me of the "check out my big amp and effects" sound of the guitars in every band I played keyboards for in high school and college (way back in the '80s, long before GarageBand, though we did practice and record music in the garage).

6   Stop playback, if you haven't already.

Now that you know how to audition and select different instrument parts, let's take a look at some additional mixing features that you can use to make choosing instrument parts even easier.

Mixing Instruments in Magic GarageBand

Auditioning instruments while listening to the other parts works well to get a feel for how the part fits with the overall sound. However, sometimes you may want to solo or mute a particular instrument before you make your final decision.

Each instrument part includes a mixer that allows you to control the volume of that instrument in the overall mix, as well as solo and mute controls.

In this exercise you'll use the mixer to help with the audition of the bass part.

1   Click the Bass to select that instrument.

2   Click the disclosure triangle on the left side of the Bass overlay to show the mixer.

3   Start playback. Feel free to choose a different part of the song for the bass audition.

4   Click the Solo button to isolate the sound of the bass.

You should hear only the sound of the bass instrument. This is a great way to hear the part clearly.

5   Choose a different bass instrument from the instrument list and listen to it.

6   Click the Solo button again to unsolo the new part.

7   Toggle the Solo button on and off as needed while you audition the remaining bass parts. Select different parts of the song to hear the bass in the Intro, Chorus, Verses, and Ending. Stop playback when you're happy with your bass selection.

If can't decide on a bass part, try the Driving bass. It has a nice presence without overshadowing the Big Stack guitar.

The good news is that there is no right or wrong choice. All of the parts sound great; that is part of the "magic" of Magic GarageBand Jam.

TIP ▸ A fast way to find a new combination of instrument parts is to click an empty part of the stage, then click the Shuffle Instruments button. Voila! Now the song has fresh sound with a different set of instruments.

Project Practice

Take a few minutes to practice what you've learned so far, and select new instruments for the drums, keyboard, and melody parts. If you like the way the song sounds as is, you can leave the default instruments and move on to the next section.

NOTE ▸ Magic GarageBand Jam automatically saves your changes to the song as you go. If you need to close the project and come back to it later, just double-click the Rock genre icon from the Magic GarageBand Jam genre list and it will open exactly the way you left it.

Setting Up Your Instrument

Now that the musicians and instruments have been selected, the last step is to choose the instrument that you'll play. Once you've set up your own instrument you can play along and even record your part.

1   Click the Grand Piano labeled My Instrument located at the center of the stage.

The default instrument for the Rock genre is a Grand Piano.

2   Click the My Instrument menu to see the choices of instruments that you
     can use and have connected to the computer.

Your choices are as follows:

▶   **Keyboard** is for using a MIDI instrument such as a piano or organ.
If you don't have an external MIDI instrument, you can also play along
using your computer's keyboard.

▶   **Guitar** is for using an instrument such as a guitar or bass that is connected through the audio in-port or another approved audio interface.
This could also include a microphone that you're using to record vocals
or other acoustic instruments.

▶   **Internal Mic** allows you to record your voice or another instrument
such as a harmonica using the computer's built-in mic.

For this exercise let's use the Keyboard setting and play a part using the
computer keyboard.

3   Choose Keyboard from the My Instrument menu, if it isn't already
     selected.

Magic GarageBand Jam includes three default keyboard choices: Grand
Piano, Electric Piano, and Arena Run.

4   Choose the Grand Piano instrument if it isn't already selected.

To play this instrument using your computer keyboard, you need to turn
on Musical Typing.

5   Click the Tuner button to turn on Musical Typing.

The Musical Typing keyboard appears below the stage. You can click the
notes on the Musical Typing keyboard to play them, or type the corresponding notes on your computer keyboard. Notice that the Tab key
works as a sustain pedal, and the (z) and (x) keys will change the octaves
higher or lower.

6   Start playback and play a few notes on your computer keyboard to hear
how they sound. Don't worry if they aren't the right notes. This is just to
illustrate how it works. When you're finished jamming, stop playback.

NOTE ▶ The My Instrument menu includes Monitor Off and Monitor On
choices. If you don't need to hear your instrument through the computer
speakers or headphones you can choose Monitor Off. This may be handy
if you want to monitor (listen to) the other instruments in your headphones, because you can hear your instrument (such as vocals or acoustic
guitar) without adding it to the mix. The Monitor Off setting is also a
good way to avoid feedback if your live mic is too close to the speakers.
The default setting is Monitor On.

Adding an Instrument

Unlike the specified instrument choices for the other parts of the song, an advantage of your instrument part is that you can choose from any sound available in GarageBand. In this exercise, you'll customize the choice and add a new sound that you can play on your computer keyboard, or with an external MIDI keyboard.

1   Click the Tuner button again to see the My Instrument keyboard instrument list.

2   Click the Customize button.

The Instrument Menu appears, showing all of the available Pianos and Keyboards instruments. Your instrument list may have fewer instruments than the one shown, which includes sounds from Jam Pack: World Music.

For this exercise, let's choose an interesting Synth Pad to add some electronic '80s texture to this Rock song.

3   Click the Pianos and Keyboards menu header to see a full list of Software Instrument categories.

4   Choose Synth Pads from the Instrument menu.

5   Choose Falling Star from the Synth Pads instrument list. Then click Done to hide the Instrument menu.

The Customize button is replaced by the Falling Star instrument in the list.

NOTE ▶ You can click the (i) information button in the upper-right corner of the Falling Star icon to show the Instrument Menu and choose a different customized instrument.

6   Click the Tuner button to turn on Musical Typing and play a few notes along with the song. When you're finished, stop playback.

The Falling Star sound is easy to work with—even if you aren't a musician. Sure, it isn't a very good choice for showing off your finger work or composing a keyboard solo, but it's perfect for adding a little excitement to the Intro and Ending of the song.

TIP ▶ The Tuner Button opens a digital guitar tuner that you can use whenever you have a Guitar connected to the computer and the Guitar setting selected in the My Instrument window.

Recording a Part

You are now two clicks away from recording a part. First you'll need to change the playback to Entire Song, then click the Record button and let the magic begin (pun intended).

When you record a part in Magic GarageBand, it's important to set the playhead position first. The recording will always start at the current playhead position.

Also, if you have a section of the song selected, you can record multiple takes of that snippet over and over, then choose the take that you like best. For this part, a single take should do the trick.

1   Change the playback setting to Entire Song, if it isn't set already.

2   Press Return to move the playhead to the beginning of the song.

3   Play the song through once from the beginning and practice playing the Falling Star part wherever you think it sounds good.

If you aren't sure when to play, remember that for a sound like this, less is more. Try playing once during the intro after the other instruments have started. Play a note again at the end of the first verse or beginning of the chorus, then another at the ending as the other instruments are playing their final notes.

Too much of this Falling Star sound will make it more of an annoyance than a musical surprise. When in doubt, keep the audience guessing, or wanting more.

4   Click the Record button to start recording.

A red recording region appears above the Control bar.

TIP ▶ If you play single notes, the name of the note and octave appears next to the Musical Typing interface. If you play multiple notes, the name of the chord appears instead.

5   Click the Play button to stop recording.

A green Software Instrument region appears above the Control bar. The horizontal lines within the region represent the MIDI note events.

If you're really unhappy with your recording and want to do it again, choose File > Undo, then repeat steps 4 and 5.

NOTE ▶ Guitar, vocals, or other Real Instrument recordings appear as purple regions.

Congratulations! You've recorded an original keyboard part. Next let's open the song in GarageBand to take a look at the finished rock song.

Opening and Saving the Song in GarageBand

Now that your Magic GarageBand song is finished, you'll need to open it in GarageBand to see the finished project, edit the arrangement, add additional tracks, save the project, or share it with iTunes.

In this exercise you'll open the finished song in GarageBand and save the finished project.

1   Click the Open in GarageBand button in the lower-right corner of the window.

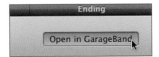

The finished song opens in the GarageBand window.

Notice that there's a timeline with a separate track for each instrument part, and that the track names correspond to the Magic GarageBand instruments that you selected earlier.

The Arrangement track at the top of the window shows each of the different sections of the song (Intro, Verse 1, Chorus, Verse 2, and Ending), and can be edited to rearrange or extend the length of the song.

The short blue regions represent the pre-recorded Magic GarageBand parts. The long green region represents the Software Instrument part that you recorded.

Let's save this project as is. Later you can re-open this project and edit, arrange, and mix this song on your own.

For this exercise, you'll do a basic save. To save the project, first you'll open the Save As window, and then you'll create a new folder to save all of your GarageBand book projects.

2   Choose File > Save As.

The Save As dialog opens.

3   Type *Magic Rock Song* in the Name field.

NOTE ▶ To expand the Save As dialog, click the downward-pointing arrow at the right side of the Save As field.

4   Click the Desktop icon on the Sidebar (left side) of the Save As window.

You've now selected the desktop as the location to save your project.

5   Click the New Folder button, located in the lower-left corner of the window.

A New Folder dialog opens.

6   Type *My GarageBand Projects* in the "Name of new folder" field. Click Create.

The new folder is created on your desktop.

7   In the Save As window, click Save.

This saving method is great for finished projects, but takes longer to save, and isn't necessary until you're ready to share the project with other iLife applications.

Your project has been successfully saved to the folder you created on your desktop.

That's it! You've created and saved a rock song. And you have a good working knowledge of the Magic GarageBand Jam interface.

Now you're ready to share your project with iTunes.

> **NOTE ▶** The song opened in GarageBand with the name "02. Rock 1." This naming convention is based on the way Magic GarageBand saves your work behind the scenes. 02 and Rock represent the genre, and 1 is the version of the Magic GarageBand Rock project you're working on. The next Rock Magic GarageBand Jam session you open and change will be "02. Rock 2" and so on. These Magic GarageBand projects are saved to User > Library > Application Support > GarageBand > Working Copies.

Sharing Your Finished Projects

Now it's time to learn how to share Magic GarageBand projects with other iLife applications and export them to iTunes where they can be downloaded onto your iPod or burned to a CD.

All of the iLife '09 applications, including GarageBand, are designed to work together seamlessly. You can write music in GarageBand and export your songs to iTunes; score your iMovie video and export it as a QuickTime movie or send it to iDVD; send your finished podcast to iWeb to publish on the Internet; or create a whole playlist of original songs to be shared with any of your applications.

Sharing with iLife Applications

You have likely experienced the ease of working across multiple iLife applications as you've completed the lessons in this book. GarageBand is no exception. The key to this integration is the Media Browser that is accessible from both iLife and iWork (as well as many other applications).

1 Choose File > Save, or press Command-S to save any changes to your project before sharing.

2 When you're ready to share your project, click the Share menu and choose one of the following options:

   ▶ Send Song to iTunes—This option places a mixed copy of the track into your iTunes library. We'll explore it fully in the next section.

   ▶ Send Ringtone to iTunes—You'll use this in Lesson 13.

   ▶ Send Podcast to iWeb—You'll use this option in Lesson 15.

   ▶ Send Movie to iDVD—You'll use this option in Lesson 17. If you don't have a video track, this option is dimmed.

   ▶ Export Song to Disk—This option guides you through saving an MP3 or AAC file to a hard drive.

   ▶ Burn Song to CD—This allows you to place a song directly onto an audio CD.

Exporting Projects to iTunes

Exporting to iTunes is as simple as choosing Share > Send Song to iTunes. Before you begin exporting, however, there are a few things you'll need to do to prepare your songs.

In the next series of exercises, you'll set your GarageBand preferences to create a playlist in iTunes. Then you'll evaluate a song to make sure that you're exporting the whole song, and you'll check the output levels for clipping. Finally, you'll export your songs to a new playlist in iTunes.

Because you'll be working with a finished, mixed song, this is a great time to practice your "ear for music" so that you can hear beyond the basics.

Setting GarageBand Preferences for iTunes

To prepare a song to export to iTunes, the first step is to set your song and playlist information in the Export pane of the GarageBand preferences. You'll continue to use Magic Rock Song for these exercises.

1   Choose GarageBand > Preferences to open the Preferences window.

2   Click the My Info button to open the My Info Preferences pane, if it's not already showing.

Next, you'll need to name your iTunes playlist, composer, and album. By default, GarageBand names the playlist and album after the registered user of the computer.

3   Type *iLife '09 Lessons* in the iTunes Playlist field. Type your name in the Artist Name and Composer Name fields. Type *iLife '09 Book Album* in the Album Name field.

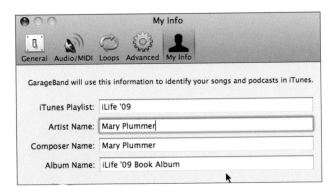

4   Click the Advanced button and make sure that the Auto Normalize check-box is selected.

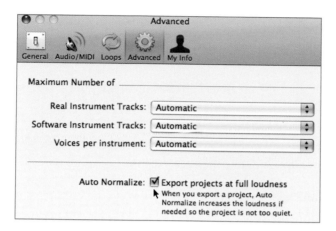

This feature is great for exporting songs to iTunes because it will automatically adjust the volume level as needed to make sure that it's loud enough. Close the Preferences window.

NOTE ▶ Although the Auto Normalize feature is good for exporting music to iTunes, you probably wouldn't want to use this feature if you were scoring video with dynamic music and sound effects that have very specific volume settings.

Now that you've set up the export information, iTunes will automatically create a playlist titled iLife '09 Lessons and include the other information in the playlist.

Evaluating the Song's Output Level

It's time to check the output levels for the song to make sure they aren't clipping. Remember, the Master Output Volume meters are located in the lower-right corner of the GarageBand window. You can use the Master Output Volume slider to raise or lower the output level as needed.

Also, because training your ears takes practice, remember to listen beyond the basic song: Check the left-to-right placement of the different instruments in the stereo field, as well as the balance between the volume levels of the different tracks.

Let's play the song and check the output levels. If the levels are too high, you'll need to lower the output. If the levels are too low, you'll need to raise the output.

If you didn't complete all of the previous exercises, open the project **Magic Rock Song.band** in the Lesson_12 folder to catch up.

1 Press Return and then the spacebar to begin playback. As the song plays, watch the Master Output Volume meters for signs of clipping.

> **NOTE ▶** If you don't see the master level meters along the bottom of the GarageBand window, increase the size of the GarageBand window. You may need to change the resolution of your monitor to make more room. You can also hide the track info if it's visible.

If you see any clipping (red) in the meters, stop playback. If you aren't sure whether you saw red, the handy clipping indicators (red dots) at the end of the meter light up to let you know that clipping did indeed happen.

You should discover red level meters and some clipping throughout the song.

2 Drag the Master Output Volume slider to -3.1 dB to lower the output volume and avoid clipping.

3 Play the song again from the beginning and check the new output level in the meters.

Be careful not to set your levels too low. Ideally, your levels should peak between the highest green and yellow portions of the meter. Fortunately, you selected Auto Normalize in the GarageBand preferences, so the levels should still output with plenty of volume for iTunes.

TIP If a song sounds like it ends abruptly, you can choose Track > Fade Out to add a fade to the master track's volume. You'll learn more about track automation and adding control points in Lesson 14.

4   Press Command-S and save the changes in your project.

Sending a Song to iTunes

When you export a song to iTunes, the entire song or cycle region, if active—from the beginning of the first measure to the end of the last region—is exported. But, remember, if you mute or solo tracks, only those tracks set to play will be exported. Let's export the song to iTunes.

1   Choose Share > Send Song to iTunes to export the song.

2   The Share dialog opens and offers several choices.

You can choose to modify the playlist information. You can also select the Compress checkbox, and then choose compression settings from the Compress Using and Audio Settings pop-up menus. If you don't select Compress, a CD-quality AIFF file will be created.

NOTE ▸ By default, GarageBand projects are sent to iTunes in AIFF (Audio Interchange File Format) at 44.1 kHz (kilohertz). This is a CD-ready format so that your songs can then be burned to an audio CD. You can also compress files to change the file type so that it can be downloaded to an iPod, or converted to another format, such as MP3, from within iTunes.

3   Click Share.

GarageBand begins to mix down your song.

The mixdown process means that all of the different tracks are mixed (at the current levels) into one stereo pair (left and right) for iTunes.

A progress alert shows the progress of the mixdown. You can cancel the export process during mixdown by clicking Cancel.

When mixdown is complete, iTunes opens with your song in the new playlist, and the song automatically plays in iTunes.

4   Press the spacebar to stop playing the song, and then press Command-Q to quit iTunes.

Once your song has been sent to iTunes, you can access it from any of the iLife applications through the Media Browser.

5   Select the GarageBand window to make it active, if it's not already active, and press Command-R to show the Media Browser. Select the Audio pane, if it's not already showing.

The iLife '09 Lessons playlist appears in the iTunes library of the Media Browser.

Your song can now be used in any of the iLife applications, including GarageBand and iMovie.

6   Save your project. When asked if you'd like to include an iLife preview, click Yes. Then close your project.

> **NOTE ▶** Any tracks that are muted at the time you export will not be included in the song. This can work to your advantage if you want to make a practice version without certain instruments in the mix.

Enjoy the song. Technically this composition was crafted by Magic GarageBand Jam, but the settings on your computer will be ready for the next song that you create in GarageBand.

Lesson Review

1.   How do you select an instrument in Magic GarageBand Jam?

2.   Can you add or change Magic GarageBand instruments?

3.   How do you isolate the sound of an instrument in Magic GarageBand?

4.   Is there a way to have Magic GarageBand change all of the instruments for you?

Answers

1.   You can select an instrument in Magic GarageBand Jam by rolling over the instrument and clicking the instrument.

2.   You can change any Magic GarageBand instrument by selecting the instrument and choosing another instrument in the menu. To add an instrument in the My Instrument category, click the Customize button and then choose an instrument from the list.

3.   To isolate the sound of an instrument in Magic GarageBand, you can turn on the Solo button in the instrument's mixer.

4.   You can have Magic GarageBand automatically change all of the instruments to a different combination by moving to an empty space on the stage, and then clicking the Shuffle Instruments button when it appears.

13

Lesson Files

After installation:

iLife09_Book_Files > Lesson_13 > VoiceRingtoneStart.band

Time

This lesson takes approximately 30 minutes to complete.

Goals

Create a loops-based ringtone

Record a Software Instrument part

Play the onscreen Music Keyboard

Send a ringtone to iTunes

Edit a Real Instrument voice track

Edit regions in the editor

Merge Real Instrument regions

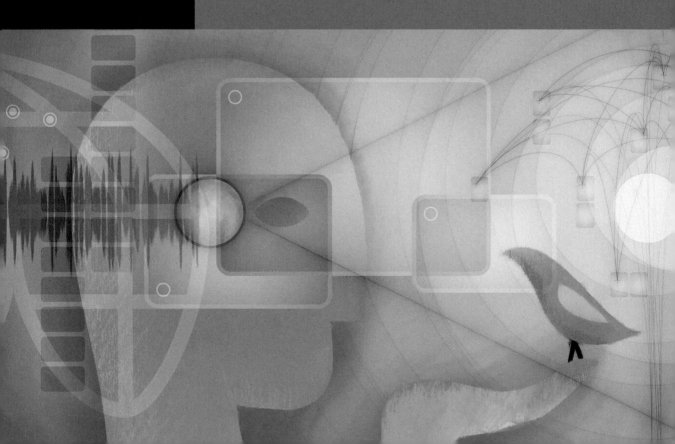

Creating an iPhone Ringtone

GarageBand includes a project preset that makes it easier than ever to create your own iPhone ringtone. In fact, this process is so simple that you're going to make two different ringtones. In the first exercise, you'll open a project template and record a new Software Instrument part to go with the pre-built music. Then you'll open a ringtone project that contains a vocal recording and edit the recording to create a fun ringtone.

Opening a Ringtone Template

You can turn any short piece of music or dialogue into an iPhone ringtone. That includes snippets of your favorite songs. Rather than create a ringtone from scratch, let's start by opening a ringtone project preset, and then choose a ringtone template.

1 Open GarageBand. In the New Project dialog, click iPhone Ringtone.

There are three ringtone templates: Example Ringtone, Loops, and Voice.

2 Double-click Loops to create a loops-based ringtone.

3 In the New Project dialog, name the project *LoopRing*, and save it to the My GarageBand Projects folder on your desktop.

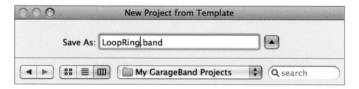

The GarageBand LoopRing project opens with everything you need already in place to finish and send the ringtone, including a yellow cycle region showing above the Timeline, the Loop Browser showing so that you can select additional loops, and a Timeline with four tracks already containing a basic Apple Loop arrangement for the ringtone.

NOTE ▶ Apple Loops are prerecorded music files that are designed to repeat (loop) over and over as a seamless pattern. Loops are commonly used for drumbeats, rhythm parts, and other repeating musical sections within a song. GarageBand includes over 1,000 pre-recorded Apple Loops that are available in the Loop Browser (Cmd-L).

4   Play the project to hear the default arrangement.

Sounds good, has a fun electronic feel, and would likely turn heads (in a good way) if it plays in a crowded restaurant. However, it would be even better if you recorded an additional part to add your own distinctive sound to the music.

Recording a New Software Instrument Part

Now that your project is set up, it's time to start recording an additional part. In this exercise, you'll record a synth part to complete the ringtone song. Don't worry if you aren't a musician; you'll still be able to play along and record.

There are three ways to play a Software Instrument in GarageBand.

▶   Connect a MIDI or USB MIDI keyboard to the computer and play the keys on the musical keyboard. (You can find instructions for connecting a keyboard in Lesson 11.)

▶   Use Musical Typing to turn your computer's keyboard into a musical instrument. (You can try this method in Lesson 12.)

▶   Use the onscreen music keyboard in GarageBand to click the keyboard keys with your mouse.

Playing the Onscreen Music Keyboard

One option for playing music with GarageBand is the onscreen music keyboard. You can use the keyboard to both play and record Software Instruments. First, let's create a new Software Instrument track that you'll use to record your part.

1   Choose Track > New Track, then select Software Instrument from the New Track dialog. Click Create.

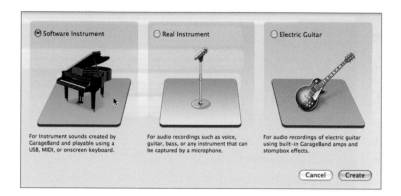

A new Grand Piano track appears below the other tracks in the Timeline. Grand Piano is the default Software Instrument; however, you can change it at any time to a different Software Instrument.

2   To show the onscreen music keyboard, choose Window > Keyboard.

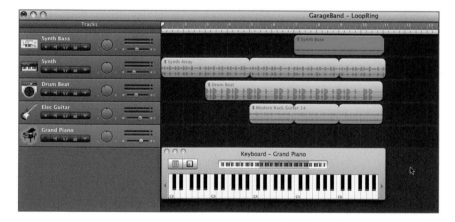

The onscreen music keyboard appears, ready to play the selected Grand Piano track.

NOTE ▶ The onscreen music keyboard works only for Software Instrument tracks.

3   Drag the lower-right corner of the keyboard down and to the right to resize it for larger keys that are easier to click.

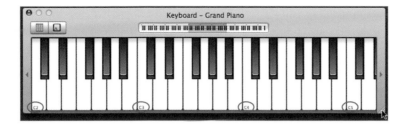

TIP ▶ The onscreen music keyboard is touch sensitive. Click the top of the keys near the top of the keyboard to play with a lighter velocity and get a quieter sound. Click the bottom of the keys near the bottom of the keyboard to play with a harder velocity and get a louder sound. You can always change the velocity of Software Instrument notes in the editor after they've been recorded.

4   Play the onscreen keyboard by clicking the notes on the keyboard.

Although you can play music this way, it's not the easiest way to create complex music arrangements. However, it will work perfectly for this ringtone composition.

Let's change the track instrument to a synth sound that works better for this project.

5   On the Track Info pane, choose Synth Leads as the instrument category (left column) and Solo Star as the instrument.

6   Click a few notes to hear the Solo Star instrument in action.

The part you'll play will be incredibly simple. Because the project is in the key of C, you'll simply click the C key (marked C2—usually the first key on a standard keyboard, including the onscreen music keyboard) and drag the pointer toward the right until you reach the C3 key an octave higher. Then you'll do it again starting with the C3 key and dragging toward the right to C4.

Your goal is to play and hold C2 for the third and fourth measures, and then drag to C3 during the fifth measure. Hold the C3 note through the sixth measure. Click C3 again and hold through the seventh and eighth measures, and then drag to C4 during the ninth measure. Hold the C4 note until the tenth measure.

7   Practice clicking C2 and dragging across the white keys to C3. Then do it again from C3 to C4. Try again while the song is playing. Choose Control > Metronome, or press Command-U to turn off the metronome during your recording.

Don't worry if you miss a key along the way, or overshoot the last note and backtrack. Whatever you do will sound fine in this composition. When you're ready, go ahead and try recording.

8   Press C to turn off the cycle region for this recording. Press Return to move the playhead to the beginning of the project.

9   Press R to start recording, and play your part. When you're finished, press the spacebar to stop recording.

Play back your recording. If you're happy, continue finishing the ringtone. If not, press Command-Z to Undo and try again.

10 Press Command-S to save your project.

Nice work. If you happen to hear that same tune including the Synth Riff as a ringtone somewhere, give that person a high five for going through the same exercise as you. Or better yet, show off your own custom ringtone. It's only a matter of time before ringtones have their own awards.

Sending a Ringtone to iTunes

When you've finished building your ringtone song, the last step is to create a cycle region the same duration as the song. That way you can hear it loop as it will when the phone rings. Then you can send the finished ringtone to iTunes.

1 Press Command-C to show the cycle region. Resize the cycle region so that it ends at the 11th measure (or at the end of the last region in the Timeline.)

2 Choose Share > Send Ringtone to iTunes.

The finished LoopRing ringtone plays in iTunes and is ready to sync to your iPhone.

3 Press Command-Q to quit iTunes.

4 Press Command-W to close the LoopRing GarageBand project.

5 Click No in the "save with iLife preview" dialog.

NOTE ▶ GarageBand adds effects, including special compressors, to ringtone projects to maximize the quality of the sound through an iPhone speaker when the phone rings.

Editing a Real Instrument Voice Track

In the next lesson, you'll work with vocal recordings for a podcast project. In this exercise, you'll edit a Real Instrument vocal region to make a special ringtone that was created as a Valentine present. You can apply this exercise's techniques to your own voice recordings whether they're voiceover, dialogue, or a special voice ringtone for whatever occasion you choose.

1 Open the project **VoiceRingtoneStart.band** in the Lesson_13 folder. Then choose File > Save As and save it to the My GarageBand Projects folder on your desktop.

2 Play the project to hear the finished Valentine's Day ringtone. Imagine hearing this ringtone in a crowded elevator. When you stop laughing, pause playback.

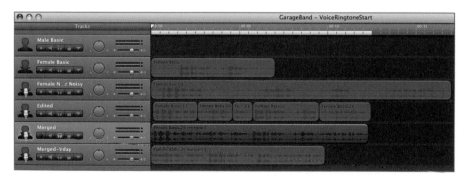

For this project, I started with the Voice ringtone template, and then changed the track instrument to Female Narrator Noisy to apply the noise reduction filter automatically to the track. We used the built-in microphone on my laptop, so the recording was extra noisy.

NOTE ▶ You can record vocals with professional microphones connected to an audio interface, a USB microphone such as the Blue Snowball, or even an iSight microphone. Make sure that you choose the correct Input source for your microphone in the System settings before recording in GarageBand.

In this case, the "female narrator" is my two-and-a-half-year-old daughter Katie. We decided to surprise my husband Klark with a ringtone on Valentine's morning.

This project includes the before and after versions of the edited recordings.

The top Female Basic track includes the initial recording. The Female Narrator Noisy track includes a second, longer recording.

The Edited track is the result of removing all of the unwanted parts of the recordings and arranging them in the track.

The Merged track includes one merged region that was created from all of the edited parts.

The Merged-Vday track is the same as the Merged, except that I removed the "Happy Valentine's Day, Daddy" from the beginning so it can be used as a ringtone beyond the month of February.

3   Mute the Merged track and Solo the Female Basic track to hear the first recording.

You can see the waveform pretty clearly in this region, so you can trim the beginning and ending right in the Timeline.

4　Drag the Timeline Zoom slider toward the right (about two-thirds into the slider) until you have a really clear view of the waveform and region in the Timeline.

Your goal with this Timeline editing is to remove most of the silence (straight horizontal lines) at the beginning and end of the region.

5　Drag the lower-left corner of the Female Basic region in the Female Basic track toward the right until you get close to the beginning of the waveform.

6　Scroll down the Timeline until you see the last half of the region.

7　Drag the right edge of the region toward the left to trim off the excess recording. Be sure to stop trimming when you get close to the waveform.

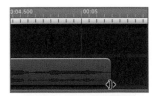

8　Press C to hide the cycle region. Play the trimmed region to make sure it sounds okay. If you accidentally trimmed some of the words, drag the lower corner outward to reveal the missing waveform.

Unfortunately, Katie had a cold the day we recorded this so the effects will eventually filter out some of the noise, but not the lovely nasal tones.

9 Unsolo the Female Basic track and Solo the Female Narrator Noisy track.

10 Press Command-S to save your progress.

Now that you've seen how easy it is to edit a voice recording in the Timeline, let's try editing within the region. For that more advanced maneuver, you'll need to work in the editor.

Editing Regions in the Editor

The editor allows you to see a much larger, more focused view of regions, making it easier to pinpoint areas that need editing. In the Timeline edit that you performed in the previous exercise, you trimmed away the parts that you didn't want. Your goal in this exercise is to select and remove all of the sections of the recording that you don't want to keep. Mainly it's me trying to direct Katie to say what I wanted her to say.

To open the editor, you can either click the Editor button (which looks like scissors cutting a waveform) or double-click the region that you want to edit.

1 Double-click the Female Basic region in the Female Narrator Noisy track to open it in the editor.

The editor appears at the bottom of the GarageBand window.

2   Drag the Editor Zoom slider to around one-third from the left for a good zoom level for this type of work. Feel free to zoom in more or less as needed.

3   Press Return to move the playhead to the beginning of both the editor and the Timeline. Then play the project and watch the waveform in the editor as it plays.

You should be able to hear the parts that need to be removed from the region.

To select part of a region in the editor, you drag to highlight the area. Once you've made a selection, you click the selection to make it a separate region. Once the separate region is selected, you simply delete it from the project. Let's try it.

4   Play from the beginning and pause after Katie says "Happy Valentine's Day, Daddy." (Just beyond three seconds in the ruler at the top of the editor.)

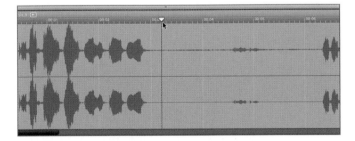

5   Click the crosshair cursor on the middle of the region in the editor, and continue holding down the mouse button while you drag right to create a selection. Release the mouse button just after six seconds in the ruler. (Just before the waveform where Katie talking starts again.)

TIP ▶   Press the spacebar after you make a selection in the editor to hear that selection. If you don't like your selection, undo and try again.

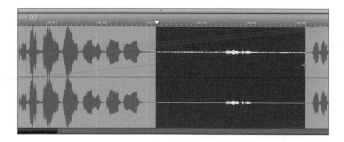

6 Press Delete to remove the selection from the region.

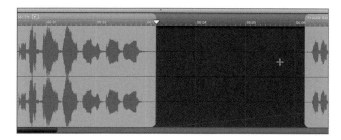

NOTE ▸ Clicking the selected area turns it into a separate region but does not delete it.

As you can see, it's pretty easy to select and delete specific areas of a region within the editor.

Project Tasks

Now it's your turn to remove the rest of the unwanted audio from the track. Scroll down through the region in the editor, and delete any of the sections that shouldn't be there. Don't forget to trim off the nasty pop at the end. When you're finished, you should have four separate regions in the Female Narrator Noisy track. Save your progress before moving on to the next section.

Merging Real Instrument Regions

The final steps to completing this ringtone are to arrange the regions and merge them into one finished region. Technically you don't have to merge them, but it ensures that you don't have excess space between regions. Merging regions is often used with musical recordings to create a finished track or section that can then be looped or duplicated more easily as a single region.

1   Press Command-E to hide the editor if it's still showing. Drag the Timeline Zoom slider to about 1/2 to match the screenshots.

2   Drag the second and third regions in the Female Narrator Noisy track toward the left until they're all touching each other in the Timeline. Feel free to overlap them slightly to cover excess silence at the end of a region.

3   Move the trimmed region from the Female Basic track down to the empty space between the third and fourth regions in the Female Narrator Noisytrack.

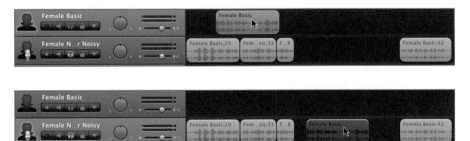

4   Move the last two regions in the track toward the left until all of the regions are next to each other in the track. Feel free to use the Edited track below as a guide for placement.

5   Double-click the track header to select all of the regions within the Female Narrator Noisy track.

6   Choose Edit > Join, or press Command-J to join the regions.

The region appears as a single merged region in the track.

7   Trim the pop from the beginning of the region in either the Timeline or the editor.

8   Save the finished project.

That's it! You've edited a voice recording in both the Timeline and the editor. You can use these techniques to edit your own recordings in the future. If you want to complete this ringtone, simply solo the track that you want to use, create a cycle region the length of the region so that it loops properly, and then choose Share > Send Ringtone to iTunes.

Lesson Review

1.   What types of ringtone templates are available?

2.   Where can you edit Real Instrument regions?

3.   When you hear a region of your song that needs to be removed, how do you isolate it?

4.   What are the benefits of merging Real Instrument regions?

Answers

1.   GarageBand comes with three ringtone templates: Example Ringtone, Loops, and Voice.

2.   You can edit a Real Instrument region in the Timeline or the Editor.

3. In the editor, drag to highlight the area. Once you've made a selection, you click the selection to make it a separate region. Then select it and press Delete to remove it.

4. To create a finished track or section that can then be looped or duplicated more easily as a single region.

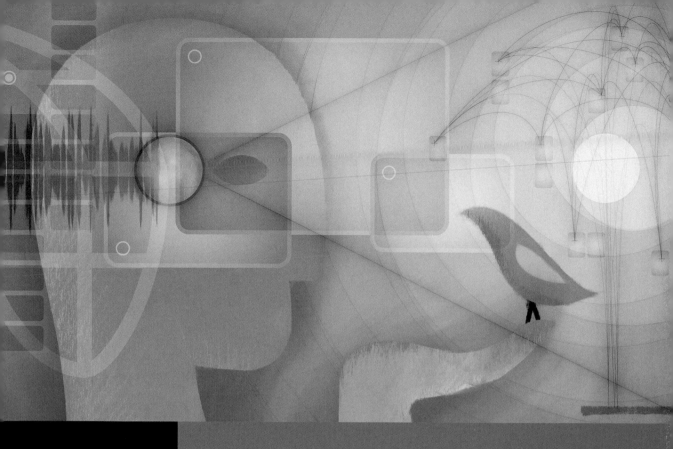

iWeb and iDVD:
Publishing with iLife

Richard Harrington is an author, Apple Certified trainer, and owner of RHED Pixel (www.rhedpixel.com), an award-winning visual communications company in Washington, D. C. that produces everything from national television commercials to entertainment podcasts. Richard's other books include *Apple Training Series: iWork '09*.

14

Lesson Files

After installation:

iLife09_Book_Files > Lesson_14 > 14_MommyCast_Start.band

iLife09_Book_Files > Lesson_14 > Podcast Photos

iLife09_Book_Files > Lesson_14 > Open.mp3

iLife09_Book_Files > Lesson_14 > Feels Like Home.mp3

Time

This lesson takes approximately 60 minutes to complete.

Goals

Create a new podcast episode

Add the Speech Enhancer effects to voice tracks and adjust them

Record a voice track

Add artwork to the Media Browser and podcast track

Edit marker regions

Crop and resize artwork in the Artwork Editor

Add a URL and URL title to a marker region

Edit a project's episode information

Lesson 14
Recording a Podcast

Podcasts are one of the most popular sources of entertainment and information available on the Internet. Podcasts are similar to radio or television shows, in that they deliver audio and sometimes video to their audience. A key difference, though, is that a podcast is not broadcast using traditional means. Rather, a person subscribes to the show (usually for free) and then it's delivered to the subscriber's computer.

Podcasts can be delivered and listened to in a variety of ways. They can, of course, be played on a computer, but they can also be sent to portable media players like iPods and iPhones, as well as to television sets via an Apple TV.

With GarageBand '09, you can create your podcast episodes and then upload them to the Internet using iWeb or another application. There are four primary types of podcasts: audio podcasts; enhanced audio podcasts with markers, artwork, and URLs; video podcasts containing a movie; and enhanced video podcasts containing a movie, markers, artwork, and URLs.

In this lesson, you'll help create a podcast for the MommyCast show, a weekly radio show for and by women. In creating this project, you'll learn how to create a new podcast episode and set up voice tracks for recording. You'll then work on an enhanced audio podcast with multiple tracks, markers, artwork, and URLs. Along the way, you'll also build an opening title sequence, edit marker regions and artwork, and record sound effects directly to the Timeline.

Creating a New Podcast Project

Setting up a new podcast project is easy. GarageBand offers a useful Podcast template right in the GarageBand welcome screen. Let's build the opening sequence to our podcasting episode.

1   Open GarageBand. If GarageBand is already open, choose File > New.

2   In the GarageBand welcome screen, choose New Project and select Podcast. Click the Choose button to create the project.

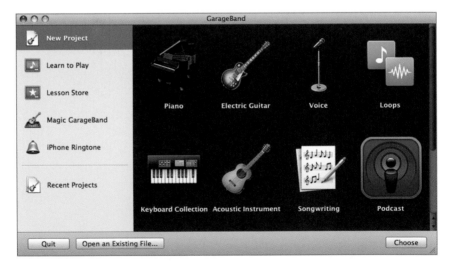

3   Name the project *Show Introduction* and save it in the default GarageBand folder (located inside your User's Music folder). Click Create.

The Podcast Template project opens, with the empty Podcast Track, editor with marker information, and Media Browser already showing. The Media Browser contains buttons for three different types of media files (Audio, Photos, Movies), a browser that lets you navigate to the media files you want to use, and a media list showing the media files in the current location.

You can use movie files to create a video podcast. Likewise, any files in the Photos pane of the Media Browser can be used as episode artwork for your podcast.

Besides the default items from your iLife media library, you can add other folders of still images and photos to the Photos pane so you can access artwork files anywhere on your computer.

Showing and Hiding the Podcast Track, Browser, and Editor

Because you're using the Podcast template from the GarageBand welcome screen, all of the basic tracks and panes needed for a podcast are already showing. However, as you work on your own podcast projects, chances are you'll need to show and hide some tracks and panes to maximize your Timeline workspace.

1   Choose Control > Hide Editor or press Command-E to hide the editor.

2   Choose Control > Hide Media Browser or press Command-R to hide the Media Browser.

The podcast template includes a Podcast Track and three pre-built audio tracks, including Male Voice, Female Voice, and Jingles. You can always add more tracks or delete unneeded tracks from the Timeline.

To make your vocal tracks easier to hear, GarageBand has automatically enabled ducking. This means that some tracks take priority as lead tracks while others function as backing tracks (as indicated by the yellow and blue arrows next to the track name). By default, the voice tracks are set as priority tracks, whereas the Jingles track is set as a backing track that will be ducked as needed to favor the voice tracks.

NOTE ▶ Whenever a sound is present on a lead track, the volume of the backing tracks is lowered. Ducking is indicated by the arrows pointing up and down next to each track's header. Click the up arrow to indicate a lead track. Click the down arrow to indicate a backing track.

3   Double-click the podcast track to select it.

The Podcast Track pane opens. Let's edit the information about this show introduction.

4   Triple-click the name below Artist and enter your own name.

5   Triple-click the name below Composer, enter the name *Matthew Ebel*, and press Return.

6   Let's switch back to the Media Browser. Press Command-R to show the Media Browser and automatically hide the Track Info pane.

7   Press Command-R again to hide the Media Browser.

Hiding the Media Browser will not make the Track Info pane reappear. When a pane is hidden to make room to show another pane in its place, the previous pane remains hidden until you choose to show it again.

Now that you're comfortable with showing and hiding the various panes you'll be using during this lesson, let's move on to setting up a microphone to record your podcast. If you don't have a microphone, you can continue to read the lesson, and an audio file will be provided.

> **NOTE ▶** A project can include either a podcast track or a movie track, but not both. If you try to show the movie track for a project that contains a podcast track, a dialog appears asking if you want to replace the podcast track with a movie track and vice versa.

Choosing Podcast Recording Equipment

Recording audio for a podcast in GarageBand can be as easy or as complicated as needed for your project. For example, if your podcast needs only one voice track (which can contain more than one speaker), you can record the narration by connecting a microphone to your computer or by using the built-in microphone (if it has one). This could be the built-in iSight camera, which includes a fully functioning microphone.

TIP ▶ You can record interviews directly to GarageBand with iChat users. Each participant will have his or her voice recorded to a track.

Voice tracks you record for a podcast are Real Instrument tracks, which means you can record a maximum of eight tracks simultaneously. To record more than one track at a time, you'll need to use an external audio interface, which is explained in more detail below.

NOTE ▶ For this lesson, most of the audio tracks have already been recorded, so you'll just need to record the show's opening. If your computer doesn't have a microphone, you can open a starter project in the Lessons folder.

Due to the popularity of GarageBand, a variety of third-party recording equipment is available. You don't have to invest in additional hardware, but most podcasters purchase a standalone microphone.

For the radio show, the podcasters recorded this episode in their home-based studio with GarageBand. The MommyCast crew uses professional radio-quality microphones, but when they started the show, they used very basic equipment.

TIP ▶ There are several manufacturers who offer USB-based microphones and interfaces that can connect to your Mac with a single USB cable. These are affordable and provide a clear audio signal for recording.

Remember, additional equipment isn't necessary to create a podcast if your Mac has an iSight camera. A separate microphone, though, is a reasonable purchase and can greatly improve the sound of your podcast.

GarageBand can work with both professional and consumer audio equipment.

NOTE ▶ Before recording, make sure that your equipment is turned on and properly connected to the computer. For more specifics on the operation of your equipment, refer to the equipment manuals.

Exploring the Vocal Track Presets

To improve the sound of a recorded voice, GarageBand includes microphone settings and vocal enhancement effects. These can be applied to a vocal track before or after recording. Let's record your voice to introduce the show.

1 In the Timeline, double-click either the Male Voice track header or the Female Voice track header, depending on your gender.

The Track Info pane appears for the selected track. Notice that the Vocals instrument category has been selected, and Female Basic (or Male Basic) is the specified preset. Let's change to a more appropriate preset designed for podcasting vocal recording.

2 Click the Podcasting category and examine the different vocal track presets.

There are five Female Voice presets: iSight Microphone Female, Female Narrator Noisy, Female Narrator, Female Radio Noisy, and Female Radio. The same presets are available for Male Voice. The presets with "Noisy" in the title include an automatic noise reduction filter to help eliminate unwanted background noise in the track. The iChat and iSight presets are made for tracks using those types of recordings.

3 In the Track Info pane, select the Female Narrator or Male Narrator preset (based on your voice).

The preset effect changes, and the Track Header's name changes to reflect the new preset.

4   Click the Edit pane in order to reveal the effect's details. This will let you tweak the preset to match your microphone type.

This preset contains several effects to enhance a standard narrator voice recording. A Bass Reduction effect can pull out the low end (or rumble) in the recording. The Reverb effect can help fill in the sound by simulating reflections of sound. Most importantly, customizing the settings for the Speech Enhancer lets you specify which type of microphone you're using. This is a helpful way to improve the recorded sound if you're using the built-in microphone on your computer.

5   Roll your pointer over the microphone icon next to the Speech Enhancer and click the Edit button to open the Speech Enhancer controls for the Female (or Male) Narrator preset.

The Speech Enhancer controls include a Reduce Noise slider, which is currently at the lowest setting. In the Microphone Type menu, you can choose the type of microphone, and in the Voice Type menu, you can select the type of voice.

6   Select the Microphone Type box, then click the Microphone Type pop-up menu to see the different choices, ranging from MacBook to iMac Intel. Choose the microphone type that best fits your recording situation. Use Generic if you're using an external microphone.

7   Choose a preset from the Voice Type menu. Try a preset that best suits the type of recording you might use in a podcast. The best for podcasting will be the Female Voice Over or Male Voice Over option.

8   Drag the Reduce Noise slider to the right to adjust for any noise in your location. For a very noisy room, drag all the way to the right.

9   Close the Speech Enhancer window.

Project Tasks

Now it's time to record the introductory voiceover for the podcast. Let's take a moment and try recording to the track you just set up.

1   Make sure the Male Narrator or Female Narrator track is selected.

2   Review the following short script:

The online community talk show, dedicated to moms in every country. We're holding the world together, one child at a time, at W-W-W Dot MommyCast Dot Com.

3 Choose Control > Metronome and deselect it.

The metronome is useful for keeping time in musical projects, but you won't need it to record podcasts.

4 Choose Control > Count In to select it. GarageBand will count you into the read with a few clicks of the metronome. When the clicking stops, recording has begun.

5 Press R to start recording and the spacebar to pause.

If you have a microphone attached or built into your computer, you can read the script aloud.

The online community talk show, dedicated to moms in every country. We're holding the world together, one child at a time, at W-W-W Dot MommyCast Dot Com.

If you aren't happy with your first try, you can stop the recording, erase it, and try again.

Working with Music and Sound Effects

Now that you know how to create a new podcast project and set up your vocal tracks, let's complete the show's opening by adding sound effects and a music track.

1 Continue working with your current podcast project or open the file **14_Show Introduction_Stage_Two.band** from the Lesson_14 folder.

2   Click the View button to show the Loop Browser.

You can now access a stinger to use at the show start. A stinger is a short musical intro that adds emphasis and captures the attention of the listener.

3   Use the following path to access a stinger: Stingers > Soft Pulsing Accent.

When you click the stinger, it begins to preview the audio. This is a useful way to audition clips. You can click other tracks to preview them.

NOTE ▸ Because GarageBand ships with several sound effects, you can quickly perform a search based on a keyword.

4   Drag the Soft Pulsing Accent stinger into the Jingles track. Be sure to drag it all the way to the left to ensure that the music begins at the start of the Timeline.

Now that you've added a stinger, let's edit the voice track and stinger so they slightly overlap.

5   Select the Female narrator track and move the playhead so that it's just before the start of your first word. You can use the visible audio wave-forms for guidance.

TIP ▸ You can use the Zoom slider at the bottom of the screen to zoom in and see the audio waveforms more clearly.

NOTE ▸ Your track may have a slightly different name depending upon how many times you recorded your script.

6 Choose Edit > Split to add an edit to the track.

By splitting the track, you can remove pieces from the audio.

7 First click an empty track to deselect the narrator, then click the first segment of the narrator track, and finally press Delete to remove it.

8 Drag the remaining narrator segment so its audio waveforms and the accent waveforms overlap slightly. This will cause the two sounds to blend together.

NOTE ▶ The track will only drag to certain positions because Snap to Grid is on. This causes the track to lock to certain points of time. Press Command-G to disable snapping and have greater control over the track's starting time.

Now that the stinger is placed, let's add a music track.

9 In the Timeline, position the playhead just before you say "Dot Com" in your narration track (approximately 11:00).

10 Open the Lesson_14 folder in the Finder, locate the file **Open.mp3**, and drag it onto the Jingles track so it lines up with your playhead (approximately 11:00).

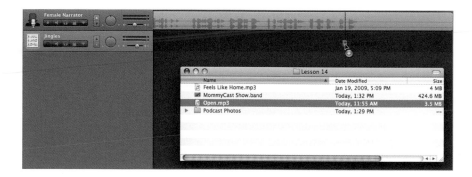

NOTE ▶ If your LCD display doesn't show the time in seconds, choose Control > Show Time in LCD.

11 Press Return to rewind, and then press the spacebar to play the project.

You'll notice that the music and sound effects automatically play lower under the vocal track. This is because ducking is enabled (as indicated by the up and down arrows next to the track names). The vocal track has been set to behave as the lead track. The jingle track has its arrow pointing down, which indicates that it's a backing track.

Let's refine the end of the narrator track so the music knows when it's okay to get louder.

12 Using the same techniques as in steps 4–6, remove any extraneous material from the end of the narrator track. You'll want to remove any portion where you're not talking so the ducking knows when the track ends.

13 Press the Return key, then click the Play button to listen to your track.

The overall volume of the Jingle track is a little high. To adjust its volume, use the track volume slider. Adjust until you find a value that balances with your voice. A negative value will work best.

NOTE ▶ If the level meters next to the narrator track occasionally light red, lower the track volume. If the track is continually red, you recorded your voice too loud and it will sound distorted.

14 If necessary, adjust the volume of your narration track by moving your track volume slider.

15 Choose File > Save As.

Name the file *Podcast Open* and save the project to the default GarageBand folder inside your User folder ([User] > Music > GarageBand). If you store the project in the GarageBand folder, it will appear in the Media Browser.

16 Close the project by choosing File > Close. When prompted, click Yes to include an iLife preview.

The preview file makes it easier to use the GarageBand project with the other iLife applications.

NOTE ▶ You can compare your work to the file **14_Podcast_Open_END. band**, which is located in the Lesson_14 folder.

Editing the Podcast

Now that you know how to set up and edit a basic podcast, we'll jump forward in time and work with a mostly completed show. You'll find a project called **14_MommyCast_Start.band** in the Lesson_14 folder, which contains two recorded Real Instrument voice tracks, one music track containing orange (imported) Real Instrument regions, and one empty podcast track. Open this project so we're both working with the same project file.

You'll notice that the ducking controls are hidden. Due to the complex nature of this project, we'll use Automation Gain to manually mix the levels of the individual tracks. But before we mix our audio, there's a little cleanup to be done.

Adjusting a Recorded Track

The recordings of both of the hosts contain a little background noise that can be removed (it's actually the microphone picking up the other host in the room). It'll be easier to make this fix by isolating each track temporarily.

1   Move the playhead to right before Gretchen speaks for the second time.

2   Press C to show the Cycle Region Ruler. A gold bar appears at the top of the Timeline.

3   Drag the cycle region so it begins just before the first waveform for Gretchen. Then drag its right edge and extend it slightly beyond the end of the first question (from :43.000 to around 1:10.000).

This will keep the audio playing in just this area as we make adjustments.

NOTE ▸ If you can't see the gold bar, drag the zoom slider to the left until the bar is visible.

4   If you don't already have the Track Info pane open for the selected track, double-click the Gretchen track header to open it. Then click the Edit tab to see the track's details. The track has the Speech Enhancer effect applied, with the Female Narrator preset.

5   Click the Edit button to open the Speech Enhancer controls.

6   Press the spacebar to begin playback of the cycle region.

7   Press S to solo the selected track (that is, to hear it independent of the other tracks).You can hear a bit of Paige's voice being picked up by Gretchen's microphone. You may not be able to get rid of all the noise, but you can certainly remove some of it.

8   Continue playback and drag the Reduce Noise slider from the lowest setting (quiet noise) to the highest setting (loud noise). Feel free to choose a setting in between that you like better.

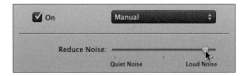

Can you hear the difference in the noise while she's talking? Press S again to unsolo the track.

9   Double-click the Paige track to select it and press S for solo. Using the same steps you just used, adjust the Speech Enhancer preset for Paige to remove Gretchen's voice.

NOTE ▸ You don't have to remove all of the background noise because the two microphones are synchronized with each other.

10 Close the Speech Enhancer dialog and pause playback.

11 Press S to unsolo the track, then press C to hide the Cycle Region Ruler.

12 Choose File > Save to capture your work.

As you can see, it's easy to apply the Speech Enhancer effects to a track before or after it's been recorded.

Importing a GarageBand Project

If you look at the entire Timeline, you'll notice a gap at the start of the project. This is where you'll place the show opening that you built at the start of the lesson. GarageBand makes it easy to import one project into another.

> **NOTE ▶** To make it easier to add one project to another, save it to the default GarageBand folder and include an iLife preview. You did both of these steps earlier in this lesson.

1 Click the Go to Beginning button to rewind your podcast to the start.

2 If it's not visible, press Command-R to show the Media Browser. Click the Audio button to show the Audio pane within the browser.

Your iTunes folder and default GarageBand folder are automatically showing in the Audio pane.

3 Click the GarageBand icon to show the contents of your GarageBand folder.

4 Scroll through the folder contents in the lower pane of the Media Browser.

Normal GarageBand project file icons look like a document (paper) with a guitar printed on it. GarageBand project files saved with an iLife preview show only a guitar icon.

5   Drag the **Podcast Open** project from the Media Browser to the beginning of the Timeline (just after the first narration) and drop it in an empty area below your music tracks.

The project file appears in the Timeline as an orange Real Instrument region. The small guitar icon in the upper-left corner of the region shows that it's a GarageBand project instead of a normal audio file.

6   Play the first part of the project to hear the Welcome and the Show Introduction as well as the start of the interview.

7   Drag the Show Introduction so the stinger happens immediately after the host says the show number.

You've successfully added a GarageBand project to the Timeline of another project. Now the song just needs to be faded out as the main show starts; we'll do that with an automation curve.

NOTE ▶ By placing one GarageBand project inside another, you can easily make modifications to the nested project and, best of all, when you save the changes, the project automatically updates in the Timeline.

Working with Automation Curves

Although GarageBand's ducking controls offer a quick way to mix between audio tracks, they don't offer precise control over audio levels. You can use harness automation curves to gradually adjust a track's volume (or other properties).

1 Click the arrows next to the Podcast Open track to show its automation curve.

Let's fade the music out gently as the main talk show begins.

2 Position your playhead where the main segment begins (around 44.000).

3 Click once on the Track Volume automation curve to add a control point.

Control points allow you to adjust the automation over time.

4 Move the playhead forward to (1:00.000) and click to add a second control point.

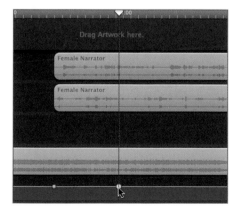

5 Drag the second control point down to −144.0 dB. The track fades out slowly.

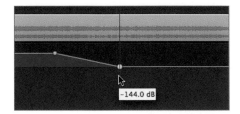

6   Move your playhead back to 35:00 and press Play to listen to your work.

The music now gently fades out as the show begins. Let's add one more fade at the end of the show.

7   Click the automation arrow to disclose the automation for the music track called "Feels Like Home."

8   Scroll the Timeline to the right to see the end of the narrator tracks.

Let's apply automation to have the music gently fade in at the end of the show.

9   Click the automation curve to add a control point at the start of the song.

10   Move forward 10 seconds, then click to add another control point.

11   Drag the first control point downward until it reads −144.0 dB.

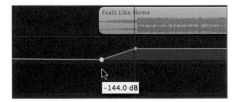

The music now fades in as the hosts finish talking

12   On your own, you can add more control points to Paige or Gretchen's tracks to control their volume. This is optional, but good practice.

13   Choose File > Save to capture your work so far.

Working with Artwork and Markers

The next step in building this podcast is to enhance it with artwork, photos, and markers. In this way, you can create a visual identity for the show and add photos of the band that will help the viewer better experience the show's subject.

Once you've added episode artwork to a podcast, the artwork appears when you play the podcast episode in iTunes (or on an iPod) and in iWeb.

Artwork added to the podcast track creates a marker region the same length as the artwork in the podcast track. Marker regions are used in podcasts to literally *mark* a specific region in the Timeline to include artwork, a chapter title, or a URL. When you publish your podcast as an AAC file, these marker regions can include information for that region in the project.

You can edit, move, and resize marker regions at any time while creating your podcast project. You can also add and edit chapter title markers and URL markers in the podcast track. In addition to the artwork used as marker regions in the podcast track, you can designate the episode artwork in the editor. The episode artwork appears in the Podcast Preview pane whenever there is no artwork for the current marker region.

Adding Artwork to the Media Browser

The artwork you'll be using for this project is in a folder called **Podcast Photos** inside the Lesson_14 folder. You can add artwork folders to the Media Browser by dragging the folders from the Finder into the Photos pane of the Media Browser.

1   In the Media Browser, click the Photos button to show the Photos pane.

2   In the Dock, click the Finder icon to open the Finder window. Locate the iLife_09_Book_Files folder on your computer's desktop.

3   In the Finder, open the Lesson_14 folder and click to select the Podcast Photos folder. Drag them to the Photos pane of the Media Browser. Return to GarageBand.

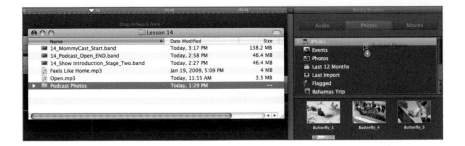

A new folder (named Folders) appears in the Media Browser.

4   Click the disclosure triangle at the left of iPhoto to hide your library, and then click the triangle for the Folders icon to view the folder's contents. Click to select the folder called Podcast Photos. This contains the artwork we'll use for the show.

5   Press Return to move the playhead to the beginning of the project.

6   Select the podcast track so you can view and edit marker regions for a podcast episode.

Adding Episode Artwork to the Project

Episode artwork represents the entire project—like a movie poster or CD cover. People will see it when they choose your podcast to download or preview. The project can have only one piece of episode artwork. Let's take a moment and assign a file as the episode artwork for this podcast.

1   If the editor isn't visible, press Command-E to show it. The editor appears for the podcast track. The Episode Artwork well on the side of the editor is currently empty.

The Podcast Preview pane shows that no artwork is available, because the playhead is at the beginning of the project where there is no artwork in the podcast track.

2   In the upper pane of the Media Browser, select the Podcast Photos folder.

The folder contains photos and graphic files. You can create title graphics using programs like Keynote, Motion, or Adobe Photoshop.

3   Select the file **MC_Album.jpg** and drag it to the Episode Artwork well.

NOTE ► If you change your mind after you've added episode artwork, just drag the artwork from the well, or you can add another piece of artwork to the well to replace the original.

Adding Artwork to the Podcast Track

Now it's time to add artwork to the show. First you'll add art to the opening introduction, then to the band interview. Let's zoom in to the Timeline for a larger view of the podcast track as you add the artwork.

1   Drag the zoom slider until the ruler shows 10-second increments.

2   Drag the file **Episode_Art.jpg** from the Media Browser to the beginning of the podcast track in the Timeline and release the mouse button.

A marker region appears and fills the empty space at the beginning of the podcast track.

NOTE ▶ If you released the artwork too far to the left or right, it won't start at the beginning of the track. Drag the beginning of the marker region toward the left until it extends to the start of the track.

3   Press the spacebar to play the podcast. When the announcer starts to discuss kids (around 53.000), press the spacebar to pause playback.

4   From the Media Browser, drag **Computer_01.jpg** into the podcast track. Drop the photo at the playhead.

5   Press the spacebar to play the podcast. When the announcer starts to discuss the kids in high school and college (around 1:12:00), press the spacebar to pause playback.

6   From the Media Browser, drag **Computer_02.jpg** into the podcast track and release the file at the playhead..

You're off to a great start, but you can further enhance the podcast by filling in some more photos. Keep in mind that although you don't have to use photos in a podcast, they can often improve the entertainment or educational value of your show. This folder contains nine computer images and six host images that you'll use to fill in the rest of the podcast.

7   Drag the photos into the podcast track and attempt to synchronize them
with the interview. There is no "right" answer as to where these should be
placed. You can use the list below for guidance, or make your own decisions.

00:00:00.000	Epsiode_Art.jpg
00:00:53.000	Computer_01.jpg
00:01:13.000	Computer_02.jpg
00:01:27.000	Paige_1.jpg
00:01:40.000	Computer_03.jpg
00:02:00.000	Computer_04.jpg
00:02:10.000	Gretchen_1.jpg
00:02:20.000	Computer_05.jpg
00:02:45.000	Computer_06.jpg
00:03:13.000	Paige_2.jpg
00:03:20.000	Gretchen_2.jpg
00:03:27.000	Computer_07.jpg
00:03:51.000	Computer_08.jpg
00:04:00.000	Paige_3.jpg
00:04:18.000	Computer_09.jpg
00:04:25.000	Gretchen_3.jpg
00:04:30.000	Nadas_Cover.jpg

8   The last piece of artwork needs to be trimmed. Scroll to the end of the
Timeline and move the pointer to the end of the artwork track.

9   Drag to the left to shorten the track until its length matches the end of
the song.

10 Press Return to rewind to the start of the show. Then, in the podcast track's header, click the Preview icon. The Podcast Preview pane opens.

NOTE ▶ You can move the window by dragging its title bar, and resize it by dragging its lower-right corner.

11 Click the Play button and watch the project and listen to the audio.

Any thoughts? A few of the pictures are cropped and can be adjusted to improve their appearance.

Resizing and Cropping Artwork

GarageBand includes a handy Artwork Editor you can use to resize and crop your artwork. To access the Artwork Editor, double-click the artwork in the project.

1 In the Marker list, click the artwork at approximately 00:01:40.000 (it's the shot Computer_03.jpg).

2 Double-click the marker's thumbnail to open the Artwork Editor.

3 Drag the photo up so the head and shoulders are visible.

4   Click the Set button to apply the change.

5   In the Marker list, click the artwork at approximately 00:02:11.000 (it's a picture of Gretchen podcasting).

6   Double-click the marker's thumbnail to open the Artwork Editor.

7   Drag the scale slider and reposition the photo so it's more tightly cropped.

Click Set to apply the change.

8   You can adjust any other shots that you'd like to improve their appearance. Then choose File > Save to capture your progress.

Good job. You've completed the podcast artwork. All that's left is to add URL markers and publishing information.

Viewing Marker Information

You can see more information about a project's markers, artwork, and marker regions in the editor. You can also select markers and update their information.

1   Close the Podcast Preview pane, then look at the Editor pane.

The marker regions are listed in chronological order from the beginning of the project. The editor includes columns that show Time, Artwork, Chapter Title, URL Title, and URL for each marker.

2 Drag the vertical scroller to scroll down through all of the project's markers.

As you can see, there are several markers in this podcast. The checkboxes in the Markers area of the editor show how the marker will be designated. Adding artwork to a marker region automatically selects the Displays Artwork checkbox for that marker.

Adding a URL to a Marker

You can add a URL to a marker region in a podcast and view the URL when you play the podcast in iTunes. Not only will viewers see the URL when they play the finished project, but they can also click the URL to open the webpage.

If you add a URL title, the title appears in the Album Artwork window of iTunes (in a published podcast) and clicking it opens the webpage for the URL. An example of a URL title would be "Check out our website."

Let's add a URL title and link to the end of the project. You'll add the URL to an existing marker region. To get there, you could navigate in the Timeline or simply double-click the marker in the editor.

1 In the editor, select the last marker in your list.

2 For the selected marker, click the URL Title field. Type *Visit The Nadas* and press Return.

3 Scroll to the right to view the URL Field. Click the URL field. Type *www.thenadas.com* and press Return.

GarageBand will automatically add "http://" to the address.

Notice the checkmark for the Display URL option after you add a URL to the marker. The URL also appears on the marker region in the podcast track to show that the marker includes a URL.

4 Open the Podcast Preview pane by clicking the Preview icon in the podcast track's header. Press Play to see the marker and its URL title appear in the Podcast Preview pane.

Click the URL title in the Podcast Preview pane to open the webpage.

Adding Episode Info to a Podcast

The last step needed to complete your podcast episode is to add the episode information, which includes the title, artist information, a description of the episode, and a parental advisory. The episode information is available when you work on the podcast in iWeb and when you view the podcast in iTunes.

1   Select the podcast track in the Timeline, then open the Track Info pane by pressing Command-I.

2   Click the Description area and type the following:

The whole family is getting on Facebook. Paige and Gretchen share some dos and don'ts as well as advice on keeping kids safe. Our song is "Feels Like Home" by The Nadas. Thanks for listening to our show!

3   From the Parental Advisory menu, choose Clean.

4   Type *MommyCast – Episode 357* in the Title field.

5   Press Command-S to save the finished podcast.

6   Play the podcast from start to finish to see the completed project.

NOTE ▸ To see a finished version of the podcast, open the project
14 MommyCast_End.band from the Lesson_14 folder.

MORE INFO ▸ To find out more about MommyCast and its hosts Paige
and Gretchen, visit www.MommyCast.com.

Congratulations! You've created an enhanced podcast and gained a good working knowledge of how to build your own podcasts. Once you've created a podcast episode, you can publish it using iWeb. You'll learn more specifics on how
to export and share your finished podcast in Lessons 15 and 16.

Lesson Review

1. Where can you add and adjust the Speech Enhancer effects for a voice
   track?
2. What must you do to a project so that it can be previewed or added to
   another project?
3. How do you crop or resize artwork in a podcast project?
4. Where do you add URL titles or URL information to a marker region?
5. Where do you edit the podcast episode information?

Answers

1. In the Track Info details area, click the Edit button to open the Speech
   Enhancer dialog and modify the effects settings on the selected track.
2. You must save the project with an iLife preview in order to preview it in
   the Media Browser and use it in another project.
3. You can crop or resize podcast artwork by double-clicking the artwork in
   the editor and modifying it in the Artwork Editor.
4. You add URL titles or URL information to a marker region in the editor.
5. You can edit a podcast episode's information in the Track Info pane for
   the podcast track.

15

Lesson Files

After installation:

iLife09_Book_Files > Lesson_15 > Bhutan

iLife09_Book_Files > Lesson_15 > Bhutan_Final_Medium.m4v

iLife09_Book_Files > Lesson_15 Bhutan_Flag.jpg

iLife09_Book_Files > Lesson_15 > Bhutan_notes.rtf

Time

This lesson takes approximately 90 minutes to complete.

Goals

Create a new website and choose a theme

Create a homepage

Position text, shapes, and images on the page

Create links to external pages

Add pages to the site

Include a Google Map on a page

Publish the site

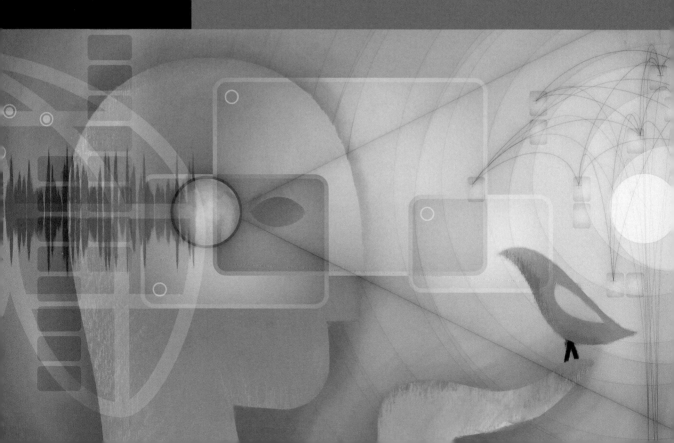

Lesson 15

Publishing a Website

Throughout this book, you've been exploring ways to express yourself with digital media. You've learned how to capture and organize your digital photos, how to make a movie and tell a story, how to create your own music, and how to record a podcast.

Now that your creative juices are flowing, wouldn't it be great to share your work with others? With iWeb you can! You can quickly and easily pull your photos, movies, and audio files into a website and post it online for others to see. There's no limit to the number of pages you can include in your site, and iWeb can incorporate anything you've created with the other iLife applications.

Deciding the Site's Purpose

Before you start building a website and sharing it with the entire world, it wouldn't hurt to develop a quick plan. Let's begin by answering two questions:

▶   What do you have to share?

▶   Whom are you trying to reach?

Although these may seem like simple questions, they'll help you assess what you have and what you want to do with it. Do you have pictures you want to share? Do you want to post highlights of your vacation with a blog? Do you have videos you think others will want to watch? Making an inventory of your website's contents will help you build the website from the ground up, just like the blueprints you'd use to build a house.

The second question relates to your audience. By identifying who you think will come to your page, you can tailor the site's appearance and content accordingly. If you're using iWeb to make a website for your business, that site will look very different from one created to share photos with friends and family.

In this lesson, you'll build a website that highlights a trip to Bhutan. The site will include a homepage that welcomes visitors, a page that shows photos from your trip, and a page to show a video that you edited in iMovie.

Choosing a Theme

Now that you've determined what you're going to say and who you want to say it to, it's time to start making other decisions. The first step is to choose is a theme. iWeb, iLife's application for creating websites, has 28 Apple-designed themes to choose from. Each theme has its own style, and the one you choose will depend upon how you answered the questions at the start of the lesson.

For example, you might choose Darkroom to share your best photos with other photo enthusiasts, or you might choose Notebook for an online journal. Which theme you choose is really a matter of personal taste, but you should keep your audience in mind. If you're designing a website for a business, you'll find many classic and modern themes to choose from. Similarly, there are lots of fun and playful themes designed for kids and teens that should match whatever "feel" you want your site to have.

Each of these site themes provides eight template pages for the various kinds of web pages you might use on your site. There are pages designed specifically for blogs, photos, videos, and podcasts as well as versatile blank pages that you can use for purposes that the other iWeb page templates don't address.

Let's start building a website! We'll begin by picking a theme.

1 Open the iWeb application.

The iWeb icon is placed in your Dock when you install iLife, but if you don't see it there, you can find it in your Applications folder. When you open it for the first time, iWeb displays a template chooser sheet. (If you don't have a MobileMe account, iWeb presents a MobileMe signup dialog that you'll need to fill out before iWeb will display the template chooser.)

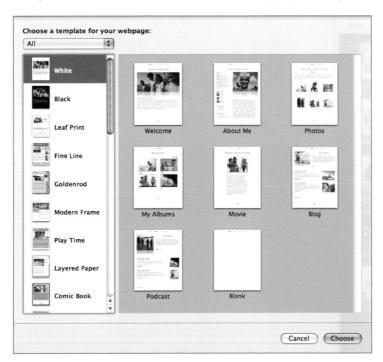

NOTE ▶ MobileMe is an online subscription service offered by Apple that offers many benefits. It can be used to store your important information in an online server, or "cloud." It can also be used as a backup location for important files. With iWeb, you can use your MobileMe account to host your website and all of its video and photo files. You can sign up for a free trial at http://www.apple.com/mobileme/.

NOTE ▶ If iWeb has been run previously, it may already have a site created, and you won't see the webpage template chooser. If that's the case, choose File > New Site to open the chooser.

2   On the left side of the template chooser, you'll see a scrolling list of themes. Scroll down the list to see the different choices you have, then scroll back to the top of the list and select the Modern Frame theme.

In the right pane, you can preview the theme. You'll see thumbnails for each of the eight templates iWeb offers.

Let's make our first page for the site.

3   Select the Welcome template and click Choose.

NOTE ▶ Although you're starting with the Welcome template, you can choose any of the templates as your first page. This first page will be the homepage for the site. You can then choose to add any kind of page to your site at any time. Additionally, you can rearrange pages in your site, so the order in which you build the pages is not important.

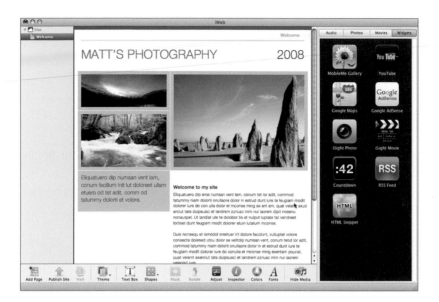

iWeb displays the Welcome page that you chose in the webpage canvas in the center. The left pane shows the sidebar, which lists the sites and pages you've created. Right now, your new website is called "Site," and its one page is named "Welcome;" you'll change these names later. The right side shows your Media in the Media Browser. If this pane is closed, click the Show Media button in the toolbar to open it. The newly added webpage contains both placeholder text and images. These will be modified or replaced with your own content as you build the website.

TIP You can change the theme of your website at any time. Select a page in the sidebar and click the Theme button to apply a new look to the page. It's a good idea to stick to one theme per website so your visitors don't get confused while they're moving between pages on your site.

Making the Homepage

The page you added to the site is the *homepage*; it's the first page that visitors will see. The homepage should help visitors get a good idea of what your website is all about with just a quick glance. This particular template page has room for three photos, a descriptive caption, and a welcome letter.

The Welcome page template you've selected contains a *navigation menu* at the top. It currently contains the name of the only page on your site right now: "Welcome." As you add pages to your site, the names of those pages appear in this menu so your visitors can click a page name to go to that page.

Modifying the Header

Let's change the header on the page so it's clear what this website is all about.

1   Double-click the *MATT'S PHOTOGRAPHY* placeholder text in the header, and type *EXPLORING BHUTAN*.

When you double-click a text box containing placeholder text, all the text is selected so you can immediately replace it by typing.

Next, let's change the colors of the page title to match the colors used in the national flag of Bhutan.

2   Select the new header text you just typed.

You need to have the text that's inside the text box selected for the next steps, which will change its color.

3   Click Colors to open the Colors window.

The Colors window offers several ways to choose colors for iWeb. One of those ways is to load an image file.

4   In the Colors window, click the Image Palettes button.

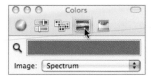

5   Near the bottom of the window, click the pop-up menu currently labeled Palette and choose "New from file."

6   Navigate to the Lesson_15 folder and select the file **Bhutan_Flag.jpg**.

The Colors window updates and shows the flag.

NOTE ▸ We'll be using the flag throughout this lesson. When you're done with the flag graphic you can click the Palette pop-up menu and choose Remove to reset the Colors window to the default spectrum graphic.

7   Click the Orange in the flag to change the text color.

8   Select the placeholder text labeled 2008 and type *2009*.

9   Select the text and change its color to the gold in the flag.

The text is updated, but it's a little hard to read.

10 Press Command-B to make the text bold.

| EXPLORING BHUTAN | 2009 |

11 Choose File > Save or press Command-S.

> **NOTE** ▸ iWeb saves all your pages and sites in a single file in your user account's Library folder: (user folder)/Library/Application Support/iWeb/ Domain. You may want to copy this file to a backup location periodically. If you're using Time Machine, then your file should already be backed up.

Adding Your Photos to the Page

Now that the title is done, let's add some great photos to this page. The goal here is to choose some of your best travel pictures to the homepage so the website's visitors are intrigued enough to explore the entire site.

Because iWeb is part of iLife, it's very easy to access your iPhoto library right from iWeb. The Media Browser shows you your entire iPhoto library. If you have Aperture (Apple's professional image management and enhancement software) installed, its entire library is also available.

1 Click the Photos button at the top of the Media Browser.

2 Click Events to see all your iPhoto Events.

> **NOTE** ▸ If you don't see a list below iPhoto, click the disclosure triangle next to the word *iPhoto*. If needed, there's a folder called Bhutan in the Lesson_15 folder that you can import into iPhoto to use for this lesson.

3 Double-click the Bhutan thumbnail.

> **NOTE** ▸ If you completed the iPhoto lessons, your screen should look like the one on the right. If your Events appear differently, you can skim the Events you see by moving the pointer over the thumbnail. The Bhutan Event contains photos of traditional dancers and countryside shots.

The Event opens to show you all of the available photos. Let's use some photos to replace the media placeholders used by the iWeb template.

TIP To quickly check if an element is a media placeholder, position your pointer over it until a help tag appears. If there's no help tag, or if the help tag doesn't identify the element as a media placeholder, then it isn't one.

4   Locate the file **PA116936.jpg** in the Media Browser.

5   Drag the file onto the large placeholder image of the desert.

The image updates with your photo.

6   Drag the file **PA137360.jpg** onto the small placeholder image of the sunset.

The photo is masked to the new shape. Let's adjust it so we see a different part of the photo.

7   Double-click the image you just added to adjust the image's mask.

Drag the photo upward to match the previous figure, and then press Return.

Let's replace the final image on the page.

8   Drag the file **PA147540.jpg** to replace the last media placeholder.

The pictures look pretty good, but the one of the open fields is a little dark and the big image on the right could be a little more saturated. Fortunately, you can fix these pictures without ever leaving iWeb.

9   Select the open fields shot and click the Adjust button in the toolbar.

10 Click the Enhance button.

11 Drag both the Saturation and Contrast sliders to the right to increase their values. A contrast value near 17 and Saturation near 61 should work well.

12 Select the horizon photo, and click Enhance. iWeb attempts to fix the image automatically.

13 Drag the Saturation slider to the right to increase the intensity of the colors. Try a value near 71 to boost the color.

You've updated all the photos on the page. Let's move on to text.

TIP ▸ If you want to add a new media placeholder to a webpage, simply select a media placeholder from any webpage on your site and then copy and paste. Choose Edit > Copy and then switch to the desired page. Choose Edit > Paste and your placeholder is ready for new media content.

Adding Text to the Page

There are several ways to add text in iWeb. You can type text into any box (or add a new text box). You can also copy and paste your text from a word processing application such as Pages (part of iWork). You can also insert your text or drag it onto a text block if it's saved as a Rich Text Format file (RTF). Let's fill in our page.

1   Double-click the text block containing "Welcome to my site."

2   Type *Adventures near the top of the world* into the text block.

3   Double-click the photos' caption and type the following text:

Join us high in the Himalayas as we visit temples, attend cultural festivals, see prayer wheels, and meet the wonderful people of the Kingdom of Bhutan.

Join us high in the Himalayas as we visit temples, attend cultural festivals, see prayer wheels, and meet the wonderful people of the Kingdom of Bhutan.

Adventures near the top of the world

Eliquatuero dip eros numsan vent lam, conum tet lor adit, commod tatummy niam dolorti onullaore dolor in estrud dunt iure te feugiam modit dolorer iure do con ulla dolor et mconse ming ex ent am, quat velenit exuti erciut tate duipsusci et landrem zzriusc inim nul laorem dipit nosenu

The text looks good. Let's finish this page by dropping in some text that's already been typed.

4 Double-click to select the placeholder text in the large text block.

5 Select Insert > Choose, then navigate to the Lesson_15 folder, choose the file **Bhutan_notes.rtf**, and click Insert.

Join us high in the Himalayas as we visit temples, attend cultural festivals, see prayer wheels, and meet the wonderful people of the Kingdom of Bhutan.

Adventures near the top of the world

The Kingdom of Bhutan is located at the eastern end of the Himalaya Mountains. It is bordered to the South, East and West by India and to the North by the Tibet. The people of Bhutan call their country Druk Yu, which means "Land of the Thunder Dragon."

While Bhutan used to be one of the most isolated nations in the world, it has opened itself to visitors in recent years. The country has balanced modernization with its cultural values. The Kingdom of Bhutan has also avoided the destruction of the environment. The country goes to great efforts to preserve the culture and landscape.

The regions of Bhutan vary greatly. The Northern region contains glaciated mountain peaks and is extremely cold. The central area of Bhutan contains the Black Mountains and a watershed between major rivers. The Southern region is covered with dense forests, river valleys, and smaller mountains.

On our trip, we visited all three regions. Come explore the beautiful country that welcomed us so warmly.

The new text replaces the placeholder text and completes the page.

TIP Although you can type and format text easily in iWeb, it's often easier to prepare text in another application and then just insert (or drag and drop) the text file. iWeb can incorporate text saved in RTF format, which can be exported from most word processing programs, including Pages and Microsoft Word.

The homepage is complete. If you haven't done so, now would be an excellent time to choose File > Save and save your work so far.

Building a Photos Page

You've already explored the web-publishing options offered by iPhoto. Although these are great ways to share your photos, iWeb offers its own useful Photos page that will match your site's other pages in style and navigation.

An iWeb Photos page can be seamlessly added to your site, and you never have to leave iWeb. As you've already seen, you can access your entire iPhoto library right from the Media Browser.

In this exercise, you'll make a Photos page to show your best pictures from your trip to the Kingdom of Bhutan. These are the same photos you used to make a book in Lesson 4.

1   Click the Add Page button at the bottom left of the iWeb window.

The New Page sheet appears, showing the available page templates from the last theme you used.

2   Select the Photos template and then click Choose.

A new Photos page opens in the webpage canvas, and a Photos page appears in the sidebar. Notice also that the Photos page appears in the navigation menu along with the site's other pages.

3   In the sidebar, double-click the name of the new page and rename it *Photo Journal*. The new name appears in the navigation menu.

4   Using the same techniques you learned when you were building the homepage, customize the page title to read *PHOTOS FROM BHUTAN 2009*.

PHOTOS FROM BHUTAN   2009

5   Add the following text to the top of the page:

Natural Beauty

Our trip led to thousands of photos. Here are some of our favorites. We hope you enjoy looking at them almost as much as we did taking them.

> **Natural Beauty**
> Our trip led to thousands of photos. Here are some of our favorites. We hope you enjoy looking at them almost as much as we did taking them.

Now that the text is done, let's add photos to the page.

Adding Pictures and Other Content to the Page

An iWeb Photos page has a large content region that is occupied by the photo grid. As you add more photos, the grid expands to show more photos. You can also rearrange the order of photos and add captions. When a visitor clicks on a photo, it's shown in the detail view that the page provides.

1   Make sure the Media Browser is open and select the Photo tab.

2   Double-click an empty area near a photo thumbnail to return to the Events view.

3   Select the Bhutan Event and drag it from the Media Browser to the photo grid on the Photos page.

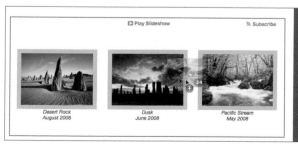

The grid updates to show all of your photos. Let's rearrange some photos.

4   In the Columns pop-up in the Photo Grid window, change the number of columns to 4.

5   Click the Album Style pop-up menu and choose the red border.

The thumbnails update to show a new border.

TIP With 21 different album styles to choose from, iWeb lets you customize the look of your site. Be sure to explore your options when you build your first personal website.

6   Try dragging the photos around to rearrange them. Move a few photos until you're happy with the order on the page.

7   Click the placeholder text below a photo and type a caption.

For this lesson, add your own descriptive captions based on the photo's content. There are no wrong answers here—just give it a try.

TIP If you need space for bigger captions, you can type up to seven lines using the Photo Grid window. To turn off captions, click a photo and set the caption lines to 0 in the Photo Grid window.

8   Let's try out the album. Double-click the thumbnail "Crowd at festival."

A detail page opens. This particular item is a movie that was stored in the iPhoto library. You can also add movies to Photos pages, which makes them truly flexible.

9 Click the Next button.

The page looks good, but you can customize it in the Inspector window.

10 Click the Inspector button in the toolbar and then select the Photos inspector (it's the second button)

11 Click the Photos button and select the checkbox next to "Allow comments."

Visitors can now comment on your pictures.

NOTE ► You must publish the site using MobileMe in order to use comments. A warning dialog likely popped up and told you this already. Click OK to close the window.

NOTE ► If you allow comments, you need to monitor them. iWeb keeps in contact with your site and tells you when new comments have appeared, and it gives you the ability to delete individual comments if someone posts an inappropriate one. Monitor the page after you publish it; otherwise, you may find inappropriate or offensive comments piling up.

On a picture's detail page, visitors are offered the option of downloading the picture. You can specify the size of the pictures visitors can download, or choose not to allow downloads at all.

12 Click the Photo Download Size pop-up menu and choose Large.

Now that the details pages are set, let's adjust the slideshow settings.

13 In the Photos inspector, click Slideshow.

You use this pane to control whether your Photos page allows visitors to view the pictures in a slideshow, and to set slideshow display options.

14 Select the checkbox next to Full Screen.

This allows visitors to enjoy an immersive slideshow experience. You'll see this slideshow when you publish the website at the end of this lesson.

Adding a Movie Page

iWeb includes a movie page template that's designed for showcasing movies on your website. It offers an area for a single movie and presents the needed controls. In fact, if your movie has chapter markers, special controls will be added when you publish the site. Let's add a movie page now.

1 In the Media Browser, select the Movies tab.

2 You should see iMovie selected and all of your movie projects below.

3 Click the Add Page button in the toolbar at the bottom of the iWeb window.

4 Choose the Movie template from the list on the right and click Choose.

A new page is added to your site.

5 Select **ATS-Bhutan - (Final)** and drag the mobile version onto the movie placeholder.

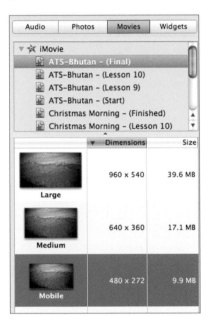

The movie is replaced by a web-optimized version from the iMovie project.

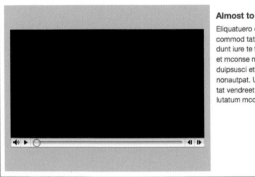

NOTE ▶ For best performance, a movie file should be no larger than 10 megabytes (MB). If you shared your movie to the Media Browser from iMovie, it's automatically compressed.

NOTE ▶ If you didn't complete the iMovie lessons yet, you'll find a file called **Bhutan_Final_Medium.m4v** in the Lesson_15 folder that you can use to complete this exercise. Just drag this movie from the Finder onto the placeholder movie.

6   Let's adjust the layout of the page. Select the text blocks to the right of the movie and press Delete to remove them from the page.

There is now room to make the movie bigger.

7   Drag the corner of the movie to resize it until it is 640 pixels wide.

This looks good and makes the movie quite large. Let's scale the gray box so it fits behind the movie as a border.

8   Click the gray box so that it's selected.

9   Drag the corner resize handle until the box is w: 660 px by h: 430 px.

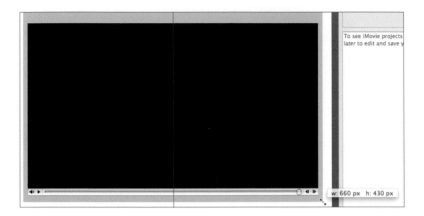

Let's align the boxes so that they're even with each other.

10 The gray box should still be selected; Shift-click the movie so that it's selected as well.

> **TIP** When you open iWeb's preferences, you can choose whether alignment guides align with the centers of objects on the page, with the edges of objects, with both, or with neither.

11 Choose Arrange > Align Objects > Centered to horizontally align the movie and box.

12 Choose Arrange > Align Objects > Middle to vertically align the movie and box.

The page looks good, but it needs its text updated.

13 Using the same techniques you used for the homepage, customize the page title to read *FESTIVAL OF THE DRAGON 2009.*

FESTIVAL OF THE DRAGON   2009

14 In the sidebar, double-click the name of the new page and rename it *Dragon Festival Movie.* Press return.

The new name appears in the navigation menu. The movie page, is complete. Let's finish the site by adding a map of Bhutan, and press return.

Adding a Map to a Blank Page

In order to give you plenty of design options, iWeb offers blank page templates. There are also nine widgets that let you add content from sites such as YouTube and Google, as well as your own content with your iSight camera and more. When you combine a blank page with one or more widgets, you've got great design options.

1   Click the Add Page button in the toolbar.

2   Choose the Blank template from the list on the right and click Choose.

A new page is added to your site.

3   In the sidebar, name the page *Map*.

4   Using the same techniques you learned in the homepage-design exercise, customize the page title to read *THE KINGDOM OF BHUTAN*.

TIP ▶ You can press Command-+ (plus sign) to make text bigger and Command- – (minus sign) to make text smaller instead of choosing those items from the Format menu.

5   Select the smaller text box and press Delete, because we need just a map on the page.

6   In the Media Browser, click Widgets.

7   Drag the Google Maps widget onto the page.

A new map is added to the page. Currently it shows Apple's headquarters (which is a nice place to visit). Let's change this to the capital of Bhutan.

8   In the Google Maps window, type *Thimphu, Bhutan* and click Apply.

The map updates. Next, let's adjust its size and zoom level so visitors can see the whole country.

9   Click the edge of the map to see the resize handles.

10 Hold down the Option key and drag the side handle to make the map larger. Use the figure for guidance.

11 Drag the Zoom slider so you can see most of the country and then drag
    on the map to position it. Use the figure for guidance.

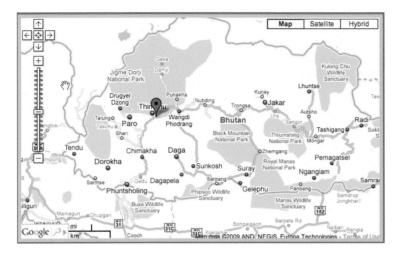

12 Click the Hybrid button to see a traditional map overlaid on top of a satel-
    lite image of Bhutan.

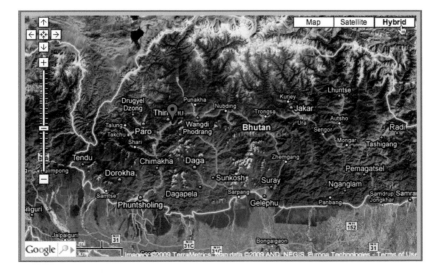

Congratulations, you've completed a website with iWeb.

Publishing the Site

Now that the site is done, you can publish it for the world to see. This is your chance to see how the site looks and works in a web browser, and to tell a few friends about it so they can visit.

Before you publish your site, you have one loose end to clean up: the name of the site and the name of the homepage.

1   In the iWeb sidebar, double-click the top item, Site.

    The name of your site is selected for editing. It needs to be changed to something less generic than the word *Site*.

2   Type *The Kingdom of Bhutan* and press Return.

3   Choose File > Save to store your work so far.

    You are now ready to publish the website.

    NOTE ▸ iWeb also keeps track of which pages you've published and which pages you haven't. The pages and sites you haven't published, or have changed since the last time you published, appear in red in iWeb's sidebar.

Publishing Your Website to MobileMe

By far the easiest way to publish your site is to a MobileMe account. If you have a MobileMe account, iWeb can send the site there with a single click of a button.

Ready? Let's publish your site.

1   Select the site in the sidebar.

    The Site Publishing controls appear in the center pane.

2   Choose MobileMe from the "Publish to" menu.

    NOTE ▶ Make sure you've signed in to MobileMe by launching System
    Preferences and updating the MobileMe preference pane.

3   Enter your email address if you'd like visitors to contact you.

4   Review the privacy settings.

    You can choose to keep a site private if you'd like to share it with only
    friends and family. This also works well if you're making a website for
    clients of your business.

5   If you're a Facebook user, you can select the checkbox next to "Update my
    Facebook profile when I publish this site."

    A new sheet opens to complete the Facebook login. You must allow iWeb
    to access your Facebook page.

6   At the lower left of the iWeb window, click Publish Site.

iWeb displays a Content Rights window with a reminder about using copyrighted material.

NOTE ▸ Clicking the Publish button is the same as choosing File > Publish. Both of these publish only any changed pages on your site to MobileMe. In addition, you can choose File > Publish All, which publishes all the pages on your site, whether they've been changed or not.

7 Click Continue.

iWeb logs into your account, prepares your site for publishing, and then begins sending your site to MobileMe. It presents a sheet telling you that the publishing is now taking place. You can continue working while iWeb sends your site to MobileMe.

8 Click OK.

You can see how the publishing process is going by looking in your sidebar: iWeb displays a small round progress indicator as it transfers your site to MobileMe.

That's it: three steps. If you select the two "Don't show this message again" checkboxes in the two sheets that iWeb displays, it will take only one step the next time you publish.

As soon as your site is published, MobileMe lets you know with one more sheet.

You can click OK to dismiss the sheet, click Visit Site Now to open Safari and view the site, or click Announce to open Mail and send an email message with the site's address to anyone you want. iWeb even prepares the email for you—all you have to do is supply the addressees.

> **NOTE ▶** Once you've published your site to MobileMe, the Visit button at the bottom of the iWeb window becomes active. You can click it at any time to visit your published site.

Let's take a look at the site you just published.

It looks almost exactly as it does in the iWeb window. If there are any discrepancies between how iWeb displays the site and how it looks in your browser, trust your browser because that's what people will be using to view your site. But keep in mind that what looks one way in your browser might look different in another browser on another computer.

NOTE ▶ Even if you own your own Internet domain, you can still publish your site to your MobileMe account and have users visit your site by
entering your domain's address. Choose File > Set Up Personal Domain
on MobileMe to have iWeb walk you through the process of setting up
MobileMe hosting of a personal domain.

To see what the finished page should look like (since we can't put a finished
version on the DVD), go to http://www.peachpit.com/ats.iLife09.

Publishing Your Website via FTP

If you choose not to publish to your MobileMe account, you can still use iWeb
to design a site and then publish your site to a web host via FTP or to a folder
on your computer, which you can then manually upload to a web server oper-
ated by your Internet service provider or other web hosting service.

1   To begin, select the site in the sidebar.

The Site Publishing controls appear in the center pane.

2   Choose FTP Server from the "Publish to" menu.

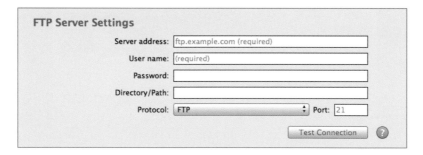

3   Enter your login information as well as the domain name for the site.

4   Click the Test Connection button to make sure your login information is
correct.

5   When ready, click Publish Site and follow the on-screen prompts to
upload the site. The process is very similar to publishing with MobileMe.

Publishing to a Folder

If you choose, you can publish to a folder right on your computer. You might use this method if you want to test the site locally, or if you need to upload it manually from another machine or at another time.

1   Select the site in the sidebar.

The Site Publishing controls appear in the center pane.

2   Choose Local Folder from the "Publish to" menu.

3   Click the Choose button to specify where you'd like the files stored.

4   Click the Publish Site button. iWeb presents the same Content Rights window that it shows when you publish to MobileMe.

5   Click Continue.

iWeb saves your site folder and presents a sheet that tells you which features work differently (or not at all) between a site published on MobileMe and one published to a folder. In particular, features that rely upon code on the MobileMe servers, such as hit counters, comments, and password protection, won't work for iWeb sites published to a folder.

6   Click the Visit Now button on the sheet to dismiss it.

Clicking the Visit Now button opens the site in your Mac's browser. This is an excellent way to check the appearance of your site in a browser before you actually publish it online, either on MobileMe or on another web hosting service.

Lesson Review

1. What are three advantages of creating a MobileMe account?
2. Where can you find themes to use in building your iWeb site?
3. How do you access iPhoto images to add them to your iWeb page?
4. What is a poster frame, and how do you select one?
5. Which is the more reliable place to preview a site you're publishing to the web: in the iWeb window, or in your web browser?

Answers

1. MobileMe can be used be used to keep your important information in an online server, or "cloud;" to provide a backup location for important files; and to host your website and all of its video and photo files.
2. In a scrolling list in the sidebar on the left side of the template chooser.
3. Open the Media Browser and click the Photos button.

4. A poster frame is the first frame shown from a movie on your website to entice viewers to watch the clip. To choose a poster frame from your movie, open the QuickTime inspector, click the movie to select it, then drag the Poster Frame slider until you find the frame you want your site visitors to see.

5. Your web browser, because that's a better indication of how your viewers will see it. But keep in mind that some viewers using different browsers, screen sizes, or screen resolutions may see your site differently.

16

Lesson Files

After installation:

iLife09_Book_Files > Lesson_16 > Web Page Graphics

iLife09_Book_Files > Lesson_16 > Web Page Podcast

iLife09_Book_Files > Lesson_16 > Web Page Text

iLife09_Book_Files > Lesson_16 > Web Page Videos

Time

This lesson takes approximately 60 minutes to complete.

Goals

Customize web page graphics

Create a blog

Add blog entries

Make a video blog entry

Create a podcast entry

Republish an RSS feed to a page

Submit a podcast to iTunes

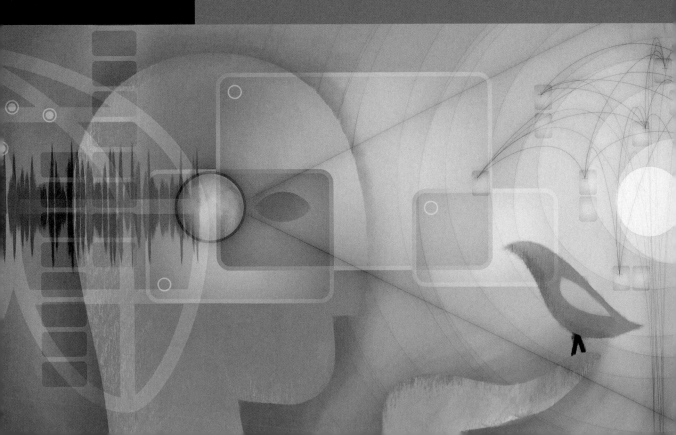

Lesson 16
Creating a Blog and Podcast

It's estimated that more than 12 million American adults currently maintain a blog. What's that? you say … what's a *blog*? Well, it's short for *web log*, which is really just a fancy way of saying an online journal. Blogs are a great way to share your thoughts, ideas, and creations with the world. The reason they're so popular is that they're easy to search and read. Plus visitors can subscribe to your blog and get automatically notified when you post something new.

Closely linked to blogs are podcasts. A podcast page is just like a blog page, but it incorporates audio or video (as a blog can, but often doesn't), and allows for people to subscribe to it in iTunes. This means new audio or video can be automatically delivered to your audience as soon as it's released. Blogs and podcasts are among the most powerful, flexible, convenient, and enjoyable ways for you to reach out to others over the Internet. If you've got something to say, chances are someone will want to listen.

In this lesson, you're going to build a website for the MommyCast team. You edited a podcast for the show back in Lesson 14. Now you'll put a website together to distribute this and other shows.

NOTE ▶ This lesson assumes you've completed Lesson 15. You'll build upon the skills learned earlier. If you haven't done Lesson 15, please complete it before proceeding with the exercises in this lesson.

Making the Homepage

As with any website, you'll want to add a homepage to this site to welcome visitors. The homepage offers up a quick overview of the website's content and mission. Let's create a custom look for this site that helps express what the MommyCast show is all about.

To get started, let's create a new site.

1   If it's not running already, launch iWeb.

2   Choose File > New Site.

The Theme chooser opens and prompts you to choose a theme.

3   For this site, choose the Modern theme.

4   Next, select the Welcome template and click Choose.

5   In the sidebar, name the site *MommyCast*.

6   Choose File > Save to capture your work so far.

Modifying the Browser Background

Each page you design in iWeb has a specific width (which by default is 700 pixels). This ensures that the page can be viewed on different-sized displays. When a visitor views your website from a browser window that is bigger than the size of your webpage, some of the browser background—the area bigger than the webpage—shows. With iWeb, you can set this to be a color, a gradient, or even an image.

> **NOTE ▶** You have to set the browser background for each page of your website individually. Be sure to pay attention to these steps, as you'll need to repeat them later in this lesson.

1 Select the Welcome page, and rename the page *Home*.

2 Click the Inspector button, and then click Page. Click Layout.

3 Click the Browser Background pop-up menu and choose Image Fill.

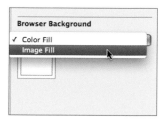

4 In the window that opens, browse to Lesson 16 > Web Page Graphics and select the file **pink_bg.jpg**. Click Open.

The image fills the browser background area of the webpage.

5 Choose File > Save to capture your work so far.

Modifying the Page Background

In addition to customizing the browser background, you can change the background color of a webpage, or even use an image as the background. This is a great way to customize the look of your site.

1   In the Page inspector, click the Page Background pop-up menu and choose Image Fill.

2   In the window that opens, browse to the Lesson_16 > Web Page Graphics folder and select the file **yellow_bg.jpg**. Click Open.

Modifying the Header

If you'd like to put something at the top of the page, you can use the header area on the page. Currently, the homepage has no header, but this is an easy fix.

1   Select the Page inspector.

2   Type a value of *90* px (for pixels) into the Header Height field.

3   Let's make it easier to see items as we lay out the page. Choose View > Show Layout.

4   In the Finder, open the Lesson_16 folder, then open the folder Web Page Graphics. Locate the file **MommyCast_Logo.png**.

5   Drag the logo into the header area of the webpage.

The logo is added to the page, but it needs to be formatted.

6   Switch to the Graphic inspector so we can remove the line from around the logo. In the Stroke area of the Inspector window, click the Line Type pop-up menu and choose None.

   MORE INFO ▶ The logo is a PNG (Portable Network Graphic) file. This particular format is designed to allow web graphics to have transparency stored with the graphic and works well for logos. You can prepare this type of file with most graphics editing software.

   The stroke is removed from the graphic. Now it's time to size the logo.

7   Drag a corner resize handle on the logo until it's 600 pixels wide.

8   Drag the logo to center it on the page. Use the pop-up alignment guides to make sure you're centering it precisely.

9   Choose File > Save to capture your work so far.

Adding Your Photos and Graphics to the Page

The page is really taking shape. Let's drop a photo in to complete the design and add one ornamental graphic as well.

1   Click the large placeholder image of two skiers to select it.

2   Choose Insert > Choose.

3   Navigate to Lesson_16 > Web Page Graphics > **Duo.jpg** and click Insert.

A photo of MommyCast hosts Paige and Gretchen is added to the page.

Let's add a decorative graphic to the page.

4   Choose Edit > Deselect All.

5   Choose Insert > Choose. A sheet opens and the last folder used is selected.

6   Select the file **Daisy_Pink.png** and click Insert.

7   Remove the border from the image using the Graphic inspector.

8   Drag the resize handle so the daisy is approximately 150 pixels wide.

9   Position the daisy near the bottom of the main photo.

10 Choose File > Save to capture your work so far.

Your first page is almost complete. Let's replace some text on the page.

Adding Text to the Page

There are two text blocks on the page that need formatting. The first is a title; the second is the body copy for the page.

1 Double-click the text block containing "Welcome to my site."

2 Type *Welcome to MommyCast* into the text block.

Let's change the font so the text matches the style of the page better.

3 Press Command-A to select all of the text in the block.

4 Click the Fonts button in the toolbar.

5 Choose Comic Sans MS, Bold to stylize the page.

Let's update the main text block by dragging and dropping.

6 Switch to the Finder and open the Lesson_16 folder, then open the Web Page Text folder and select the file **We are MommyCast.txt**.

7 Drag the text file onto the large text block.

The new text is added to the page. You can format it so it's easier to read.

8   Double-click the large text block and press Command-A to select all of its text.

9   In the Font panel choose Comic Sans MS, Regular, 18 pt.

10   Open the Colors window by clicking the Colors button in the toolbar.

11   Change the text color to a very dark gray.

12   Choose Edit > Deselect All.

13   Press Command-S to save your work.

Building a Blog

A blog is a great way to keep a site fresh and up to date. iWeb blogs provide the features and components that every blog needs:

▶ A main page that lists the most recent entries and gets updated automatically when a new entry is added

▶ The blog entries themselves, including links that allow the reader to move from one entry to the next

▶ An archive of entries, so that even when older entries have dropped off the main page, readers can still find them

You can also enhance your text posts by adding photos, video, or audio. Visitors can subscribe so they're notified whenever something new is posted. If you publish your site to MobileMe, you can also let visitors comment on your blog.

In this exercise, you're going to add a blog and then add three entries.

1   Click the Add Page button at the bottom of the iWeb window. In the sheet that appears, choose the White theme, click Blog, and then click Choose.

   NOTE ▶ We're mixing two themes here, but they're both very similar in design.

   iWeb creates a new blog for you consisting of a main page, an Entries page, and an Archive page. The Entries page appears in the webpage canvas.

   Before you start adding entries, you need to customize the three pages iWeb has created to have the same look as the rest of the site.

2   In the sidebar, click Blog.

3   Rename the Blog page *MommyCast Video*.

   This page is the one visitors see when they click it in the site's navigation menu. You'll begin customizing this page first.

4   Select the Page inspector and click Layout. Click the Browser Background pop-up menu and choose Image Fill. The last-used fill is added
to the page.

5   Drag the photo **portrait.jpg** from the Lesson_16 > Web Page Graphics
folder onto the large placeholder image.

Double-click the masked image and drag it downward so the heads show
through in the masked area.

6   Double-click the text "My Blog" and type *MommyCast Video*.

7   Change the font to Comic Sans MS, Bold, 36 pt.

8   Navigate to the Web Page Text folder and drag the text file **Welcome to our
blog.rtf** onto the large text block at the top of the page.

The RTF file contains formatted text including a web link.

TIP ▸ If you'd like to create your own web links, highlight text on the canvas and use the Link inspector.

9   Press Command-S to save your work.

Formatting the Archive and Page

The next page to format is the Archive page, where old blog entries get indexed. You'll format it in a way similar to the last page.

1   In the sidebar, click Archive. The Archive page appears in the canvas.

2   Select the Page inspector and change the Browser Background to the **pink_bg.jpg.**

3   Change the "Blog Archive" text to *MommyCast Video Archive* using Comic Sans MS, Bold, 36 pt.

    NOTE ▸ Once you have a blog set up in iWeb, you seldom need to bother with the Archive page or the main page; iWeb updates them itself, every time you add a new entry. This allows you to spend your time creating entries.

Creating Entries

Now that the blog is set up, you can start to add entries. Each story, video, or audio clip you post should be a single entry.

1   In the sidebar, click Entries.

2   Select the Page inspector and change the Browser Background to the **pink_bg.jpg.**

3   Change the "My Blog" text to *MommyCast Video* using Comic Sans MS, Bold, and 36 pt.

4   Double-click the placeholder text "Day of Longboarding" and type *Happy New Year!*

5 Double-click the date and change it to *Thursday, January 1, 2009*.

6 Drag the text file Lesson_16 > Web Page Text > **Happy New Year.rtf** onto the main text block.

7 Drag the picture **New_Year.jpg** onto the placeholder image. This particular post does not have a video, but our next two will.

You have successfully built your first entry. Let's build two more quickly.

Creating a Video Post

The next entry we'll create is a video post about moms and video games.

1 Click the Add Entry button and name the new page *Moms & Gaming*.

2 Format the Page Title (MommyCast Video) and Browser Background as you did for the previous entry. Drag the text file **Gaming.rtf** onto the blog entry and set the date to *Tuesday, March 3, 2009*.

3 In the Lesson_16 folder, open the Web Page Videos folder, the drag the video **Gaming.m4v** onto the media placeholder.

4 Size the video to be 560 pixels wide.

That looks good, but let's change its poster frame.

5 Select the QuickTime inspector and drag the poster frame slider until the mom is seen lying on the couch playing a video game.

6   Let's save some time on our last blog post. Select the Moms & Gaming entry and press Command-D to duplicate the post.

The page title and background are carried from the last design. All you need to do now is update the content of the entry.

7   Name the entry *Kids & Snacking* and date it Friday, May 15, 2009.

8   Select the show description text and delete it. Then add the file **Snacking.rtf**.

9   Update the video with the file **Kids_Snacking.m4v**, then update the movie's poster frame to a shot of a kid snacking.

TIP ▶ If you want more options for pictures and videos, iWeb has them. You can drag the iSight Photo or iSight Movie widget to record a picture or video with your computer's built-in iSight. Just drag a widget on top of the media placeholder and follow its instructions.

Now that we have a few entries, let's check out the main blog page.

1   Click MommyCast Video in the sidebar.

2   Click to select the Kids & Snacking title, and change the font to Comic Sans MS, Bold, 24 pt.

All of the entries update.

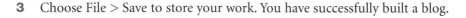

3   Choose File > Save to store your work. You have successfully built a blog.

> **NOTE** ▶ You can allow or block comments and attachments using the Blog & Podcast inspector.

Making a Podcast

What, exactly, is a podcast? It's the web equivalent of a radio or TV broadcast; a single podcast is called an *episode* and a group of them is called a *series* or *show*. People can subscribe to podcasts using a variety of applications, including iTunes. In addition, with iWeb you can not only publish podcasts on your MobileMe website, you can also submit them to the iTunes Store, where they'll be available to the hundred million people who use iTunes.

> **NOTE** ▶ iWeb's Podcast page template includes a subscription link that allows visitors to your site to subscribe directly to your podcast series, so that every time you publish a new episode, the subscribers receive it automatically in their iTunes library. However, any blog page can be a podcast page if it has an audio or video media file in its media placeholder. The benefit of keeping your podcasts separate from the blog is that every entry will have an episode to download. This is a better experience for the audience members looking at your show in the iTunes Store.

In this exercise, you'll take the podcast file you created with GarageBand in Lesson 14 and create a new podcast page and entry.

1   In iWeb, click the Add Page button.

2 Select the White theme, select the Podcast template, and click Choose.

The Podcast template is very similar to the blog template, but it adds an iTunes Subscribe button instead of an RSS Subscribe button.

3 Open GarageBand and then open the GarageBand podcast project that you created in Lesson 14.

> **TIP** ▶ If you skipped Lesson 14, you'll find a copy of the file here: Lesson_16 > Web Page Podcast > **14_MommyCast_End.band**.

4 Choose Share > Send Podcast to iWeb.

The Send Podcast to iWeb command in GarageBand is designed to send the podcast episode directly to a new entry in your site. GarageBand presents a sheet in which you choose how to prepare the episode for delivery to iWeb.

5 Choose AAC Encoder from the Compress Using pop-up menu.

In this instance, you need to use the AAC format because this is an enhanced podcast with pictures and a web link.

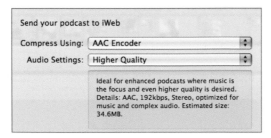

6 The rest of the defaults are fine, so click Share.

GarageBand processes the file and creates an audio mixdown of the show. The process can take a few minutes depending on the length and complexity of the project, but a series of progress sheets appear to keep you informed about what GarageBand is currently doing.

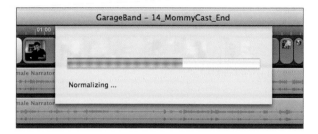

Once the file is compressed, GarageBand asks you to specify which blog or podcast you want to receive the episode.

7 Select the Podcast page and click OK.

Matching the Podcast Section to Your Site's Style

Now that the podcast page is added, let's format the podcast section to match the rest of the site.

1 Rename the podcast page *MommyCast Audio*.

2 Reformat the page title and Browser Background to match other pages on the site.

3 Replace the page body text with the file **podcast.rtf**.

The new text overlaps the Subscribe button and search field.

4 Click the Subscribe button, then Shift-click to also select the search field, and then drag both buttons down so they aren't obscured by the text.

5 Replace the large media placeholder with the graphic file **Globe.png**.

6 Change the episode title font to Comic Sans MS, Bold, and 24 pt.

Refining and Archiving Your Entries

Your podcast page is complete. Now let's clean up the Entries and Archive pages.

1 In the sidebar, select the Entries page for MommyCast Audio.

2 Delete the placeholder entry "Sounds at the beach."

3 Format the Episode 357 page to match the other pages in your site, being sure to change the background, title, and fonts to match as well.

4 Adjust the Archive page title to read *MommyCast Audio Archive.*

5   Format the background and fonts to match.

You've successfully completed the podcast page. We'll submit it to iTunes in a moment.

Publishing the Site

You learned about publishing in our last lesson, and that's the next step for this site. Let's get the site online so it's ready to launch, and then we can submit the podcast to iTunes.

1   Choose File > Save to capture your work.

2   Click the site title in the sidebar.

3   Choose your desired publishing option, MobileMe or FTP server.

   NOTE ▸ You learned about setting up a MobileMe or FTP account in Lesson 15.

4   Enter the required information.

5   Click Publish Site.

6   Click Continue to dismiss any warning dialogs.

   You'll now need to wait a few minutes as the site uploads, because you're uploading large video files. iWeb can continue this process in the background while you keep reading.

To see what the finished page should look like (since we can't put a finished version on the DVD), go to http://www.peachpit.com/ats.iLife09.

Adding the Podcast to iTunes

If you'd like to get a much larger audience, then the best place to put your podcast is in the iTunes store. This way it can be easily found by all of the visitors to the store.

1   Select the MommyCast audio page in the sidebar, then select the Blog & Podcast inspector and click Podcast to see the Inspector window's podcast settings options.

The Podcast pane of the Blog & Podcast inspector offers two sections. One is for the entire the Podcast Series, and the other is for the current entry called the Podcast Episode.

2   In the Podcast Series section of the Inspector window, in the Series Artist field, provide the name of the author or artist responsible for the series, and then provide a contact email address in the Contact Email field.

NOTE ▶ The email address is not made public, but it is used by Apple's iTunes Store staff so they can contact you about your series.

3   Make sure the Allow Podcast in iTunes Store checkbox is selected.

You can also optionally indicate whether the series should have a Clean or Explicit label when it's listed among the Store's offerings by making a choice from the Parental Advisory pop-up menu.

4   Select the Entries page in the sidebar and choose the entry MommyCast – Episode 357.

5   The information in the Podcast Episode area of the Inspector window is filled in automatically.

6   Choose File > Submit Podcast to iTunes.

iWeb requests some additional information about the podcast.

7   Enter the following information for your podcast:

MommyCast is a family-friendly weekly talk show for and by women. Hosts Paige and Gretchen talk about parenting and the never-ending issues that come with motherhood. This is real talk by real moms. But MommyCast is not just for moms! Dads love MommyCast, too.

8 Enter *KDCP Productions* in the Copyright box.

DO NOT click Publish and Submit.

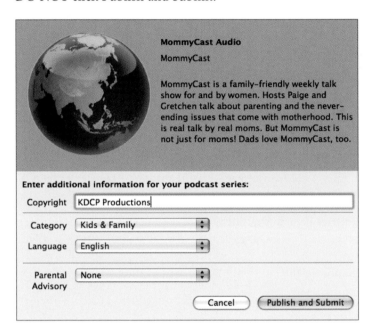

Because this is not actually *your* podcast, click Cancel.

In the future, when you're publishing your own podcasts, iWeb will publish the site and prompt you to follow a few instructions in the iTunes Store to complete the submission process.

You've done it: You've successfully created a blog and podcast and are ready to publish to the global community. Get to it! Let's see your creativity in action.

Lesson Review

1. What is a blog?
2. What is the most important thing to remember about allowing comments on a blog?

3. What's the difference between a podcast page and a blog page?

4. What's the most efficient way to create a new blog entry when you've customized the page template?

5. What is the difference between the blog Archive page and the blog main page?

Answers

1. A blog is short for "web log" and is a series of webpages containing a set of entries that present personal observations, announcements, or insights, organized by date.

2. You must remember to monitor the comments frequently in order to delete inappropriate or offensive comments.

3. A podcast page and blog page are very similar. A podcast page offers an iTunes Subscribe button, whereas a blog page offers an RSS Subscribe button.

4. If you've customized a page template for your blog, you can make additional entries quickly by duplicating an existing entry and changing its content.

5. The blog's main page lists summaries of only the most recent blog entries, whereas the Archive page lists all of the blog's entries and doesn't provide a summary for each entry.

17

Lesson Files   After installation:

iLife09_Book_Files > Lesson_17 > ATS - Bhutan (Final for DVD).m4v

iLife09_Book_Files > Lesson_17 > BhutanMenuMusic.m4a

Time   This lesson takes approximately 90 minutes to complete.

Goals   Learn DVD concepts and terminology

Create an iDVD project

Modify the DVD menu screens

Add a slideshow to the DVD

Burn a DVD

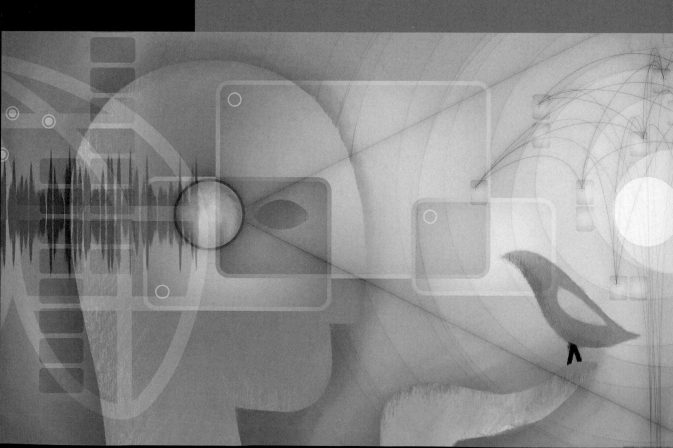

Making a DVD

iLife makes it very easy to take your songs and pictures and movies and put them on the web. And the web *is* a great entertainment destination— if you have a high-speed Internet connection and a home entertainment system connected to it. That's why, when it comes to relaxing and engaging home entertainment, there's much to be said for simply popping a DVD in your player and curling up on the sofa with a bowl of popcorn and a remote control.

iDVD is the iLife application that you use to make DVDs of your other iLife creations. The popcorn is optional.

Exploring iDVD

At one time the acronym *DVD* stood for *Digital Versatile Disc*, and iDVD is certainly versatile. Making a DVD with iDVD can be a complex creative undertaking requiring a lot of time, thought, planning, and ingenuity—or it can be as simple as making a couple of menu choices, sticking a recordable DVD into your Mac's optical disc drive, and clicking a button.

The work you'll do in this lesson falls somewhere between a complex creative undertaking and the super-simple click-and-burn solution. Before you begin, though, it will help if you take just a few minutes and get to know some basic iDVD concepts, along with some of the names and functions of the tools that iDVD offers.

Although the purpose of using iDVD is to make a shiny DVD that you can play in your DVD player or on your Mac, what you're actually making as you work is an iDVD *project*. Each iDVD project is stored in its own *project file*, which you can store anywhere on your Mac. iDVD remembers the last project you worked on, and it opens that project's project file when you launch iDVD.

If iDVD can't find the last project you worked on, it shows you this window when it launches, and it displays this window when you close the project that you're currently working on:

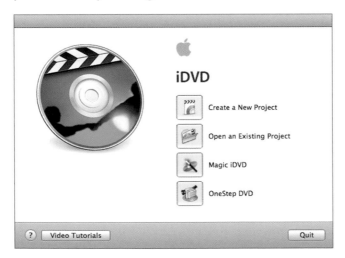

What the first two buttons in the main pane of this window do are obvious. Here's what the other two buttons do.

Magic iDVD

This button offers a quick way to create a DVD containing multiple movies and photo slideshows. You simply drag movies and sets of photos into the main iDVD screen, choose a design theme for the DVD, and click a button—at which point iDVD creates a complete project, ready for you to use to burn a DVD or to further customize. Magic DVD is a great way to get a running start when assembling a DVD project. In fact, you'll use Magic iDVD to begin your project in this lesson.

OneStep DVD

This is an even simpler way to use iDVD. Connect your video camera to your Mac, click this button, and iDVD takes the video from your camera and prepares a DVD from it.

Exploring the iDVD Main Window

Nearly all the work you do when creating an iDVD project happens in the iDVD main window.

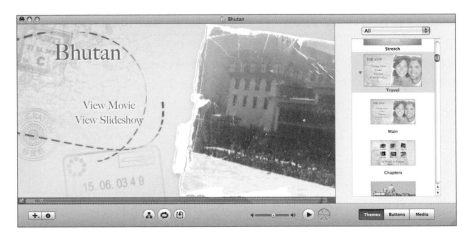

On the window's right side is a pane that displays various collections available to you as you build your projects. The first collection shown in this pane is a list of *theme families* that you can use as the basis for your project. These are similar in many ways to the themes that you use in iWeb when you design a site, or in iPhoto when you create a book, card, or calendar.

DVD Menus

On the window's left is the main area where you build your project. This area normally presents a DVD *menu*.

DVD menus do not look or act like the menus you use in Mac applications. A DVD menu refers to an entire screen that you see when you view a DVD. On the other hand, DVD menus do serve a similar function: They provide you with a way to choose an item in order to cause something to happen, such as starting a movie playing or showing a slideshow.

Menu Buttons

The items that you interact with on a DVD menu are called *buttons*, even though they may not always look like buttons.

Although they look like text labels,
these are DVD menu buttons

You typically use the DVD player's remote control to move among the menu buttons on the DVD menu and to pick one—usually by clicking a real, physical button on the player's remote control. (If you use your Mac's DVD Player application to view a DVD on your Mac, you can navigate among the menu buttons on the DVD's menu with the simulated DVD remote control that DVD Player provides.)

The appearance of a DVD menu's buttons is set initially by the theme family that you choose when you create a DVD project. You can change a button's appearance with the Buttons pane, which you access by clicking Buttons below the pane on the right of the iDVD window. The Buttons pane contains a collection of button styles you can apply to DVD menu buttons.

Aspect Ratios

Many of the theme families you can use in iDVD come in two sizes: the 4:3 aspect ratio used by standard television sets, and the 16:9 widescreen aspect ratio used by modern HDTVs. You choose the aspect ratio for your project when you create it from scratch, though you can change it at any time. iDVD also chooses the appropriate aspect ratio for your project when you create it by sending a movie to iDVD from another iLife application.

DVD Submenus

In addition to coming in two aspect ratios, many iDVD theme families offer three menu themes: one for the main menu, one for *chapters submenus,* and one for *extras submenus.*

When a movie on the DVD is marked with chapter markers, such as the movie you made with iMovie in an earlier lesson, you can add one or more chapters submenus. You use a chapters submenu to pick the chapter in the movie that you want to view.

You add an extras submenu when your DVD contains additional material, such as the behind-the-scenes production videos that many commercial DVDs offer in addition to the main feature.

Both extras submenus and chapters submenus appear onscreen when you choose the menu buttons on the main DVD menu that link to those sub-menus. You establish those links when you construct your iDVD project.

Motion Menus

A number of iDVD themes provide animation, just like many commercial DVDs. Menus with animation are known as *motion menus.*

On a motion menu, a playhead appears in a *scrubber bar* at the bottom of the DVD menu in the iDVD window (it doesn't appear, of course, on the final DVD that you make).

The scrubber bar and playhead with the intro at the left

You can position the playhead by dragging it left or right to see different parts of the animation. The shaded areas that may appear at the left and right of the scrubber bar indicate the presence of *intros* and *outros* in the animation. These are sequences of animation that appear respectively when the menu first appears onscreen, and when the menu leaves the screen.

Drop Zones

Depending on the theme family, iDVD menus and submenus may also contain one or more *drop zones.*

Drop zones are sections of the DVD menu that contain an image, slideshow, or movie. Drop zones add visual interest to the menu, and frequently show small scenes taken from the content of the DVD itself. You can change the contents of a drop zone by dropping your own media into the drop zone as you build your project.

Motion Button

Finally, iDVD can play a motion menu's animation as you work. However, this can be distracting. You can stop and start the motion menu playback by clicking the Motion button at the bottom of the iDVD window.

Okay, enough preliminary information. Let's build something!

Starting Your iDVD Project

The project you're about to build uses a movie that you've seen before in a previous lesson: the Bhutan movie. The version you'll use has had chapter markers added to it.

1   Open iDVD, and then click Magic iDVD. The Magic iDVD window appears.

2   At the top left of the window, in the DVD Title box, replace the proposed title with *Bhutan*.

3   At the right, above the Choose a Theme thumbnails, click the pop-up menu and choose All. The Magic iDVD window displays many more theme thumbnails.

4   In the Choose a Theme thumbnails, click Travel.

You have to scroll a little to the right to see the Travel theme. The Travel theme is appropriate for the Bhutan movie.

5   On your Desktop, open the iLife09_Book_Files folder and the Lesson_17 folder inside of that, and then drag the **ATS - Bhutan (Final for DVD).m4v** file to the Drop Movies Here strip in the Magic DVD window.

A thumbnail of the movie appears in the strip.

6   Near the lower right of the window, click Create Project.

A progress sheet appears as iDVD creates the project. The Magic iDVD window changes to become the Bhutan project window, displaying the project's main DVD menu. The Motion menu button in the window is active, so the menu is animated, and you hear the default music associated with the Travel theme.

7   Click the Motion menu button to stop the music and the animation.

The Motion menu button becomes gray. Take a moment to enjoy the silence, then notice that the main menu screen has a menu button with the name of the file that you dragged into the Magic iDVD window. This button leads to a submenu from which you can either play the whole movie or choose a scene to play. Before you explore that submenu, though, you need to change the menu button's text to something more informative.

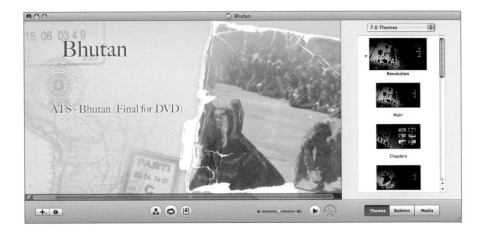

8   In the iDVD window, click the ATS – Bhutan (Final for DVD) menu button, and then click the text inside the menu button.

The text inside the menu button is selected, and a formatting panel appears near the button. You can use the formatting panel to change the typeface, style, and size of the menu button's text.

NOTE ▶ Don't double-click a menu button to edit its label—instead, click once to select the button, and then click a second time. Double-clicking a menu button causes iDVD to perform the action associated with that menu button. For example, double-clicking the ATS – Bhutan (Final for DVD) menu button causes iDVD to show the submenu to which the button links.

9   Change the button's text to *View Movie.*

Navigating Your Project with the Map

Now that you have the main menu's menu button label squared away for the moment, you should take a look to see where that menu button currently leads.

1   At the bottom of the iDVD window, click the Map View button.

iDVD displays a navigation map of the project. In the map, the main menu, each submenu, and the movies they lead to are displayed as boxes with connecting lines so that you can see which ones are connected to which. For example, the Bhutan menu (marked with a folder icon by its title) links to the the ATS – Bhutan (Final for DVD) menu, which is linked to a Play Movie item and a Scenes 1-5 menu.

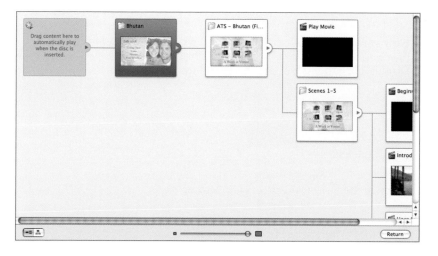

The Play Movie item is labeled with the name of the menu button that leads to it and is marked with a clapboard icon, which indicates that it's a movie. The Scenes 1-5 menu is a chapters submenu which, in turn, links to five movies; the menu buttons on the chapters submenu are labeled with the names that the chapter markers were given in iMovie.

NOTE ▶ The five movies connected to the chapters submenu are actually one single movie. Each button on the chapters submenu points to a specific time in the movie. Clicking a chapters button plays the movie starting at that time.

2   On the toolbar below the map, drag the slider a third of the way to the left.

The map changes size so that you can see more of the items without scrolling.

TIP ▶ You can also change the orientation of the map with the buttons at the left side of the map toolbar.

NOTE ▶ If iDVD spots a potential problem with a menu, a yellow caution icon appears on the menu in the map. A help tag appears that describes the problem when you place your pointer over the caution icon. If you have a menu with an empty drop zone, iDVD warns you about it.

Now you're going to use the map to navigate your iDVD project.

3   Double-click the ATS – Bhutan (Final for DVD) menu.

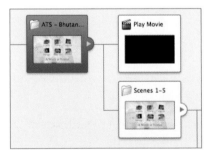

The ATS – Bhutan (Final for DVD) menu appears in the iDVD window. When you double-click an item in the navigation menu, iDVD displays that item in its window.

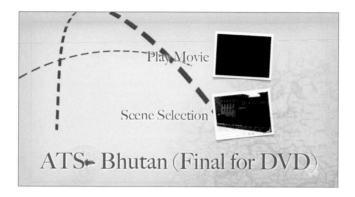

Now that you're here, you can change the title label at the bottom of the menu to something better.

4   At the bottom of the menu, double-click the large ATS – Bhutan (Final for DVD) text label, and then type *Bhutan Movie*.

Unlike a menu button, you can double-click a text label on a menu to edit it.

5   Change the font size of the label to 48.

Once the label becomes shorter you can see the left arrow menu button, which takes you back to the main menu.

6   Click the left arrow menu button. This button is a standard part of the submenu and is not easily editable; a single click takes you back to the main menu.

> **TIP** ▸ You can make such a button editable if you drag it slightly so that it shows a selection rectangle.

7   Choose File > Save (Command-S).

In the next exercise, you'll change the project's theme temporarily. You should always save your project before you make major changes to it. In fact, you should develop the habit of saving your project regularly.

Switching Themes

When you created your project with Magic iDVD, you chose the theme for the DVD. This choice was not irrevocable: In this exercise, you'll see how to change themes—and then change them back.

1   If the Themes collection isn't showing in the right pane of the iDVD window, click the Themes button in the window's lower right.

2   Choose 7.0 Themes from the pop-up menu at the top of the pane, then scroll down the pane and click the Center Stage theme family.

A sheet appears telling you what happens when you switch a project's theme family: The theme for all menus in the project will change. If you like, you can click the disclosure triangle at the sheet's lower left to read additional information.

3   Click OK.

iDVD changes the theme of the menu shown in the window; it also changes the theme of any submenus in the project. As a result, the menu buttons and text label move and change appearance.

4 Choose Edit > Undo Set Theme (Command-Z).

Because you haven't done anything else, such as modify an item or chosen to view a different menu, the Undo command restores the Travel theme.

NOTE ▶ If you have done something else after changing the theme, you can revert to the file that you saved at the end of the previous exercise. Close the current project without saving, and then, in the iDVD window that appears, click Open an Existing Project and reopen the project that you previously saved.

Editing Drop Zones

Magic iDVD filled the drop zones in your project automatically when it created the project. You can change the contents of any of the project's drop zones. In this exercise, you'll change the contents of the single drop zone that appears on the main menu.

1 If you aren't on the project's main menu, navigate there.

2 At the bottom of the iDVD window, click the Drop Zone button.

The drop zone editor appears in the main pane of the iDVD window, listing all the drop zones on the current menu, as well as the menu itself along the bottom of the pane. The pane at the right of the iDVD window now displays the iLife Media Browsers. iDVD shows the Media pane automatically when you edit drop zones, because you usually fill drop zones with media from your iLife Media Libraries.

3 At the top of the iDVD window's right pane, click Photos, click iPhoto in the list below, and type *PA116936* in the pane's search field.

The Media Browser shows you the picture that matches the search term. It's in the Bhutan Event in iPhoto.

4 Drag the picture from the Media Browser into the first (and only) drop zone shown in the iDVD drop zone editor.

The drop zone in the editor shows a small version of the picture, and the main menu displayed above it shows a larger version of the same picture in the menu's drop zone.

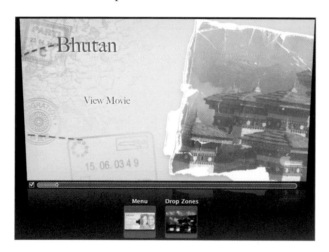

NOTE ▶ Drop zones can contain either a movie, a single picture, or a group of pictures that are displayed as a slideshow.

5   At the bottom of the iDVD window, click the Drop Zone button again.

The drop zone editor goes away and the main menu again fills the left pane of the iDVD window.

Editing the Main Menu

As you may have noticed, the Travel theme plays a bouncy clarinet tune when you click the Motion menu button. You'll change this music and make some other minor adjustments as well.

1   With nothing selected in the main menu, choose View > Show Inspector.

The semi-transparent Inspector window appears showing the Menu Info Inspector. The Inspector window will show a different inspector for each item you select in the current menu. When nothing is selected, the Inspector gives you options for modifying characteristics of the entire menu—in this case, the project's main menu. The Loop Duration slider in the Inspector's Background is set all the way to the end, meaning the entire audio file will play when the motion menu is playing.

2   On your desktop, open the iLife09_Book_Files folder and the Lesson_17 folder inside of it, and then drag the **BhutanMenuMusic.m4a** file to the Audio well in the Inspector.

When the motion menu plays, it will play the complete contents of the music file. You'll fix that next.

3   Drag the Loop Duration slider left to the 28-second mark.

As you drag, a help tag above the slider shows the current time setting of the slider. If your menu has movies in its drop zones, the slider also controls how long they'll play. The duration slider shows the duration of the longest media in the menu, whether in a drop zone or background audio or movie.

4   In the Audio section of the Inspector, slide the main volume slider to the left until it's above the first tick mark.

You can choose to showcase the audio by raising the volume, which is better for complete songs, or to make it into something more like an ambient sound by lowering it, which is more suitable for short sound loops.

5   At the bottom of the iDVD window, click the Motion menu button, listen to the music play, and then click the Motion menu button again.

6   In the Buttons section of the Inspector, click the Highlight swatch.

A Colors window appears. The button highlight color shows you which menu button is currently selected when you view the DVD; you can change the highlight color specified by the menu's theme to a different one.

7   Use the Colors window to pick a different menu button highlight color, such as a medium green.

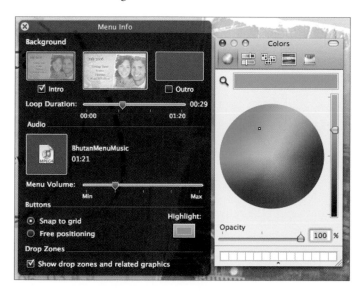

When you view the DVD, the View Movie button on the main menu will use the new highlight color when you select the button.

8   Choose File > Save (Command-S) to save your project, as you should whenever you make significant changes.

9   Close the Inspector and the Colors windows.

Previewing the DVD

Before moving on to the next design exercise, you can take a moment to use iDVD's preview feature to get an idea of how the DVD will play.

1   At the bottom of the iDVD window, click the round Play button.

The Play button turns the iDVD window into a preview window and brings up the iDVD remote control window so you can experience using the DVD as a viewer would. The View Movie button is highlighted, and the menu music you added plays.

2   Click the enter button on the remote control.

The Bhutan Movie menu appears. It still has the clarinet music and the red highlight color: Each menu has its own music and highlight color.

You might want to change this menu to use the same music and highlight color you used on the main menu before you burn your DVD.

TIP ▶ When you preview a DVD, take written notes on a pad of paper or in a text editor window when you see things that don't work or look the way you want. That way, you have a record of all of the things you need to change.

3   Click the down arrow button on the remote control.

The Scene Selection menu button highlights.

4   On the remote control, click enter.

The preview window shows the Scenes 1-5 menu. Again, note that the menu music and the highlight color don't match the main menu.

5   Use the remote control's arrow buttons to move to the Introduction menu button, and then click the remote control's enter button.

The movie begins playing, starting at the scene you picked.

NOTE ▶ You can also use your mouse to click the menu buttons directly in the preview window. However, using the control gives you a better sense of how users will experience the DVD.

6   On the remote control, click menu.

The Scenes 1-5 menu appears again in the preview window.

7   On the remote control, click title.

The DVD's main menu appears in the preview window.

8   On the remote control, click exit.

The remote control goes away and the iDVD window replaces the preview window.

9   Optionally, using the techniques you've learned, modify the menu music and the highlight color of the Bhutan Movie and the Scene Selection menus to match the main menu.

If you make these changes, remember to save your work.

Adding a Slideshow to the DVD

DVDs are not just for video. You can also add slideshows of still images to your DVD. The pictures you use in the slideshow can come from anywhere on your Mac, but it's easiest to get them from your iPhoto library, which, as you've already seen, can be displayed in the iDVD Media Browser.

You'll use the pictures in the Bhutan Event from iPhoto to create the iDVD slideshow.

1   Navigate to the main menu, and then, at the bottom left of the iDVD window, click the Add (+) button.

A menu appears, offering items that you can add to the current menu.

2   Choose Add Slideshow from the menu. A new menu button appears on the main menu.

3   Using techniques you've learned earlier, change the text of the menu button label to *View Slideshow*, then double-click the Slideshow menu button.

The iDVD slideshow editor appears in the left pane of the iDVD window, and the Media Browser's Photo collection appears in the right pane.

4   Type *PA* in the Media Browser's search field. The Bhutan pictures appear in the bottom panel of the Media Browser. By a stroke of good fortune, all of the pictures in the Bhutan Event have titles that begin with those letters.

> **TIP** ▶ When you have iPhoto pictures that you want to use in a DVD slideshow, you can give them special titles or keywords in iPhoto, and then quickly find them in the Media Browser when you're constructing your iDVD project.

5   Select all the Bhutan pictures in the Browser, and then drag them to the left pane of the iDVD window.

iDVD lays out the picture thumbnails in the slideshow editor pane. A number appears at the lower right of each thumbnail to indicate its position in the slideshow.

6   Drag the first picture in the slideshow to the left of the third picture.

Rearranging the order of slides in an iDVD slideshow is a simple matter of dragging the slides into the order you prefer.

7   From the folder in which you found it earlier in this lesson, drag the **BhutanMenuMusic.m4a** file to the Audio well in the slideshow editor toolbar below the slideshow thumbnails.

An icon representing the file appears in the well, and the Slide Duration pop-up menu on the left of the toolbar now reads Fit To Audio, indicating that the slideshow will last exactly as long as the audio's duration.

NOTE ▶ In addition to the Fit To Audio choice and choices for specific numbers of seconds, the Slide Duration menu also offers a Manual setting. When this is chosen, the slides won't advance automatically; instead, you use the DVD remote control to move from one slide to another when you view the DVD.

8   In the toolbar, click the Transition pop-up menu and choose Fade Through Black.

As the slideshow plays, each slide will fade out before the next one fades in. Other transitions are available on the Transition menu that involve motion. You can control the direction of the motion for those transitions with the directional controller to the right of the Transition menu.

9   Click the preview button at the bottom of the iDVD window.

The preview window replaces the iDVD window, the iDVD remote control appears, and the show begins playing, using the audio and transition that you set. You can use the Pause button on the remote to stop the show, and the left and right arrow buttons to move among the slides. When the slideshow finishes, the main menu of the DVD appears, still in preview mode.

10 Click exit on the remote control window. The main menu of the iDVD project appears.

> **NOTE ►** If you click exit before the slideshow ends, you see the slideshow editor instead of the main menu. To get back to the main menu of the DVD, at the right of the slideshow editor toolbar, click Return.

11 Choose File > Save (Command-S).

> **TIP ►** You can also add a slideshow created in iPhoto to a DVD by choosing Share > Send to iDVD from within iPhoto. The iPhoto slideshow is added not as still pictures but as another movie to the DVD.

Modifying Menu Buttons

Next you'll change the way that the menu buttons on the main menu display highlights.

1 In the main menu, choose Edit > Select All Buttons, and at the lower right of the iDVD window, click Buttons.

The Buttons palette appears in the window's right pane. You can use the menu above the palette to change what the palette displays. The items above the line in the menu provide choices suitable for text menu buttons. The items below the line add motion graphics in frames to the buttons.

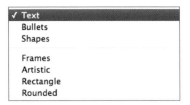

2   If it isn't already chosen, choose Text from the pop-up menu at the top of the pane.

In this set of choices, the graphical items appear with the selected buttons only when the buttons are highlighted; you can select the topmost item in the palette to remove any highlight graphic currently associated with the selected buttons.

3   Click the only available line in the palette.

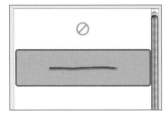

This highlight line appears beneath both selected buttons in the highlight color you previously selected in this lesson.

4   At the lower left of the iDVD window, click the Inspector button.

The Inspector window opens. It shows the options for changing buttons, because buttons are the items that are selected on the main menu. The iDVD Inspector window is context-sensitive, showing only the options for the currently selected objects.

5   In the Inspector window, move the Size slider to the right to increase the size of the highlight line.

The Size slider affects the highlight line, not the text, which can be changed by adjusting its type size with the pop-up menu in the Inspector window's upper right.

6   Choose Edit > Select None. The highlight lines disappear, because they're visible only when a button is highlighted.

You're almost ready to put your DVD into production.

Adding Photo Files to the DVD

If you have one or more DVD slideshows in your project, you can add the photo files that make up those slideshows to the DVD. When the DVD is inserted into your Mac, you can open up the DVD in the Finder and access those files directly.

1   Choose iDVD > Preferences. In the Preferences window, at the top, click Slideshow.

2   Select "Always add original photos to DVD-ROM contents."

3   Close the Preferences window.

TIP ▶ You can add other files to the DVD as well by choosing Advanced > Edit DVD-ROM Contents.

Burning the DVD

When your iDVD project looks the way you want, you can burn a DVD in your Mac's optical drive. But before you actually burn your iDVD project to a DVD, you should make a few final checks.

NOTE ▶ If your Mac doesn't have a DVD burner, or if you don't happen to have a recordable DVD available, just read through this section.

1   Click the Map View button at the bottom of the iDVD window.

It's always good to take one last look at the map to see if there are any warning icons you need to deal with, and to make sure that the DVD menu structure is arranged the way you want it.

NOTE ▶ You can use the map orientation buttons at the bottom left of the map to flip the map between horizontal and vertical orientations, and you can use the Size slider beneath the map to change the size of the map's thumbnails so you can see more of the map.

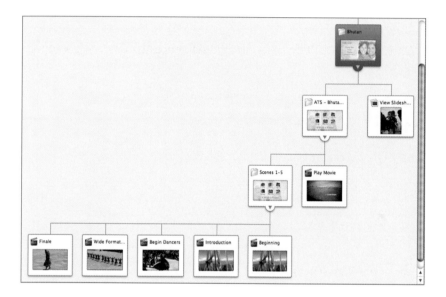

2 Click Return at the bottom right of the navigation map, and then choose Project > Project Info.

The Project Info window appears. The Capacity bar near the top of the window shows you how much space on the DVD your project will take, and it shows the amount of space taken by each kind of media in your project. Use the Media area at the bottom of this window to see which files iDVD will use when it creates the DVD, and to check whether they're all available. If a checkmark doesn't appear in the Status column for a particular file, iDVD couldn't find the file. This can happen if the file has been moved or changed after you added it to the project. To fix this, move the file back or replace it in your project with a different file.

NOTE ▶ If you don't see the Media area, click the disclosure triangle at the bottom of the window.

You can also use the Project Info window to change the encoding method used for the DVD, to specify whether it's NTSC video (for U.S. televisions) or PAL (European television systems), to change the project's aspect ratio, and to choose whether the DVD is to be burned on a single-layer or dual-layer DVD.

NOTE ▶ The encoding methods are Best Performance, High Quality, and Professional Quality. Best Performance is the fastest method, but it can fit less material on the DVD than the other two methods. When Best Performance is chosen, iDVD can encode your media (that is, convert it into the format used by DVDs) in the background as you work on your project; background encoding is not available for the other two methods.

3 Select the text in the Disc Name field and change it to *Bhutan_DVD*, and then close the Project Info window.

When you create the project with Magic iDVD, iDVD automatically chooses a name for the disc you burn that's the same as the name of the project file. When you change the disc name, the name you specify is converted to uppercase when the disc is created. You can use only letters, numbers, and spaces in disc names (spaces are converted to underscores).

4 Get a recordable DVD disc and click the Burn button at the bottom of the iDVD window.

The button opens up to show the standard Mac disc-burning icon, and iDVD requests that you insert a blank disc.

5 Insert the blank disc into your Mac's optical disc drive.

After a few seconds, iDVD detects the disc and begins the disc-burning process. This process can take anywhere from a few minutes to several hours, depending on the amount of material you've included in the project and the encoding method you've chosen. A sheet appears to keep you informed of the current stage of the disc-burning process, along with an estimate of how long it will take. You can cancel the process at any time, but canceling renders the recordable disc you inserted useless.

NOTE ▶ When iDVD finishes burning the DVD, it ejects the disc and gives you the opportunity to burn another copy. The second and subsequent copies may take less time to burn than the first because iDVD doesn't have to encode the material again.

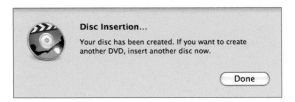

TIP ▶ If you need to move your project to another Mac to burn it, or to give it to someone else to work on, you can choose File > Archive Project. This places all the media needed by the project into the archived project file.

Once the DVD is burned, you can quit iDVD, put the disc back into your Mac, and play it with your Mac's DVD Player application.

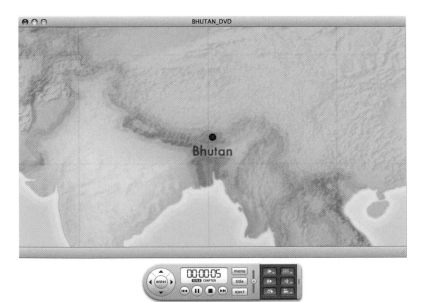

Or, even better, you can pop some popcorn, turn off your iPhone's ringer, and enjoy your evening at the movies.

Lesson Review

1. What is a OneStep DVD?

2. What is a DVD menu?

3. What aspect ratios does iDVD use for DVD projects?

4. What is a submenu?

5. What is a drop zone?

6. How can you use the navigation map?

7. What are intros and outros?

8. Why is there a dividing line in the pop-up menu on the iDVD Buttons palette?

9. What's the difference between an iPhoto slideshow that you share with iDVD and a slideshow that you create in iDVD?

Answers

1. A OneStep DVD is a DVD created by hooking up a video camera to your Mac: iDVD burns the video recorded on the camera to a DVD in one step.

2. A DVD menu is a screen that presents you with buttons you can select using your DVD player's controls, to perform actions such as playing a movie or presenting another menu.

3. iDVD can create projects using the 4:3 aspect ratio used by standard television sets and the 16:9 aspect ratio used by widescreen televisions.

4. A submenu is a secondary menu screen, accessed from another menu. iDVD can create chapters submenus and extras submenus. Chapters submenus are used to present scene selections based on the chapter markers you set in a movie with another application such as iMovie or GarageBand, and extras submenus can be used to offer viewers bonus material, such as slideshows or additional movies.

5. Drop zones are areas on a DVD motion menu that present images, slideshows, or short video clips to provide visual interest; they have no other function.

6. The navigation map shows where each menu leads in your iDVD project. It shows which media files are accessed from each menu, so you can see the path that a user must follow to get to particular sections of the DVD. The map also displays icons that alert you to possible problems, such as menu buttons that don't lead anywhere, or drop zones that lack media.

7. An intro is a brief bit of animation that plays when a DVD menu first appears onscreen; an outro is animation that plays when the menu leaves the screen. Not all themes offer intros or outros.

8. The items above the line in the menu provide choices suitable for text menu buttons and button highlight graphics. The items below the line add motion graphics in frames to the buttons.

9. An iPhoto slideshow is sent to your iDVD project as a movie, containing the audio and all of the video effects. iDVD treats it like any other video file. An iDVD slideshow uses the individual photos that you provide along with the transitions and audio that you specify. iDVD also can automatically include the original photo files for the slideshow on the DVD-ROM when you burn the DVD.

Index

Apple Certification
Fuel your mind.
Reach your potential.

Stand out from the crowd. Differentiate yourself and gain recognition for your expertise by earning Apple Certified Associate certification to validate your iLife '09 skills.

How to Earn Apple Certified Associate Certification

As a special offer to owners of *iLife '09,* you are eligible to take the certification exam online for $45.00 USD. Normally you must pay $65.00 USD to take the exam in a proctored setting at an Apple Authorized Training Center (AATC). To take the exam, please follow these steps:

1 Log on to ibt.prometric/apple, click Secure Sign-In (uses SSL encryption) and enter your Prometric Prime ID. If you don't have an ID, click First-Time Registration to create one.

2 Click Continue to verify your information.

3 In the Candidate Menu page, click Take Test.

4 Enter iLife09EUPP in the Private Tests box and click Submit. The codes are case sensitive and are only valid for one use.

5 Click Take This Test, then Continue to skip the voucher and enter your credit card information to pay the $45 USD fee.

6 Click Begin Test at the bottom of the page.

7 When you finish, click End Test. If you do not pass, retake instructions are included in the results email, so do not discard this email. Retakes are also $45.

Reasons to Become an Apple Certified Associate

- **Raise your earning potential.** Studies show that certified professionals can earn more than their non-certified peers.

- **Distinguish yourself from others in your industry.** Proven mastery of an application helps you stand out from the crowd.

- **Display your Apple Certification logo.** Each certification provides a logo to display on business cards, resumes and websites. In addition, you can publish your certifications on Apple's website to connect with schools, clients and employers.

Training Options

Apple's comprehensive curriculum addresses your needs, whether you're an IT or creative professional, educator, or service technician. Hands-on training is available through a worldwide network of Apple Authorized Training Centers (AATCs) or in a self-paced format through the Apple Training Series and Apple Pro Training Series. Learn more about Apple's curriculum and find an AATC near you at training.apple.com.

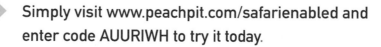